WHAT REPTILE?

BARRON'S

WHAT REPTILE?

A Buyer's Guide for Reptiles and Amphibians

Chris Mattison

Editor: Philip de Ste. Croix
Designer: Philip Clucas MSIAD
Production management: Consortium, Suffolk
Print production: 1010 Printing International Ltd (tbc)
Printed and bound in China
9 8 7 6 5 4 3 2 1

The Author

Chris Mattison, B.Sc., has an honors degree in zoology from the
University of Sheffield and specializes in the natural history of
reptiles and amphibians. He has written more than 20 books,
including *Bearded Dragons* (Interpet Publishing, 2011), and many
magazine articles on reptiles and amphibians, other wildlife topics,
and nature photography. Over the years he has made many field
trips to various parts of the world, including several visits to
North, Central, and South America; the Galapagos Islands;
southern Africa; East Africa; Southeast Asia; Borneo; Australia; and
Madagascar, to study and photograph wildlife. He has lectured to
audiences in England, Scotland, Wales, Sweden, Finland, Holland,
and the United States on the natural history of reptiles and
amphibians and nature photography.

Acknowledgments

I have accumulated information
about reptiles and amphibians
in captivity over many years and
through many publications, websites,
lectures, and private conversations. I
would therefore like to thank all the
many people, too numerous to
mention, who have been generous with
information of this kind over the years. Thanks
are also due to the following people and
organizations that have loaned me animals to
photograph. Many of the animals were
provided by Craig Robinson, Neil Hardwick,
Sean Allingham, and Wayne Swift at Wharf
Aquatics, Pinxton, and several more came
from Andrew Gray and Adam Bland at the
University of Manchester. In addition, John
Armitage, Jason Barnard, John and Linda Bird,
David Birkbeck, David Burbage, Ben Cornick,
Alan Drummond, Toby Mace, Ben Middleton,
John Pickett, and Fred Rassineux kindly
allowed me to photograph reptiles and
amphibians from their private collections.
Finally, Philippe Blais, Alan Francis, Nick
Garbutt, and Gretchen Mattison were with
me on several field
trips and helped
me hunt for
specimens to
photograph. Nothing
would have been
possible without
the help of all
these people.

CONTENTS

Introduction   8

Newts and Salamanders

Introduction	10-11	Tiger salamander	16-17	Marbled newt	21
Axolotl	12-13	Japanese red-bellied newt	18	Fire salamander	22-23
Marbled salamander	14	Smooth, or common, newt	19	Chinese crocodile newt	24
Slimy salamander	15	Sharp-ribbed newt	20	Taliang knobbly newt	25

Frogs and Toads

Introduction	26-27	Waxy frog	46	Yellow poison dart frog	61
Dwarf aquarium frog	28	Budgett's frog	47	Tomato frog	62
African clawed frog	29	White's tree frog	48-49	Asian bullfrog or Asian	
Oriental fire-bellied toad	30-31	South American horned		painted frog	63
Yellow-bellied toad	32	frogs	50-51	Spotted reed frog	64
Painted frog	33	Square-marked toad	52	Tinker reed frog	65
Common spadefoot toad	34	Plains toad	53	Mascarene grass frog	66
Couch's spadefoot toad	35	Western green toad	54	African bullfrog	67
Asian horned frog	36	Bumblebee toad	55	Bright-eyed frog	68
Marbled tree frog	37	Marine or cane toad	56	African grey tree frog	69
European tree frog	38	Green and gold poison		Golden mantella	70-71
American green tree frog	39	dart frog	57	Asian foam-nest tree frog	72
Barking tree frog	40	Black and yellow poison		Mossy frog	73
Grey tree frogs	41	dart frog	58	Pied mossy frog	74
Cuban tree frog	42	Blue poison dart frog	59	Spotted puddle frog	75
Amazonian milk frog	43	Phantasmal poison		Northern leopard frog	76
Red-eyed leaf frog	44-45	dart frog	60	European common frog	77

CONTENTS

Turtles and Tortoises

Introduction	78-79
Common snapping turtle	80
Spotted turtle	81
European pond turtle	82
Wood turtle	83
Common map turtle	84
Mississippi map turtle	85
Yellow-bellied turtle	86-87
Yellow-margined box turtle	88
Horsfield's tortoise	89
Red-footed tortoise	90
African spurred tortoise	91
Leopard tortoise	92
Chinese soft-shell turtle	93
Hermann's tortoise	94-95
Razorback musk turtle	96
Common musk turtle	97
Matamata	98
Pink-bellied shortneck turtle	99

Lizards

Introduction	100-101
Mountain horned dragon	102
Frilled lizard	103
Common garden lizard	104
Thai water dragon	105
Eastern water dragon	106
Rankin's bearded dragon	107
Inland bearded dragon	108-109
Red Niger Uromastyx	110-111
Chinese butterfly lizard	112
Helmeted chameleon	113
Veiled chameleon	114-115
Panther chameleon	116-117
Short-tailed leaf chameleon	118
Green anole	119
Brown anole	120
Collared lizard	121
Green iguana	122-123
Desert horned lizard	124
Western fence lizard	125
Tokay gecko	126-127
Turkish gecko	128
Viper gecko	129
Mourning gecko	130
Electric blue day gecko	131
Painted big-headed gecko	132
Neon day gecko	133
Giant day gecko	134-135
Madagascan leaf-tailed gecko	136
Eastern spiny-tailed gecko	137
Crested gecko	138-139
Leopard gecko	140-141
Fat-tailed gecko	142
Frog-eyed gecko	143
Zimbabwe girdle-tailed lizard	144
Pink-tongued skink	145
Fire skink	146
Sandfish	147
Giant blue-tongued skink	148
Red-eyed crocodile skink	149
Argentine black-and-white tegu	150
Steppe lizard	151
Six-lined long-tailed lizard	152
Southern alligator lizard	153
Glass lizard	154
Water monitor	155
Spiny-tailed monitor	156-157

Snakes

Introduction	158-159	Grey-banded kingsnake	183	Gopher snake	193
Children's python	160	Common kingsnake	184-185	Pine snake	194
Green tree python	161	Milk snake	186-187	Aesculapian snake	195
Carpet and diamond python	162-163	Sonoran mountain kingsnake	188	Leopard snake	196-197
Borneo blood python	164	Baird's rat snake	189	Checkered garter snake	198
Malaysian blood python	165	Corn snake	190-191	Plains garter snake	199
Burmese python	166-167	American rat snake	192	Common garter snake	200-201
Reticulated python	168-169			Rough green snake	202
Ball python	170			Brown house snake	203

Introduction 158-159
Children's python 160
Green tree python 161
Carpet and diamond
  python 162-163
Borneo blood python 164
Malaysian blood python 165
Burmese python 166-167
Reticulated python 168-169
Ball python 170
Sunbeam snake 171
Dumeril's boa 172
Emerald boa 173
Common boa 174-175
Rainbow boa 176
Rosy boa 177
Kenyan sand boa 178
Common egg eating snake 179
Mandarin rat snake 180
Red-tailed green rat snake 181
Western hognose snake 182

Grey-banded kingsnake 183
Common kingsnake 184-185
Milk snake 186-187
Sonoran mountain
  kingsnake 188
Baird's rat snake 189
Corn snake 190-191
American rat snake 192

Gopher snake 193
Pine snake 194
Aesculapian snake 195
Leopard snake 196-197
Checkered garter snake 198
Plains garter snake 199
Common garter snake 200-201
Rough green snake 202
Brown house snake 203

Index of common names 204-205
Index of Latin names 206-207

INTRODUCTION

■ *What Reptile?* is a buyer's guide to some of the popular reptiles and amphibians that may be found in pet shops or on the lists of specialist dealers and breeders. The purpose of this book is to give you enough information to decide which species, if any, you can care for adequately and enjoyably. Just keeping something alive is not particularly enjoyable; you should aim to make your chosen reptile thrive and, if possible, breed.

■ It is important to understand that the list is made up of those species that are often available to reptile keepers. *This does not necessarily mean that they are recommended, or suitable, for captivity.* Some of the species that appear in the trade are sought by specialists but are not suitable for beginners. Other species may be easy to keep, but only if you have the right conditions and some prior experience of keeping exotic pets. For example, species that can best be kept in outside enclosures or greenhouses, or those that need very large cages or expensive specialized equipment, are not for everyone.

■ At a time when wild populations of all sorts of animals are under pressure, the trade in wild-caught amphibians and reptiles, especially rare species and species that cannot be kept properly, should not be encouraged. Wherever possible, species that are widely bred in captivity should be preferred over

those that are only available from wild-caught stock. For starters, these are likely to be healthier and free from parasites. They will also adapt better to captivity and be less easily stressed. And finally, if someone else has bred them, there is no reason why you cannot breed them too, and for many people this is the most rewarding part of keeping exotic animals.

■ The information given is just a starting point; before purchasing any species it is essential to do as much research as possible. Here, I give basic information on housing, creating a suitable environment, and breeding a wide range of species—just enough to help

SIZE OF ACCOMMODATION

Where sizes are suggested for terrariums or enclosures in the **What Accommodation?** *entries, the dimensions follow the formula – length by width by height (as example below).*

$$24 \times 18 \times 12 \text{ in}$$
LENGTH   WIDTH   HEIGHT

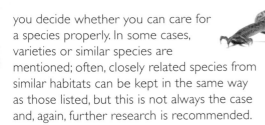

you decide whether you can care for a species properly. In some cases, varieties or similar species are mentioned; often, closely related species from similar habitats can be kept in the same way as those listed, but this is not always the case and, again, further research is recommended.

■ I have tried to indicate the approximate costs of buying, setting up, and maintaining each species. It is very difficult to be precise about all these factors as it will depend on where you buy your animals, what age they are, what variety they are, whether you decide on a basic setup or an elaborate one (some enthusiasts spend more on their plants, for instance, than on their animals), whether you grow or collect their food or whether you buy it, and numerous other factors. So please bear all this in mind when assessing the potential cost of buying and keeping a new animal.

COST GUIDE

The colored bars indicate approximate costs in the broad price bands indicated here.

	Less than $16	$16 – $80	$80 – $160	$160 – $320	$320 or more
Cost					
Setup cost					
Running cost					

■ The cost of maintenance includes food, supplements, electricity, and consumables such as lamps. The estimated costs are per animal for a one-month period. In many cases, a pair or a small group of the same species can be kept at the same cost, or only a little more, than a single animal. The species accounts should be read in ■ conjunction with the introductory sections at the beginning of each group: newts and salamanders; frogs and toads; turtles and tortoises; lizards; and snakes. These sections often contain information that applies to all the animals in the relevant group. For quick reference various key symbols are included at the beginning of each entry.

These give the following information:

- ▨ Carnivorous
- ▨ Herbivorous
- ▨ Omnivorous
- ▦ Captive-bred stock available
- ▨ UV lamp required
- ☑ Suitable for beginners

Newts & Salamanders

■ Newts and salamanders are tailed amphibians: in zoology there is no distinction between newts and salamanders, but in general use the word "newt" is often reserved for the species that spend several weeks or months in water. Newts and salamanders, of which there are 619 species, are found mostly in the northern hemisphere: North America, Europe, and Central Asia. There are a few species in South America, Africa, and Southeast Asia, but none in Australasia. Almost without exception they prefer cool, moist habitats and are secretive creatures, venturing out at night to find food or mates. During the day, or in dry weather, they remain hidden under logs, amongst leaves, or in burrows. A few species are totally aquatic, but these are not often kept in captivity (with the exception of the axolotl, which is the larval form of an otherwise terrestrial species). Most terrestrial species migrate to ponds and other bodies of water to breed, often in the spring, and some species develop crests and fins at this time of the year.

■ All newts and salamanders are carnivorous, feeding on soft-bodied invertebrates such as earthworms and slugs, and insects such as crickets and grasshoppers. They will not eat prey that is not moving. Their larvae, or tadpoles, are also carnivorous, feeding on small aquatic invertebrates such as *Daphnia* and insect larvae. The length of time taken to reach metamorphosis varies from a few weeks to a year or more, and some individuals fail to metamorphose at all, becoming sexually mature while still retaining larval characteristics such as gills, a phenomenon usually referred to as neotony.

■ Keeping newts and salamanders has to take all this into account, and their accommodation will need to be moist and cool. Natural substrates such as leaf litter, which may be sterilized if required but is probably not necessary, sphagnum moss, or simply soil can be used. On the other hand, artificial substrates such as coconut fiber or bark chippings may also be used, and some hobbyists have experimented with products such as the clay beads used in hydroponic plant culture, which retain moisture while not becoming waterlogged. During the breeding season, those species that breed aquatically (often the ones called newts) will require an aquatic setup, which is, in its simplest form, an aquarium with a substrate of gravel, a few aquatic plants, and a rock or piece of wood emerging from the surface. This can be kept clean with a filter or by manually changing a proportion of the water at regular intervals. Aquatic plants are essential for some species to attach their eggs to.

■ Many amphibians can be kept outside in a greenhouse, cold frame, or open-air enclosure, at least for part of the year, and they will require less time than those kept indoors and are more likely to breed. A garden pond should be an essential accessory for everyone interested in amphibians if they have the space for one, even if only to encourage native species, many of which are threatened by loss of habitat and breeding sites.

■ Several species of newts and salamanders—for example fire salamanders, marbled newts, and others—are widely bred in captivity, and these are good choices for beginners.

Axolotl

Left: Juvenile axolotls have proportionately large heads.

PROFILE

The axolotl is the larval form of a species of salamander, *Ambystoma mexicanum*, that never metamorphoses. They retain their caudal fins and large, feathery gills for their entire lives but become sexually mature in this state. They never leave the water, although they do come to the surface to gulp air occasionally. They are almost extinct in the wild and are found only in a complex of heavily polluted lakes in Central Mexico, near Mexico City. Because they are so easily bred in captivity, however, there is a huge captive population, and axolotls are among the most commonly seen amphibians in pet shops.

WHAT temperament?
Good display animals that rarely hide.

easily ingest small pieces of gravel accidentally, which may harm them. A bare aquarium with nothing on the bottom other than some large rocks or sunken wood is probably the best arrangement, though not particularly attractive. The water can be kept clear with a filter, although regular water changes are usually necessary as well, as they have large appetites. Floating plants such as Java moss, *Vesicularia dubyana*, can be attached to pieces of waterlogged wood or rocks to brighten up the tank's appearance.

WHAT environment?
Water temperature between 59°F (15°C) and 68°F (20°C). They will tolerate higher temperatures for a few days but prolonged periods above 72°F (22°C) should be avoided. Cooler temperatures, as low as 50°F (10°C), are not a problem, although they will be less active. Lights are not strictly necessary, but if plants are included in the aquarium, some form of lighting may be necessary. Direct sunlight should be avoided.

HOW much time?
Ten minutes a day with occasional longer periods to service the aquarium.

WHAT varieties?
Axolotls come in several "flavors." The wild-type is dark grey or brown, with paler flecks, and there are also albinos (white with pink eyes), leucistic examples (white with black eyes), "golden" axolotls (cream-colored with pink eyes), piebald axolotls (white with patches of black or brown), and several intermediate forms. Their care is exactly the same regardless of the type. In addition, there is at least one other

WHAT accommodation?
An aquarium measuring about 24 x 12 x 12 in (60 x 30 x 30 cm) is suitable for one or two adults, but larger aquariums are preferable. They need a substrate of large pebbles or rocks; because of their feeding method they can

Above: The golden form of axolotl arose from captive-bred stock and has been selectively bred. There are a number of other color varieties. The three pairs of featherly external gills are retained for the duration of the axoltl's life.

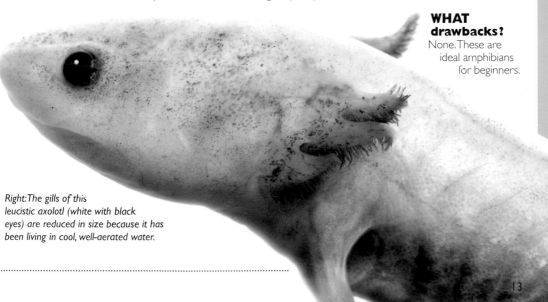

Mexican species of axolotl, *A. andersoni*, which is also rare and endangered in the wild, but occasionally available through captive breeding, although they are expensive and not widely available at this time. Unlike *A. mexicanum*, this species occasionally metamorphoses spontaneously.

Left: This is a wild-type axolotl, but it is slightly paler than normal.

WHAT care?
Daily feeding and checking for temperature, water level, etc.

WHAT food?
Almost anything; axolotls will eat fish, aquatic insect larvae, chopped earthworms, and pieces of lean meat and are extremely voracious. They will also get used to eating fish pellets as long as they are not the floating kind used for pond fish; trout pellets are ideal but should not be fed exclusively. Juveniles will eat *Daphnia*, bloodworm, *Tubifex* worms, mosquito larvae, etc. If they are not fed regularly they often bite limbs off one another and, although these grow back in time, having axolotls with one or more limbs missing is not ideal.

HOW easy are they to breed?
Very easy. Feeding them well and varying the water temperature usually does the trick.

WHAT drawbacks?
None. These are ideal amphibians for beginners.

Cost			
Setup cost			
Running cost			

Size: 8–10 in (20–25 cm) but up to 16 in (40 cm)

Distribution: Mexico

Life span: At least 20 years

Right: The gills of this leucistic axolotl (white with black eyes) are reduced in size because it has been living in cool, well-aerated water.

Ambystoma opacum

Marbled salamander

PROFILE

A small, stocky species with a flattened head and cylindrical body. Males have a pattern of white bands over a dark grey background, whereas the bands in females are grey. Its digits are unwebbed, and it lives and breeds on the land.

allowed to hibernate during the coldest months, when only minimal care is required.

Below and bottom of page: The marbled salamander, Ambystoma opacum, is a small and attractive member of the tiger salamander family. Males tend to have brighter markings than females.

Cost			
Setup cost			
Running cost			

Size: 3.5–4 in (9–11 cm)

Distribution: Eastern North America

Life span: Unknown; probably many years

WHAT temperament?
Nocturnal and secretive. They dislike being handled.

WHAT accommodation?
A glass terrarium of about 24 × 12 in (60 × 30 cm) is suitable for a small group. The substrate should be leaf-litter deep enough for the salamanders to burrow into, and with plenty of pieces of bark for them to hide under.

WHAT environment?
Cool temperatures, up to about 68°F (20°C) in summer and down to 41°F (5°C) in winter. Individuals from the south of their range may be less tolerant of cold conditions.

HOW much time?
Five to ten minutes a day, but regular daily attention is required during the active periods. Can be

WHAT varieties?
No varieties other than the color difference between males and females, noted above. There are several related species but these are rarely available.

WHAT care?
The cage should be thoroughly sprayed every day and not allowed to dry out, but it should not become waterlogged. If necessary, they will go one or two days without food, and if food tends to remain in the cage for

more than a day, the quantity should be reduced. If they are allowed to hibernate, food should be withheld altogether, but occasional spraying will still be necessary.

WHAT food?
Small insects such as crickets, as well as earthworms. Feeding takes place mostly at night. All meals should be dusted with vitamin and mineral supplements.

HOW easy are they to breed?
In the wild they breed in the autumn, laying their eggs in small depressions that later fill up with rain water, at which point the eggs hatch and development begins. This would be difficult, though not impossible, to replicate.

WHAT drawbacks?
Captive-bred young are rarely available.

Plethodon glutinosus

Slimy salamander

PROFILE

A small, slender salamander with a sticky, rather than slimy, skin. It is black in color, with small scattered spots of white, silver or yellow. Several closely related species go under the same name but their care is similar. They are secretive, spending most of their time below ground in burrows or under logs or rocks, emerging at night, especially after rain, to feed. Their sticky skin is due to mucus that they release to protect themselves from predators. Although not toxic, this substance is difficult to remove.

soil or leaf litter, with several pieces of bark scattered on the surface as hiding places. Acidic substrates, such as peat and moss, should be avoided.

WHAT environment?
Cool and humid. Temperatures over 68°F (20°C) cause stress to this species.

HOW much time?
Five to ten minutes a day. Ideally they should be disturbed as little as possible as they are easily stressed.

Cost			
Setup cost			
Running cost			

Size: To 6 in (15 cm)
Distribution: Eastern North America
Life span: Unknown; probably several years

WHAT care?
Daily light spraying and feeding twice a week. As these salamanders are nocturnal, spraying and feeding is best done in the evening, when they are most likely to be actively hunting.

WHAT food?
Small crickets and earthworms. A vitamin and mineral supplement should be added to every feed.

HOW easy are they to breed?
Rarely attempted.

WHAT temperament?
Secretive and shy, preferring not to be handled.

WHAT accommodation?
A terrarium with a floor area of 18 x 8 in (45 x 20 cm) is adequate for two or three individuals. Height is irrelevant as they do not climb, but it should be covered. A plastic box makes a good terrarium for this species. The substrate should be

Above: The slimy salamander is an elongated, glossy species that prefers damp and dark conditions. They are easy to keep but secretive in their habits. In the wild they emerge to feed at night.

WHAT varieties?
Several similar species are almost indistinguishable.

WHAT drawbacks?
Interesting but very secretive and not easy to handle. Captive-bred stock is rarely available.

Ambystoma tigrinum

Tiger salamander

PROFILE

A heavily built salamander with small, bulbous eyes and a flattened head. It has rubbery skin with distinctive folds across its body and variable markings consisting of white, cream, or grey spots, bars, and blotches on a dark grey or olive background, depending on subspecies. Its legs are short and powerful and its digits are not webbed. It lives on land except when breeding, and occurs naturally under a wide range of conditions.

WHAT temperament?

Nocturnal in the wild but adapts to diurnal activity in captivity. Very responsive, especially when there is the prospect of food! Will often take food from the hand.

Above: The barred form, Ambystoma t. mavortium.

can hide. The cage should be thoroughly sprayed regularly and not allowed to dry out; it also should not become waterlogged. Good ventilation is essential. Larvae (tadpoles) are available sometimes, and they can be cared for in the same way as axolotls; in fact, some do not metamorphose but become gilled adults, like the Mexican axolotl.

few hours at a time. For breeding it is probably necessary to hibernate them at 41–50°F (5–10°C) for two or three months in the winter. At this time, an opportunity to burrow will help to avoid extremes.

HOW much time?

Ten to fifteen minutes a day, but regular daily attention is required during the active periods. Can hibernate during the coldest months, when only minimal care is required.

WHAT accommodation?

A large terrarium of at least 11 ft² (1 m²) in floor area for a pair or small group of adults. Height is not so important as it rarely climbs. The substrate can be leaf litter or bark chippings, covered with a thick layer of natural moss and pieces of bark under which it

Above: The blotched form of the tiger salamander, A. t. melanostictum.

WHAT environment?

Very undemanding, tolerating temperatures between 41°F (5°C) and 77°F (25°C) but should not be exposed to higher temperatures for more than a

WHAT varieties?

There are up to eight subspecies recognized and the Californian tiger salamander, *Ambystoma californiense*, is sometimes recognized as an additional subspecies, *A. t. californiense*. The most colorful forms are the barred tiger salamander, *A. t. mavortium*, and the blotched tiger salamander, *A. t. melanostictum*, but there is a great deal of variation,

Cost				
Setup cost				
Running cost				

Size: Normally 3–6 in (7.5–16 cm) but exceptionally to more than 14 in (35 cm)

Distribution: North America

Life span: Many years; at least up to 20

even among individuals from the same area. All subspecies are attractive and make good pets. The spotted salamander, *A. maculatum*, is similar, but its markings consist of more rounded yellow or orange spots.

Above: A well-marked example of the blotched form. All forms are variable in color and markings.

WHAT care?

Spraying and feeding daily while active. If necessary, they will go one or two days without food, and overfeeding should be avoided.

WHAT food?

Insects such as crickets, and also earthworms

Right: The spotted salamander is slightly less heavily built than the tiger salamander.

and slugs. Food should be dusted with a vitamin and mineral supplement. They are active

hunters that usually respond immediately to the presence of food in their cage.

HOW easy are they to breed?

Captive breeding is rarely attempted but ought to be straightforward. It would be necessary to move them to an aquatic tank in the spring after they have first been conditioned and then hibernated. In cooler climates, outside enclosures containing a small pond would probably be the most effective way of inducing them to breed.

WHAT drawbacks?

Captive-bred young are rarely, if ever, available. Some forms are endangered, and numbers of all subspecies are declining due to a variety of factors. They are occasionally cannibalistic, so it is not a good idea to keep large and small individuals together in the same terrarium.

Cynops pyrrhogaster

Japanese red-bellied newt

PROFILE

A dark brown newt with a bright red or orange underside. Their skin is rough, and there is a pair of raised glands (parotoid glands) at the back of the head. The tail is flattened from side to side and ends in a small filament. Males have a purplish tinge during the breeding season, when they are aquatic, but this disappears later in the year when they become terrestrial.

WHAT temperament?

Good display animals if kept in an aquatic environment, but they sometimes refuse to feed in the water after the breeding season (spring). If kept on land, they are nocturnal and secretive.

WHAT accommodation?

An aquarium of about 24 × 12 × 12 in (60 × 30 × 30 cm) is suitable for a pair or a small group of adults. They require a substrate of gravel or small pebbles and some aquatic plants such as pondweed, *Elodea*, for the females to lay their eggs on. A small island of rock or bark is necessary so that they can come out of the water occasionally. This way, keeping them in an aquatic setup throughout the year is possible, provided the water does not become too warm. Heating is not required, but the water should be kept clear with a filter.

WHAT environment?

Water temperature between 59°F (15°C) and 68°F (20°C). Cooler temperatures are tolerated, but higher temperatures are best avoided.

HOW much time?

Ten minutes a day with occasional longer periods to service the aquarium.

WHAT varieties?

There are six subspecies recognized but distinguishing them is difficult. Not to be confused with the smaller Chinese fire-bellied newt, *Cynops orientalis*, which has smoother skin.

WHAT care?

Daily feeding and checking the temperature, etc.

WHAT food?

Aquatic invertebrates such as bloodworms, *Daphnia*, and mosquito larvae, as well as chopped earthworms.

Cost		
Setup cost		
Running cost		

Size: 3.5–5 in (9–13 cm)
Distribution: Japan
Life span: Unknown; certainly many years

Above: The red-bellied newt is appropriately named, but there are a number of other species with similar colors.

HOW easy are they to breed?

They often breed when first imported but getting them to breed in subsequent years can be difficult. A period of hibernation seems to be an essential part of conditioning.

WHAT drawbacks?

None.

Lissotriton vulgaris 🗒☑

Smooth newt or Common newt

PROFILE

A small European newt that changes shape and color during the breeding season. Males develop a high scalloped crest, and their undersides become bright orange with large dark spots. At this time they are completely aquatic, living in small ponds and ditches. Outside of the breeding season they lose their crest, leave the water, and live under logs and rocks.

WHAT temperament?

Shy when kept terrestrially but become tame in an aquarium.

WHAT accommodation?

A glass aquarium of about 24 × 12 × 12 in (60 × 30 × 30 cm) is suitable for a small breeding group. It should have a sand or gravel substrate and plenty of aquatic plants, especially pondweed, to which females attach their eggs. Once they leave the water they are more difficult to accommodate. In areas where they occur naturally, they can be introduced to a small garden pond, where they will often naturalize.

WHAT environment?

Cool conditions are required, between 50°F (10°C) and 68°F (20°C). They prefer clear, well oxygenated water.

HOW much time?

Five to ten minutes a day, with occasional longer periods

needed to maintain the aquarium, clean filters, etc.

WHAT varieties?

There is some variation between individuals and several subspecies have been described from Eastern Europe. There are a number of other small newts, such as palmate newts, *L. helveticus*, Carpathian newts, *L. montandoni*, and Bosca's newt, *L. boscai*, that have similar requirements although they are not often available.

WHAT care?

Daily feeding.

WHAT food?

Small aquatic invertebrates, especially *Daphnia*, mosquito larvae, and bloodworms.

HOW easy are they to breed?

Breeding takes place in the spring, and the females need to be conditioned before they enter

Cost*			
Setup cost			
Running cost			

Commercial trade is illegal over much of the area in which they occur, but they can sometimes be obtained from friends with ponds in their gardens. The price shown is for the Carpathian newt, which is available sometimes through the pet trade.

Size: 4 in (10 cm)

Distribution: Most of Europe and parts of Asia

Life span: To 20 years or more in captivity

hibernation. In suitable localities, natural breeding in outdoor ponds is by far the best arrangement.

Above: During its terrestrial phase, the smooth newt loses all traces of its dorsal crest and is sometimes mistaken for a lizard. Its skin is velvety in texture, however, and it lacks scales.

WHAT drawbacks?

Difficult to feed once they leave the water. They can be given whiteworms and small earthworms, but are very labor-intensive.

Sharp-ribbed newt

PROFILE

A large newt with a wide, flattened head and small eyes. The body is stocky and there is a row of poison-containing warts down each flank, often dull orange in color. These warts mark the ends of the ribs, which sometimes pierce the skin and protrude through it, acting as a means of defense. The overall color is olive green with darker spots, and the skin is rough. This species is highly aquatic and normally leaves the water only when its pond dries up.

WHAT temperament?
Very tame and always on the lookout for food. Individuals may fight over food but rarely injure one another.

WHAT accommodation?
An aquarium of 24 x 12 x 12 in (60 x 30 x 30 cm) is suitable for an adult pair although very large adults may outgrow this size eventually. The water should be at least 4 in (10 cm) deep and heavily planted with aquatic plants such as *Elodea*, and with a substrate of large gravel.

WHAT environment?
Maximum water temperature is 73°F (23°C). Minimum water temperature is 41°F (5°C). They may be moved to a terrestrial terrarium during hibernation and will then be ready to breed as soon as they are introduced to water in the spring.

HOW much time?
Five to ten minutes a day.

WHAT varieties?
None: although there are two related species from North Africa, they are rarely seen in captivity.

WHAT care?
Daily feeding and general maintenance of the aquarium. A filter can be used, but strong currents should be avoided. Manual cleaning with a siphon is usually necessary on a regular basis.

WHAT food?
Anything. Very greedy newts that will tackle even large earthworms as well as waxworms, mealworms, and other insects.

Cost		
Setup cost		
Running cost		

Size: 6–12 in (15–30 cm) and very heavy-bodied

Distribution: Spain & Portugal

Life span: 25 years or more

Above: Ribbed newts rarely leave the water voluntarily.

HOW easy are they to breed?
Very easy. One method is to hibernate them out of water and introduce them to an aquarium containing cool, clear water; after which breeding usually takes place within 24 hours.

WHAT drawbacks?
None; not the most attractive of amphibians, but they have plenty of character and the advantage of being easy to care for.

Left: The ribbed newt's small eyes and obviously flattened head are characteristic of the species.

Triturus marmoratus

Marbled newt

PROFILE

A medium-sized newt with velvet-like skin and very distinctive coloration. They are bright green with black marbling. Males have a high crest of black and cream during the breeding season; females and juveniles have an orange stripe along the center of their back. The colors are brightest when they are living on land, and they only become aquatic during the breeding season.

WHAT temperament?
Secretive and mostly nocturnal when living on land, but showy when aquatic.

WHAT accommodation?
An aquarium of 24 × 12 × 12 in (60 × 30 × 30 cm) is suitable for a pair or trio of adults, both when terrestrial and aquatic. During the aquatic phase the water should be densely planted with pondweed; during the terrestrial phase use a substrate of soil or leaf litter with bark to provide hiding places.

WHAT environment?
Temperature 50–77°F (10–25°C). A cool winter rest is needed before they will breed. During the terrestrial phase their terrarium should be well ventilated. This species may be kept outdoors in a suitable terrarium or greenhouse

HOW much time?
Five to ten minutes a day, plus

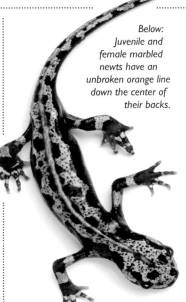

Below: Juvenile and female marbled newts have an unbroken orange line down the center of their backs.

Cost		
Setup cost		
Running cost		

Size: 5–6 in (12–15 cm)

Distribution: Portugal, Spain, and parts of France

Life span: 10 or more years

terrestrial or aquatic); *Daphnia* and bloodworms when aquatic; crickets, waxworms, etc. when terrestrial.

HOW easy are they to breed?
Difficult to breed. They require a period of hibernation followed by transfer to an aquatic setup

extra for cleaning, etc. Require no attention during hibernation.

WHAT varieties?
The southern marbled newt, *Triturus pygmaeus*, is smaller but similar in color. It is not generally available.

WHAT care?
Feeding while aquatic, spraying and feeding while terrestrial.

WHAT food?
Small earthworms (when

Above: Male marbled newts have a black and orange line down their backs outside of the breeding season.

with lots of plants. Rearing the larvae is relatively easy.

WHAT drawbacks?
Sometimes difficult to obtain. Try to source captive-bred young as they will be better adapted to captivity.

Salamandra salamandra

Fire salamander

PROFILE

A stocky, jet black and yellow salamander with short limbs and two distinct glands behind its eyes. Its tail is rounded in cross-section and is slightly shorter than its head and body length combined. Markings are extremely variable, depending on where they come from, with many subspecies, but they usually consist of yellow (sometimes orange or red) stripes, spots or blotches on a shiny black background. It lives on the land—usually damp, shady places—and is nocturnal. Females give birth to living young, either as aquatic larvae, which they deposit in shallow water, or, in some populations, to fully developed terrestrial young.

Above: Larval fire salamanders do not develop the yellow coloration until they are almost ready to leave the water.

them unsupervised under any circumstances.

WHAT accommodation?

A large terrarium of 5 to 11 ft² (0.5 to 1m²) in floor area is suitable for a pair of adults or a group of sub-adults. The best substrate is beech or oak leaf litter, to a depth of about 4 in (10 cm), covered with moss and pieces of bark. If a water bowl is included, it should not be too deep as the adults are poor swimmers. Heating is unnecessary, as is lighting. Larvae (tadpoles) need an aquatic envi-

ronment. Housing fire salamanders outside is easily possible in cooler parts of the world, and their enclosure should contain a pile of logs and a small pool with sloping sides in which the females can deposit their larvae.

WHAT environment?

Cool and moist: the temperature needs to be below 68°F (20°C). Lower temperatures, down to almost freezing, are tolerated by most forms, but 41°F (5°C) should be regarded as a minimum to be on the safe side. Hibernating fire salamanders will not feed. The substrate should be kept slightly moist (not waterlogged) by regular spraying.

HOW much time?

Five to ten minutes a day during their active periods. Can be

WHAT temperament?

Very nocturnal but becomes active in the evenings and even during the daytime in captivity. The large glands behind its head (parotoid glands) produce a strong, sticky, poisonous substance that can kill dogs and other small animals, but captive animals can be handled safely as long as normal precautions are followed; you must wash your hands after handling them, and small children should not be allowed to handle

Above: The Corsican fire salamander, Salamandra corsica, has characteristic round yellow spots.

allowed to hibernate during the coldest months, when only minimal care is required.

WHAT varieties?

Highly variable with up to fifteen subspecies recognized, some of which are very rare. Differences between them include general size and body shape, and the extent and pattern of the yellow markings. Among the most attractive are the spotted fire salamander, *S. s. salamandra*, from Central and Eastern Europe; the Pyrenean form, *S. s. fastuosa*; the northern European striped salamander, *S. s. terrestris*; and the Italian form, *S. s. gigliolii*. The Corsican fire salamander, *S. corsica*, is now a separate species, characterized by evenly spaced round spots, and the Alpine salamander, *S. atra*, is completely black.

WHAT care?

Spraying and feeding two or three times a week while active. If necessary, they will go for long periods without food, especially if kept at lower temperatures.

WHAT food?

Earthworms are a favorite, but they also eat crickets and other small insects. They will learn to take food from the hand.

HOW easy are they to breed?

Breeding in indoor terraria is very unpredictable, but they will breed annually in a well-designed outdoor

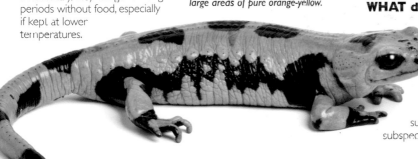

Above: Portuguese fire salamanders, S. s. gallaica, have small yellow markings.

Below: The Italian fire salamander has large areas of pure orange-yellow.

Cost		
Setup cost		
Running cost		

Size: 6–10 in (15–25 cm)
Distribution: Throughout Europe (not the UK). Related species in western Asia and North Africa
Life span: Can live for over 50 years in captivity

enclosure. Subspecies should be kept separately or they will interbreed.

WHAT drawbacks?

None, provided the warning regarding their poisonous secretions is heeded. Always buy captive-bred juveniles, of which there is a plentiful supply, as many subspecies are endangered.

Tylototriton kweichowensis

Chinese crocodile newt

PROFILE

A large newt with rough, warty skin and a distinctive pattern of orange and black. The orange is a warning color and marks a row of poison glands down the center of the newt's back and along each flank. The tips of its fingers are also orange. Mostly terrestrial but moving to shallow water to breed in the spring.

WHAT temperament?

Secretive and nocturnal at first, but soon becoming tame and more easily seen. The skin produces poisonous substances, so they should not be handled more than is necessary and not by young children.

WHAT accommodation?

A glass terrarium measuring 40 x 12 x 12 in (100 x 30 x 30 cm) is suitable for a pair or small group.

They climb well so a mesh lid should be fitted. The terrarium should include a small pool and a substrate of soil or leaf litter, with pieces of wood, bark, and flat stones under which the newts will hide. No heating or lighting is required. It is important not to overcrowd them as they are prone to fungal infections.

WHAT environment?

Temperature at 50–68°F (10–20°C), slightly cooler during hibernation. The substrate needs to be damp but not waterlogged, and ventilation must be good.

HOW much time?

Five to ten minutes a day.

There are several similar species of crocodile newts. Emperor newts, T. shanjing (upper), and Chinese crocodile newts, T. kweichowensis, are quite similar.

Cost				
Setup cost				
Running cost				

Size: 6–8 in (15–20 cm)
Distribution: China
Life span: At least 10 years

WHAT varieties?

There are several similar species available occasionally, including *T. verrucosus*, the emperor or mandarin newt, sometimes labeled as *T. shanjing*. This species is not quite as colorful as *T. kweichowensis* and is much more aquatic.

WHAT care?

Daily feeding and spraying.

WHAT food?

Earthworms, waxworms, crickets, etc. Every meal should be dusted with a vitamin supplement.

HOW easy are they to breed?

Not widely bred. A period on land, followed by a cool period and then a period in water would probably be required.

WHAT drawbacks?

None, apart from the lack of captive-bred stock.

Tylototriton taliangensis

Taliang knobbly newt

PROFILE

A dramatic-looking newt that is entirely matte black except for the tips of its fingers and a small raised lump behind its head, which are bright orange. The underside of its tail is also orange. There is a raised bony ridge down the center of its back and a lower ridge down each flank. The skin is rough and dry, and the head is greatly flattened.

WHAT temperament?

Nocturnal and prefers to hide during the day.

WHAT accommodation?

A glass terrarium measuring 24 × 12 × 12 in (60 × 30 × 30 cm) is suitable for a pair or small group. The terrarium should include a water area with a rocky pool and a terrestrial area with a substrate of soil or leaf litter, with pieces of wood, bark, and flat stones under which the newts will hide. No heating or lighting is required.

WHAT environment?

Cool and moist. A maximum temperature of 68°F (20°C) is required, but less is better, down to 50°F (10°C) at least. They prefer subdued lighting.

HOW much time?

Five to ten minutes a day.

WHAT varieties?

Another form of black knobbly newt, *T. asperrimus*, is sometimes available. It is similar but is not so flattened in shape and lacks the orange marking behind the head.

Below: The Taliang knobbly newt has a dragon-like appearance and is slow-moving. Its natural history is only poorly known, but it does quite well in captivity if kept cool.

WHAT care?

Daily feeding and spraying. Little is known about this species, so some experimentation might be necessary to reach the ideal conditions.

WHAT food?

They love earthworms but will also eat other invertebrates. However, they move very slowly, so lively food items such as crickets may not be suitable.

Cost			
Setup cost			
Running cost			

Size: 6–8 in (15–20 cm)

Distribution: China, where related species occur.

Life span: Probably to 20 years or more

HOW easy are they to breed?

Some form of hibernation, followed by transfer to a shallow aquatic environment would probably be necessary.

WHAT drawbacks?

Captive-bred animals are not available, and wild-caught stock is sometimes in poor condition. This newt is best avoided except by experienced amphibian keepers.

Frogs & Toads

■ As with newts and salamanders, there is no scientific distinction between frogs and toads. They are all tailless amphibians belonging to the order Anura. The term "toads" tends to be reserved for dry, warty species such as those belonging to the widespread Bufonidae family, several of which are listed in this book.

■ Frogs and toads have an almost worldwide distribution, and there are 5,966 species known, according to the latest figures. Most species live on the land except when breeding, but there are totally aquatic species as well as terrestrial species that breed on land. The life cycle of typical frogs is well known. It consists of eggs known as frog spawn—tadpoles that grow legs and then absorb their tails before developing lungs and leaving the water to live on the land until it is their turn to breed. Terrestrial-breeding frogs are mostly tropical and lay small batches of eggs in damp places where they complete their development without turning into free-living tadpoles. Anyone hoping to breed frogs must obviously find out what type of life cycle their species has.

■ All these factors must be taken into account when setting up a terrarium for frogs, and these may be aquatic setups (aquariums) or terrestrial setups, or they may include a land and a water area. Many frogs climb—they are known as tree frogs or reed frogs, and these require taller terrariums than those that live on the ground or burrow. Burrowing species require a good depth of loose, friable substrate into which they can dig. Suitable substrates are leaf litter or a mixture of sand and leaf litter or coconut fiber (coir). Many frogs can be accommodated in elaborately planted terrariums, and these can make attractive additions to the home, especially if they include running water and living plants. Setups of this type are almost obligatory for housing poison dart frogs, which are among the most desirable species for experienced enthusiasts. Others need much simpler setups, however, and the type of accommodation, its size, and costs, should be taken into account when choosing a suitable species of frog.

■ With just two possible exceptions that don't concern us here, all frogs and toads are carnivorous, and their diets range from tiny springtails and mites that live among leaf litter to large vertebrates such as rodents, fish, and other frogs. Some species actively hunt for their prey, whereas others sit and wait for it to stray within range, and then pounce on it. Most frogs and toads eat small insects such as crickets and cockroaches, of which there is a steady supply through the pet trade. Because these insects are cultured artificially, they may lack certain vitamins and minerals, and these can be added by dusting them with a suitable supplement, of which there are many on the market. As most species are nocturnal (poison dart frogs being notable exceptions), it is better to feed them in the evening so that they eat their prey insects before all the vitamin powder has been cleaned off. Similarly, if the food insects, especially crickets, are fed on a variety of food such as chick crumbs, and vegetables such as carrots, they will have a higher nutritional value than those that are simply used straight out of the container in which they were purchased.

■ A good number of frog species are bred in captivity, including charismatic examples such as the South American horned frogs, *Ceratophrys* species, African bullfrogs, fire-bellied toads, White's tree frogs, and others. These are all good choices for the beginner. Many different poison dart frogs are also bred in good numbers, but the care of these is not so straightforward and it is probably better to stay away from them until some experience has been gained with more robust (and less expensive!) species.

Hymenochirus boettgeri

Dwarf aquarium frog

PROFILE

A small, totally aquatic frog from tropical Africa that will live in an aquarium. It is flattened from top to bottom and holds its arms and legs out to the side. Its back, limbs, and head are brown or tan in color with many small black spots and covered in small granular warts.

WHAT temperament?
Lively and active during the day and night.

WHAT accommodation?
An aquarium measuring about 18 x 10 x 10 in (45 x 25 x 25 cm) will house a small group. It will need a good cover as the frogs are inclined to climb or jump out otherwise. The substrate can be aquarium gravel, with pieces of rock for them to hide under. Plants can be rooted in the gravel or species such as Java moss, *Vesicularia*, can be free-floating or attached to pieces of driftwood. They can be kept with tropical fish, but care should be taken to see that the fish do not eat all the food before it reaches them.

WHAT environment?
A temperature of 68–77°F (20–25°C) is required, and this is best provided with a small aquarium heater and thermostat. A filter can be used to keep the water clean,

but avoid too much disturbance as these frogs come from still water habitats.

HOW much time?
A few minutes each day for feeding, occasional longer periods for servicing the aquarium.

WHAT varieties?
Another species, *Hymenochirus curtipes*, has been available sometimes, but the differences between them are minimal and their care is identical. Most aquarium frogs seen in pet shops will be *H. boettgeri*.

WHAT care?
Daily feeding.

WHAT food?
Live bloodworms and *Daphnia* are the best food, but they will sometimes take good quality frozen (but not freeze-dried) bloodworm or similar products. Fish flakes or fish sticks are not suitable.

HOW easy are they to breed?
Difficult. Getting them to spawn is a problem, and the tadpoles are minuscule and require very tiny live food.

WHAT drawbacks?
None, other than the lack of captive-bred stock.

Cost				
Setup cost				
Running cost				

Size: 1–1.5 in (3–4 cm)	
Distribution: Equatorial Africa	
Life span: 10 years; possibly more	

Above: Dwarf aquarium frog, Hymenochirus boettgeri.

Xenopus laevis

African clawed frog

PROFILE

Not legal in some states. A totally aquatic frog (or toad) with a pear-shaped body, smooth skin, hugely webbed hind feet, and small front feet. Its eyes are small and peer upwards. Grey or greyish-brown in color with a paler underside. The back is mottled with lighter and darker blotches. It usually floats just below the surface, with its front legs held out to each side, and uses its fork-like front claws to stuff food into its mouth.

WHAT temperament?

Usually placid and always looking for a feeding opportunity. Will take food from forceps and the fingers, occasionally, as it is not a delicate feeder.

WHAT accommodation?

An aquarium of about 24 × 12 × 12 in (60 × 30 × 30 cm) is suit able for an adult pair. It must be covered as they occasionally leap out and cannot survive long on a dry floor. A substrate of gravel is suitable and there should be somewhere for them to hide, such as half a clay flowerpot. Plants are a waste of time as the frogs will uproot them.

WHAT environment?

Tropical but undemanding. A temperature of about 73°F (23°C) suits them but they will not die if it falls as low as 50°F (10°C). This species has become established in warmer parts of the United Kingdom, as well as southern United States, where it is a pest.

HOW much time?

Five to ten minutes a day; longer for occasional aquarium maintenance.

WHAT varieties?

An albino, or "golden" clawed frog, is widely available, and there are several other species, all similar.

WHAT care?

Daily feeding and general maintenance of the aquarium. A filter can be used, but clawed frogs are messy feeders, and manual cleaning with a siphon is usually necessary on a regular basis.

WHAT food?

Earthworms and pieces of lean meat. They can be trained to eat

Cost					
Setup cost					
Running cost					

Size: 4–6 in (10–15 cm)
Distribution: Southern Africa
Life span: 20 years; possibly more

pool pellets, turtle pellets, and other processed food.

HOW easy are they to breed?

Not easy. Adding cold water sometimes stimulates them to go into amplexus (the mating embrace), but eggs are rarely laid.

WHAT drawbacks?

They cannot be kept with other aquatic animals such as fish, as they will eat them.

Above: The African clawed frog comes in several color forms: this is the wild type.

Bombina orientalis

Oriental fire-bellied toad

This is an almost unbelievably colorful little toad. Its back is bright green (sometimes brown) with regular black spots and lines. Its underside, by contrast, is brilliant red with black markings. The purpose of its brightly colored underside is to warn predators of the distasteful substances that it produces in its skin and secretes from the many rounded warts on its back and limbs. The toad's behavior, when it feels in danger, is to arch its back and raise the palms of its hands and feet to show the bright patches of skin. Captive individuals rarely, if ever, display and do not produce toxins, although, as with all amphibians, you are strongly advised to wash your hands thoroughly after handling them. Children should not be allowed to handle them unsupervised. This species spends a lot of time in the water and typically hangs motionless at the surface with just its eyes and nostrils exposed. If it is disturbed, or if It senses food, it springs into action, using its large hind feet to swim to cover, or toward its prey.

WHAT temperament?

It quickly adapts to new surroundings although it sometimes remains nervous. Providing places for it to hide when it feels in danger will help to overcome this.

WHAT accommodation?

An aquatic setup measuring 24 × 12 × 12 in (60 × 30 × 30 cm) is suitable for a pair or small group of up to four adults. Half the floor area should be water of about 2–4 in (5–10 cm) in depth. Floating plants and pieces of driftwood will provide cover for the frogs. The land area can be a piece of flat rock or slab of cork bark or tree fern. Alternatively, the bottom of the terrarium can be divided into two compartments with a piece of glass and one side filled with gravel and topped off with moss and pieces of wood or bark.

WHAT environment?

This species prefers a temperature of 68–77°F (20–25°C), which can be attained with a heat mat under the terrarium or a spotlight directed at a basking place

Left and above: The fire-bellied toad's brilliant red underside is intended to warn predators that it is poisonous.

in the land section. It will tolerate occasional falls in temperature. The water can be kept clean by a small filter, but a 50% water change should be carried out every two weeks to prevent the buildup of harmful chemicals in the water.

HOW much time?
Five to ten minutes a day and up to one hour every two weeks for cleaning and terrarium maintenance, depending on the complexity of the setup.

WHAT varieties?
Oriental fire-belled toads may have bright green or greyish-brown backs. They are all the same species and their care is identical. The related giant fire-bellied toad, *Bombina maxima*, comes from China, is slightly larger, and has a very warty back. It is grey in color with an orange and black underside. It seems to prefer cooler conditions, but otherwise its care is similar to the oriental fire-bellied toad. This species is only rarely available.

WHAT care?
Daily feeding and regular water changes.

WHAT food?
Insects such as crickets, waxworms, and small earthworms. Try to provide a variety.

HOW easy are they to breed?
Breeding only takes place if the toads have had a cooler period of about two months during the winter. 59–68°F (15–20°C) seems to be cool enough to condition them and they need to be

kept on land, in moss, at this time. Warming them back up and putting them in water is often enough to induce

them to spawn. Raising the tadpoles is straightforward, but the newly metamorphosed toadlets are very small and need equally small food, such as hatchling crickets.

WHAT drawbacks?
None; these are excellent amphibians to keep, even for beginners.

Cost		
Setup cost		
Running cost		

Size: 2 in (5.5 cm)

Distribution: Southeast Asia

Life span: To 15 years

Left: The upper side is green, which provides camouflage when it is viewed from above.

Left: The giant fire-bellied toad is the largest in the genus and has a particularly warty back. The stocky forearms indicate that this individual is a male.

Bombina variegata

Yellow-bellied toad

A small semi-aquatic toad from Europe. It is grey or olive above, and its underside is yellow and black; some individuals have more yellow than others, and this depends partly on the subspecies, of which there are three. This active little toad lives in shallow bodies of water, often temporary ditches, etc. It prefers warm conditions but will tolerate cold.

WHAT temperament?
Very lively and amusing. It can be shy but overcomes its shyness if food is on offer.

WHAT accommodation?
An aqua-terrarium of 18 × 8 × 8 in (45 × 20 × 20 cm) with about 2 in (5 cm) of water and places to climb out is suitable for a small group of up to six adults. A more elaborate setup is possible, but they spend most of their time floating at the water's surface. Alternatively, they can be kept outside in the summer, in a shallow pool within an enclosure, or in a greenhouse.

WHAT environment?
A water temperature of 68–77°F (20–25°C) is ideal but they will tolerate much colder conditions. Their water must be changed occasionally.

HOW much time?
Five to ten minutes a day, with longer periods for cleaning and terrarium maintenance.

WHAT varieties?
The three subspecies are difficult to tell apart. There is another species, *Bombina pachypus*, from southern Italy, which is slightly larger. The fire-bellied toad, from northern Europe, is distinguished by a red and bluish-black underside. The latter two species are rarely seen in captivity.

Cost			
Setup cost			
Running cost			

Size: To 1.5 in (4 cm)
Distribution: Most of Europe (not Great Britain)
Life span: To 15 years; possibly longer

WHAT care?
Daily feeding and regular water changes.

WHAT food?
Insects such as crickets and small waxworms, and other small insects and spiders from the garden.

HOW easy are they to breed?
They often breed if kept in outdoor enclosures, after a cool period in winter. Raising the tadpoles is straightforward, but the young are very small at first.

WHAT drawbacks?
None. This species is a pleasure to keep, and captive-bred young are sometimes available.

Left: The yellow-bellied toad,
Bombina variegata, *is an undemanding European species that can be kept in very simple setups. It is easy to keep and breed.*

Discoglossus pictus

Painted frog

PROFILE

The painted frog is a small, sticky species with a scattering of small warts over its body. It is very variable in color and may be brown, greenish, yellow, or red, but always has a black mark behind its eyes, covering the eardrum. It lives in or around ponds, ditches and slow-running rivers and streams. The "original" painted frog, *D. pictus*, has been divided up into several similar species, so it can be difficult to find out which are being offered.

WHAT temperament?
Active in the day and at night. It spends much of its time in shallow water with just its head showing.

WHAT accommodation?
A terrarium measuring 24 × 12 × 12 in (60 × 30 × 30 cm) is a minimum size for one or two adults. One divided into equal land and aquatic areas is suitable, there should be somewhere, such as a piece of curved bark for them to hide on the land, and the water should be densely planted. They can also be kept outside in a greenhouse or cold frame.

WHAT environment?
Room temperature is adequate, and the lighting should be subdued.

HOW much time?
Five to ten minutes a day.

WHAT varieties?
There are several species of painted frogs from other parts of Europe and North Africa; they are similar in appearance and easily confused, but their requirements are the same.

WHAT care?
Daily feeding and occasional cleaning.

WHAT food?
Insects such as crickets, dusted with a vitamin and mineral supplement.

Below: The painted frog is variable, but all forms are attractive and do well in captivity.

HOW easy are they to breed?
They breed readily in outdoor enclosures, but breeding in a terrarium could be more difficult.

WHAT drawbacks?
Hard to obtain, although a number of breeders produce young every year.

Cost			
Setup cost			
Running cost			

Size: 2–3 in (5–8 cm)
Distribution: Europe and North Africa
Life span: Unknown; probably at least 5 years

Pelobates fuscus

Common spadefoot toad

PROFILE

A plump toad with smooth skin and huge, golden-colored eyes. It may be brown, grey, sand-colored or reddish, and the markings on its back are similarly variable. Like other European spadefoot toads, it lives in flat areas of sand dunes, heaths, open woods, and cultivated fields. It spends most of its life below the surface and burrows backwards, using the sharp-edged "spades" on its hind feet. It emerges at night, especially in wet weather, to feed and breed.

WHAT temperament?

Very adaptable and tolerant of a limited amount of handling in captivity.

WHAT accommodation?

A terrarium measuring about 24 × 6 × 6 in (60 × 15 × 15 cm) is ideal for an adult pair or group of juveniles. Height is not as

important as floor area, and the substrate should consist of at least 4 in (10 cm) of sandy soil. Pure sand is not as satisfactory as a mixture of sand and loam. A few pieces of flat slate or bark will help the substrate to retain moisture locally when the rest of the terrarium is dry. Alternatively, they can be kept outside in a cold frame or greenhouse.

WHAT environment?

Room temperature is suitable, ranging from about 59–73°F (15–23°C). The substrate should never be allowed to dry out completely, but neither should it become waterlogged.

HOW much time?

Five to ten minutes a day.

WHAT varieties?

No varieties, but the western spadefoot toad, *P. cultripes*, is sometimes available and can be cared for in the same way.

WHAT care?

Daily feeding and checking the water content of the substrate.

Cost			
Setup cost			
Running cost			

Size: 2–2.5 in (5–6 cm), females larger than males

Distribution: Central and eastern Europe

Life span: Many years

Above and left: The common spadefoot toad is an interesting and attractive toad, but it spends most of its time beneath the surface in a burrow and is therefore not a good display species.

WHAT food?

Small insects such as crickets and cockroaches.

HOW easy are they to breed?

Captive breeding takes place regularly. They require a dry spell followed by plenty of water.

WHAT drawbacks?

They only emerge onto the surface at night.

Scaphiopus couchii

Couch's spadefoot toad

PROFILE

A North American desert toad that spends much of its life below ground, using the horny "spades" on its hind feet to dig backwards into the soil until it is completely hidden. It emerges during rain to breed and feed. It is yellowish-brown or yellowish-green in color, with blotches of darker brown markings. The females are more boldly marked than the males. Both sexes have bright yellow eyes.

WHAT temperament?
A placid toad that is highly nocturnal and rarely seen on the surface during the day.

WHAT accommodation?
A terrarium of 24 × 12 × 12 in (60 × 30 × 30 cm) is suitable for a pair or small group. The substrate should be sandy soil, to a depth of at least 4 in (10 cm), and a few pieces of bark or cork can be scattered on the surface. There is no need for a water bowl if the substrate is kept moist.

WHAT environment?
A temperature of 59–77°F (15–25°C) is suitable, but cooler conditions are tolerated.

HOW much time?
Five to ten minutes a day.

WHAT varieties?
There are other species of American spadefoot toads, which all require similar conditions.

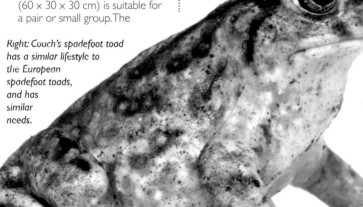

Right: Couch's spadefoot toad has a similar lifestyle to the European spadefoot toads, and has similar needs.

Cost				
Setup cost				
Running cost				

Size: 2–3 in (5–8 cm)

Distribution: North America (south-central states and south into Mexico)

Life span: Unknown

WHAT care?
Daily feeding, which should be done in the evening. Do not feed if food from the previous night is still in the terrarium. Otherwise, regular checking to ensure that the substrate does not dry out.

WHAT food?
Insects such as crickets and cockroaches.

HOW easy are they to breed?
Difficult. It would be necessary to allow them to remain underground in cool, dry conditions for several weeks or months before raising the temperature and inundating the terrarium with water.

WHAT drawbacks?
Secretive and rarely seen. Captive-bred individuals are rarely, if ever, available.

Megophrys nasuta

Asian horned frog

PROFILE

A strange but interesting frog from Southeast Asia, with a leaf-like shape and coloration, short legs, a pointed snout, and a horn-like projection over each eye. It is a rainforest species, extremely well camouflaged among dead leaves, and with a wide mouth that can accommodate large prey.

Above: The Asian horned frog is a strange species; its shape imitates dead leaves.

Cost			
Setup cost			
Running cost			

Size: 3.5–6 in (9–16 cm), females almost twice as large

Distribution: Southeast Asia

Life span: Not known; at least 10 years; probably longer

WHAT temperament?

Adapts well to captivity provided the correct conditions are provided.

WHAT accommodation?

A large terrarium measuring at least 24 × 12 × 12 in (60 × 30 × 30 cm) is suitable for one or two individuals. A substrate of sand or loam, covered with a deep layer of dead leaves and some logs or bark to hide under, is sufficient. Much larger terrariums are preferable, though, and these should incorporate an area of running water if you hope to breed them.

WHAT environment?

Tropical. 77°F (25°C) in the day, 68°F (20°C) at night are ideal, but they will tolerate cooler conditions if they are healthy. Humidity needs to be high at all times, but ventilation should be good.

HOW much time?

Ten to fifteen minutes a day.

WHAT varieties?

None. There are related species, but none of them appear in the pet trade.

WHAT care?

Daily feeding, which should take place in the evening, spraying once or twice per day; general terrarium maintenance.

WHAT food?

Large insects such as crickets and cockroaches, which should be dusted with a vitamin and mineral powder at each feed.

HOW easy are they to breed?

Very difficult. Elaborate artificial streams are required and the tadpoles are specialized and hard to rear.

WHAT drawbacks?

Lack of a supply of captive-bred young, and wild-caught individuals are often in poor condition.

Left: This photograph of a pair of Asian horned frogs in amplexus shows the great size discrepancy between males and females.

Dendropsophus marmoratus

Marbled tree frog

PROFILE

This species is fairly new on the pet scene but is interesting and easily cared for. Its main characteristic is its camouflage pattern: although this is sometimes thought to be an imitation of a bird dropping, it is more likely that it disguises the frog when it is resting on weathered and lichen-covered branches. The underside is more brightly colored, being black and bright yellow in males and slightly less colorful in females. It occurs in the Amazon Basin and requires tropical conditions.

Above: The marbled tree frog is strictly nocturnal, foraging for small insects during the hours of darkness.

WHAT temperament?
Nocturnal but rests in full view during the day, often on a surface that it resembles, making it an interesting exhibit.

WHAT accommodation?
A tall or cube-shaped terrarium measuring about 18 × 18 × 24 in (45 × 45 × 60 cm) is suitable for a pair or small group. This should be set up with a substrate that holds moisture such as leaf litter or coconut fiber; branches and vines for the frogs to climb on; and some plants, preferably living varieties such as creeping figs and bromeliads.

WHAT environment?
Moist tropical: the ideal temperature seems to be around 73–77°F (23–25°C) during the day but this can be allowed to drop at night. Frequent spraying is necessary and the cage should be well-ventilated.

HOW much time?
Five to ten minutes a day.

WHAT varieties?
None as far as is known.

WHAT care?
Daily feeding and spraying.

WHAT food?
Small insects such as crickets and flies. Meals should be dusted with a vitamin and mineral supplement and offered in the evening, before they can clean off the powder.

Cost			
Setup cost			
Running cost			

Size: 1–1.5 in (2.5–3.5 cm)

Distribution: South America

Life span: Not known

HOW easy are they to breed?
Not known. They would probably require a rain chamber and small pool in which to spawn.

WHAT drawbacks?
None, but captive-bred young do not appear to be available at the moment.

Above: The mottled pattern provides excellent camouflage when the frog is resting on lichen-covered surfaces.

Hyla arborea

European green tree frog

PROFILE

A bright green tree frog with expanded "sticky" toes. It has a brown stripe along its flank, which distinguishes it from closely related species. This species can change color rapidly, turning brown or buff, and some individuals have spots on their backs. Its call is loud and raucous, and repeated many times. One calling male will soon set off any others within earshot.

WHAT temperament?

A lively tree frog that is often active during the day and adapts well to captivity.

WHAT accommodation?

A tall terrarium, measuring about 24 in (60 cm) high, is ideal. It should contain branches and plants, preferably living, for the frogs to climb and hide among, although they will spend much of the time adhering to the glass walls of the terrarium. A pool of water will

Left: Many tree frogs have expanded discs at the ends of their toes.

prevent them from drying out. Lights will be necessary if living plants are included.

WHAT environment?

Not delicate; a temperature of 64–77°F (18–25°C) will suit them most of the time and they will tolerate much cooler conditions. Room temperature is usually perfectly adequate. They can be kept outside in a greenhouse in northern Europe.

HOW much time?

Five to ten minutes a day.

WHAT varieties?

There is a bright blue mutation that occurs very rarely in wild populations. There are

Cost			
Setup cost			
Running cost			

Size: 1.5–2 in (4–5 cm)

Distribution: Northern, central and eastern Europe, parts of Spain and Portugal

Life span: At least 10 years; possibly as long as 20

also at least three other European tree frogs, all of which differ only slightly from each other. They all require similar conditions.

WHAT care?

Daily feeding and spraying.

WHAT food?

Insects and spiders. They are especially fond of flying insects, including house flies.

HOW easy are they to breed?

Frequently bred outdoors in greenhouses and conservatories, and occasionally indoors in large terrariums. A period of cooling in winter seems to be important, followed by warmer conditions in spring.

WHAT drawbacks?

They can be noisy (to say the least). Captive-bred animals should be obtainable.

Left: The European green tree frog, Hyla arborea.

Hyla cinerea

American green tree frog

PROFILE

A medium-sized tree frog with expanded toe pads typical of this family. It is bright grass-green above with a very distinctive cream stripe along each flank, although this is absent in some individuals. It occurs in a variety of habitats and is sometimes seen on windows at night, hunting insects that are attracted there by lights. Males have a quacking or "quenk-quenk" call that can be quite loud. Humid weather can start them off but so can noises outside their terrarium (one of mine used to call every time I started to use a typewriter).

Cost			
Setup cost			
Running cost			

Size: 1–2 in (3–5.5 cm)

Distribution: Southeastern United States

Life span: Unknown; probably 10 years or more

HOW much time?

Five to ten minutes a day; slightly longer for terrarium maintenance.

WHAT varieties?

None, other than minor variation between individuals.

WHAT temperament?

Usually settles well in captivity, although it is most active at night.

WHAT accommodation?

A tall terrarium, measuring at least 24 in (60 cm) high, is necessary, and this should contain branches and leafy plants for the frogs to climb and hide among. A pool of water will safeguard them from drying out.

WHAT environment?

A temperature of 68–77°F (20–25°C) will keep them active and feeding well but lower temperatures are tolerated for short periods. Humidity should be kept fairly high at all time. Lights are only necessary if living plants are included.

WHAT care?

Feeding every day and spraying at least once each day.

WHAT food?

Small insects such as crickets as well as other insects and spiders that can be caught outdoors.

HOW easy are they to breed?

Hardly ever attempted, but it should not be difficult. They would require a cool period followed by higher temperatures and simulated rain.

WHAT drawbacks?

Only wild-caught individuals are available. Some people object to the loud calling, whereas others enjoy it.

Above and top: The American green tree frog is an attractive grass-green species with a distinctive cream line running down its flanks.

39

Hyla gratiosa

Barking tree frog

Size: 2–2.5 in (5–6.5 cm)

Distribution: Southeastern United States

Life span: Unknown; probably at least 10 years

PROFILE

A stocky, bright green tree frog with round brown spots over its back and limbs. It sometimes changes to a dark green or brown overall coloration, but the spots remain. Its skin is slightly pebbled. It is mainly arboreal but occasionally burrows into sand or soil to avoid dry conditions. Its name is a clue to its call, which is a single, loud, raucous bark, which is easily mistaken for a dog.

WHAT temperament?

Adapts well to captivity and displays well, although it is most active at night.

WHAT accommodation?

A tall cage, measuring at least 24 in (60 cm) high, containing stout branches, and one or two strong plants is ideal. The substrate can be soil or a peat substitute, or a mixture of either of these with sand. A pool of water will protect them from drying out.

WHAT environment?

A temperature of 68–77°F (20–25°C) will keep them active, but lower temperatures are tolerated for short periods. Humidity should be fairly high, although they avoid dry conditions by burrowing. Lights are only necessary if living plants are included.

HOW much time?

Five to ten minutes a day, plus extra time for terrarium maintenance.

WHAT varieties?

None. There is some variation in color between individuals.

WHAT care?

Feeding every day and spraying at least once each day.

WHAT food?

Small insects such as crickets, dusted with a vitamin and mineral supplement at each feeding.

Right: Barking tree frog, Hyla gratiosa.

Above: This is a stocky tree frog that sometimes burrows to avoid dry conditions. It needs a large terrarium with plenty of sturdy plants and branches. It has a loud barking call.

HOW easy are they to breed?

Hardly ever attempted. A period of cooling would probably be required, followed by a warmer, more humid spell.

WHAT drawbacks?

Only wild-caught individuals are available. The loud calls may disturb some people.

Hyla versicolor and *Hyla chrysoscelis*

Grey tree frogs

PROFILE

These two tree frogs are identical to look at, but their calls differ. They are pale grey, mottled with darker grey, sometimes with greyish-green patches, which makes them well camouflaged when they are resting on lichen-covered branches. When they move, however, they expose a bright orange patch of skin on their thighs. They are highly arboreal and hardly ever come down to the ground, and this has to be taken into account when caring for them.

WHAT temperament?
They are not nervous and seem to adapt well to captivity, although they are not often seen due to their camouflage coloration.

WHAT accommodation?
A tall terrarium measuring at least 24 in (60 cm) high, with branches (preferably lichen-covered) for them to rest on. Epiphytic plants such as Spanish moss, *Tillandsia usneoides*, are very suitable for this type of setup.

WHAT environment?
A temperature of 68–77°F (20–25°C) will keep them active but they tolerate much colder conditions, down to 50°F (10°C) if necessary. It seems likely that the southern species, *Hyla chrysoscelis*, is less tolerant of the cold than the *H. versicolor* (which, of course,

is not much help if you don't know which species you have). The humidity is not so important, provided they are not allowed to dry out completely; they can be kept fairly dry if they are cooled off for any reason.

HOW much time?
Five to ten minutes each day.

Cost			
Setup cost			
Running cost			

Size: 2–2.5 in (5–6.5 cm)

Distribution: Eastern North America

Life span: Unknown; probably 10 years or more

WHAT varieties?
No varieties, but two species are involved and both are "grey" tree frogs. *Hyla chrysoscelis* is known as the southern grey tree frog, and *H. versicolor* is known as the eastern grey tree frog. Unless you know where they came from it is impossible to be sure of their identity.

WHAT care?
Daily feeding and occasional spraying.

WHAT food?
Small insects such as crickets, and

Above: Grey tree frogs are often available and make good subjects for a planted, naturalistic terrarium.

sweepings (tiny insects gathered from the wild).

HOW easy are they to breed?
Hardly ever attempted.

WHAT drawbacks?
Little or no supply of captive-bred individuals.

Osteopilus septentrionalis

Cuban tree frog

This tree frog is usually brown or tan in color but sometimes green or very pale beige. Females grow very large and will eat almost anything they can fit into their mouths, including smaller frogs, so this species should be kept separately from other tree frogs. It has been accidentally introduced into Florida, where it has spread and become very common. They are very adaptable and will live under a range of conditions.

WHAT temperament?
Adapts well to captivity, although they are nocturnal and hide away during the day, emerging in the evening to look for food.

WHAT accommodation?
Large cages measuring at least 24 × 24 × 24 in (60 × 60 × 60 cm) are required for a pair or small group. The substrate can be coconut fiber or leaves, and large branches and leafy plants are necessary to give them places to hide. A large water bowl can be included.

WHAT environment?
A temperature of 73–82°F (23–28°C) is ideal, but they will easily tolerate much lower temperatures for short spells. Daily spraying will raise the humidity, but they can withstand quite dry conditions for short periods of time.

HOW much time?
Five to ten minutes per day.

Above and below: The Cuban tree frog is a large, variable, and very adaptable species that is easily cared for in a large terrarium.

WHAT varieties?
None, although the species is variable in color.

WHAT care?
Daily spraying and feeding three or four times per week.

Cost			
Setup cost			
Running cost			

Size: 3–5 in (8–12 cm), females are larger than males

Distribution: West Indies, including Cuba, and Florida. Now spreading into Georgia

Life span: Unknown, but at least 10 years

WHAT food?
Large insects such as crickets, wax-worms, and cockroaches, dusted with a vitamin and mineral powder.

HOW easy are they to breed?
Rarely bred in captivity, although the reasons for this are unclear; perhaps they are considered to be too common to be worth the effort.

WHAT drawbacks?
None, although they must be kept separately from other small amphibians.

Trachycephalus resinifictrix

Amazonian milk frog

PROFILE

Also known as the clown frog, this species has bands of white or very pale grey on a brown or greenish background. Juveniles are more strikingly marked than adults, in which the bands tend to break up into blotches. This bright coloration is a warning to predators that the frog can produce a milky, poisonous secretion from its skin, which is the reason for its common name. They live and breed in holes in large rain forest trees.

WHAT temperament?
Adaptable and calm. Nocturnal but may become active in the evening.

WHAT accommodation?
A terrarium of at least 12 × 18 × 24 in (30 × 45 × 60 cm) high is suitable for two or three frogs. The substrate can be coconut fiber, leaf litter, or a mixture of both. A water bowl should be included, and there should be stout branches and living or artificial plants to give them somewhere to hide and rest.

WHAT environment?
Tropical. A daytime temperature of 73–77°F (23–28°C) is required, but this can be allowed to fall to 68°F (20°C) at night. A fairly high humidity should be maintained, but good ventilation is important.

HOW much time?
Five to ten minutes a day.

WHAT varieties?
None.

WHAT care?
Regular feeding and spraying. The water in the bowl should be changed whenever it is dirty.

WHAT food?
Insects such as crickets, dusted with a vitamin and mineral powder.

HOW easy are they to breed?
They are bred in captivity but need specialized conditions. A regime of dry conditions followed by a spell in a rain chamber is necessary, and they should be given a container with a small entrance hole and a few centimeters of water to simulate the tree-holes in which they breed naturally.

WHAT drawbacks?
None. The milky secretions are poisonous in wild individuals, precautions should be taken after handling them.

Cost			
Setup cost			
Running cost			

Size: 2.5–4 in (6–10 cm), females are larger than males

Distribution: Amazon Basin

Life span: Probably 10 years or more

Above: This species is placid and can be handled easily. Its skin contains a milky toxin, however, so it is not a suitable pet for children.

Above: The Amazonian milk frog is a colorful species that has proved to be quite easy to breed in captivity, if the right conditions are provided.

Agalychnis callidryas

Red-eyed leaf frog

This frog epitomizes tropical rain forests, especially those of Central America. It is a stunningly beautiful, bright green frog with blue and cream flanks and large, brilliant red eyes. There is some geographical variation in the colors and patterns on its flanks and thighs. This is a fairly large frog, with long, thin legs and large sticky pads at the tips of its toes. It is well camouflaged when resting on leaves during the day, and its eyes have a secondary eyelid that has an intricate pattern of gold filigree. It lives in the canopy of rain forests, descending only to breed. Like all the leaf frogs, this species lays its eggs on leaves hanging above forest pools. When the tadpoles hatch, they wriggle down the leaf and drop off into the water below. The adults are poor swimmers and can drown if they are trapped in deep water.

The leaf frogs belong to the family that contains many other species of tree frogs, the Hylidae, but they are placed in a separate subfamily, the Phyllomedusinae. They have special requirements in captivity, being large and completely arboreal. They have a large following, however, and although breeding some species is a challenge, captive-bred young of several species are available occasionally.

WHAT temperament?

Very calm and slow-moving, but normally active only at night.

WHAT accommodation?

Very large, tall terrariums are required. One measuring at least 24 in (60 cm) high, with a floor area of 24 × 18 in (60 × 45 cm) is about right for a group of three or four adults. It should be furnished with tough-leaved house plants such as *Philodendron* and *Anthurium* species. The frogs will spend the day on a large leaf or on the sides of the terrarium, becoming active in the evening. The substrate can be leaf litter, soil, or coconut husk (coir), which should be pressed down. Alternatively, the floor can be left bare and the plants placed in flower pots. Young frogs need smaller

Top: Spurrell's leaf frog is a close relative but not common in captivity.

Left: The red-eyed leaf frog is arguably the most spectacular of all species.

terrariums, with a floor covering of paper towels at first so that they can find their food easily.

WHAT environment?

Tropical. A temperature of 73–82°F (23–28°C) is needed during the day, and it can be allowed to fall to around 68°F (20°C) at night. High humidity is required, and this can be achieved in large cages by using automatic misting systems.

HOW much time?

About fifteen minutes each day for feeding, spraying, and general maintenance. Longer periods, up to a whole day or more, will be required for a complete terrarium overhaul, the exact time depending on the complexity of the setup.

WHAT varieties?

None, apart from regional variations in pattern. Related species that are sometimes available include Spurrell's leaf frog, *Agalychnis spurrelli*, and several members of the genus *Phyllomedusa*, such as the tiger-legged monkey frog, *P. hypochondrialis*.

WHAT care?

Feeding every one or two days and spraying daily (unless an automatic system is installed). Juveniles need to be fed every day.

Cost				
Setup cost				
Running cost				

Size: 2–2.5 in (5–6 cm), females are larger than males

Distribution: Central America, from southern Mexico to Colombia

Life span: At least 10 years in captivity

Left: The tiger-legged monkey frog, P. hypochondrialis, from South America.

WHAT food?

Insects such as crickets and waxworms, always dusted with a vitamin and mineral supplement. Flying insects such as flies and moths and spiders are particularly useful.

HOW easy are they to breed?

Breeding requires a special "rain chamber" with a system comprising a pump and sprinkler bar that can be timed to operate for up to an hour twice each day. The water should drain into a reservoir containing the pump, where it will be re-circulated. Large pot plants should be positioned in the chamber for egg-laying.

WHAT drawbacks?

Rather delicate regarding temperature, but otherwise no real problems provided captive-bred individuals are obtained in the first place.

Phyllomedusa sauvagii

Waxy frog

A leaf frog with a difference! This species comes from the dry Chaco region of South America and protects itself from drying out by coating its body in a waxy secretion that it wipes over its skin using its hind legs. It is green in color with a well-defined white line along its flanks and others on its underside. It is arboreal, like the other species, and lays its eggs on leaves overhanging water.

WHAT temperament?
Very placid and adaptable. Nocturnal.

WHAT accommodation?
A tall terrarium, measuring at least 24 in (60 cm) high and 18 × 18 in (45 × 45 cm) floor area is the minimum for a pair or a small group of juveniles. A substrate of coir, orchid bark, or leaf litter is required, as well as several stout branches and a living or artificial plant for the frogs to climb on.

WHAT environment?
A daytime background temperature of 68–77°F (20–25°C) is required, and this can be supplemented during part of each day by a spotlight to create a basking area rising to 86°F (30°C) at the top of the cage. Humidity is important, but this species prefers to be drier than most other leaf frogs. The substrate should not be allowed to dry out completely. Ventilation is very important.

HOW much time?
Five to ten minutes a day.

WHAT varieties?
No varieties of this species, but the giant waxy frog, *Phyllomedusa bicolor,* is similar but larger. Its natural habitat is much more humid, however.

WHAT care?
Feeding every two or three days and occasional spraying.

Cost				
Setup cost				
Running cost				

Size: 2–3 in (5–7 cm), females larger than males

Distribution: Northern Argentina and Paraguay, east Bolivia, southern Brazil

Life span: Unknown; probably 10 years or more

Above: Waxy frogs tolerate dry conditions.

WHAT food?
Insects such as crickets and flies, dusted with a vitamin and mineral powder.

HOW easy are they to breed?
Difficult. They need a long, dry period followed by some time in a rain chamber.

WHAT drawbacks?
Captive-bred young are rare and therefore expensive.

Above: This frog has a characteristically slow, deliberate gait.

Lepidobatrachus laevis

Budgett's frog

PROFILE

Budgett's frog is related to the horned frogs, *Ceratophrys*, and its basic body plan is similar—a stocky body, wide head, and large mouth. They lack the horns, however, and their skin is very smooth. Their eyes are positioned on top of the head, looking up, so that they can see while they are partially submerged. They are grey in color with a network of orange or tan lines over the back. This species lives in temporary pools in a region that has a dry season; if its pond dries out, it burrows down and forms a cocoon around itself to prevent desiccation, reappearing on the surface only when fresh rains flood the pond again.

WHAT temperament?
Usually placid but may be aggressive; some individuals bite.

WHAT accommodation?
A semi-aquatic terrarium is required. One measuring about 12 × 24 × 24 in (30 × 60 × 60 cm) is suitable for a single adult, and the land area should contain a deep substrate such as sphagnum or coconut fiber. The water area needs no substrate and should be easy to clean.

WHAT environment?
A temperature of 68–77°F (20–25°C) is ideal, but lower and higher temperatures are tolerated for short periods.

HOW much time?
Five to ten minutes a day.

WHAT varieties?
No varieties, but there are two other species in the genus, rarely seen in captivity.

WHAT care?
Feeding once or twice each week and partial or total water changes whenever the water becomes dirty.

WHAT food?
Large insects such as crickets and locusts, as well as earthworms. All meals should be dusted with a vitamin and mineral powder. Some Budgett's frogs will take small mice, which should be thoroughly thawed and offered with feeding forceps.

HOW easy are they to breed?
Breeding is very difficult without access to hormones.

WHAT drawbacks?
Excellent pets, but some may bite.

Cost			
Setup cost			
Running cost			

Size: 3–4 in (8–11 cm), females are larger than males	
Distribution: South America	
Life span: Unknown, but at least 5 years	

Left: Budgett's frogs have extremely wide mouths, to say the least!

Litoria caerulea

White's tree frog

PROFILE

This Australian species is one of the more rotund tree frogs, a characteristic that has given it the alternate name of "dumpy frog." It has short, stocky limbs and large discs on the tips of its fingers. Like other Australasian tree frogs, their pupils are horizontal; tree frogs from other parts of the world have vertical pupils. There is an elongated fold of fatty flesh behind its eyes that can grow very large in older individuals, partly covering the tops of the eardrums. They are naturally bright green, although many captive-bred strains are bluish-green or even greyish-blue, and they can change their color to a limited degree. Their skin can secrete a waxy substance to prevent them from drying out during very hot weather. They are nocturnal and rest during the day with their limbs tucked under their body. This is a very adaptable species that is often found in

Above: White-lipped tree frogs, Litoria infrafrenata, *are from the same part of the southern hemisphere as White's tree frogs. They are large but not as heavily built. They are more active.*

houses in Australia, as well as in holes in trees and other more natural situations. It therefore adapts well to captivity, and its personality has made it a very popular pet. It is bred in fair numbers, and captive-bred young are often available at a reasonable price. They grow quickly and are usually easy to rear.

WHAT temperament?

Slow and deliberate in their movements. They seem to tolerate handling more than many other frogs. Naturally nocturnal but may become active during the day when food is available.

WHAT accommodation?

A large terrarium is required. It should be at least 24 in (60 cm) high, and the floor space should be 24 x 18 in (60 x 45 cm) for two or three specimens. The substrate can be leaf litter or coconut fiber (coir), and they will also require stout leaves and branches to rest on, preferably toward the top of the terrarium. A small water bowl will prevent them from drying out.

WHAT environment?

Hot and fairly dry. A daytime background temperature of 68–86°F (20–30°C) is required, and humidity can be relatively

Left: White's tree frog, Litoria caerulea.

Right: This species has sticky pads on its toes; juveniles tend to climb more than adults, which can become obese.

low for this species. The substrate should not be allowed to dry out completely, however, and ventilation is very important.

HOW much time?

Five to ten minutes a day.

WHAT varieties?

There are no varieties of this species, but the white-lipped tree frog, *Litoria infrafrenata*, is quite similar and is sometimes available. It is not as placid as White's tree frog, however, and requires a large cage and lots of cover; otherwise it is inclined to damage its snout by leaping into the glass sides of the terrarium.

WHAT care?

Daily feeding. Large adults can become obese, however, and their feeding can be reduced to once or twice each week until they return to normal. They can be sprayed each day, but the atmosphere in the terrarium should dry out between sprayings. The substrate should retain some moisture, and a small bowl of water should be present all the time.

WHAT food?

Insects, including crickets, in large quantities. These are greedy frogs and they will take almost anything that they can catch. Every meal should be dusted with a vitamin and mineral powder.

HOW easy are they to breed?

They are bred regularly, but some strains seem to be getting weak; perhaps fresh genetic stock would help. They require a regime of gradual drying out followed by some time in a rain chamber. Females lay up to 500 eggs, and the tadpoles are easy to raise.

Below: This is one of the best tree frogs for beginners as it tolerates a range of conditions.

Cost					
Setup cost					
Running cost					

Size: 2.5–4 in (6–11 cm), females are larger than males

Distribution: Northern half of Australia, parts of New Guinea and introduced into New Zealand

Life span: 10 years or more; the record is 21 years

WHAT drawbacks?

None, other than the problem of weak and poorly colored captive-bred stock; they should be bright green, but captive-bred individuals are often dull bluish-grey. Wild individuals are rarely available because most of their range is within Australia, which does not allow the export of wild animals.

South American horned frogs

PROFILE

These frogs have become one of the most popular pet frogs owing to their personalities, ease of care, and attractive coloration. They are also known as "Pac-man frogs." There are a number of species, of which the two most likely to be encountered are the Argentine horned frog, *Ceratophrys ornata* (also known as Bell's horned frog), and Cranwell's horned frog, also known as the Chacoan horned frog, *Ceratophrys cranwelli*. Confusingly, *C. cranwelli* is also known as the Argentine horned frog in some publications. Others are of uncertain parentage, including the so-called "fantasy" horned frog, which is, apparently, a hybrid between *C. cranwelli* and another species, the Surinam horned frog, *Ceratophrys cornuta*. Fortunately, the care of all the species and varieties that are likely to occur in the pet trade is similar. The horns that give them their names are only present in some species and vary in size.

Above: All the South American horned frogs are burrowers by nature that ambush their prey.

WHAT temperament?

Horned frogs adapt well to captivity given the correct conditions, which is why they have become so popular.

WHAT accommodation?

Horned frogs can be almost as wide as they are long, and their mouths reach from one side of their head to the other. Males and females are roughly the same size. Horned frogs must be kept in individual terrariums; they have huge gapes and will attempt to eat other creatures as large as themselves, including other members of the same species. Suitable terrariums depend very much on the size of the frog. Juveniles need only a floor space of about 8 × 16 in (20 × 40 cm) but they will soon outgrow this size and eventually require a terrarium measuring at least 12 × 24 in (30 × 60 cm). Height is not important as they do not climb, but the terrarium should be covered to prevent other pets from getting in. As they are burrowing species, they require a suitable substrate such as sphagnum, coconut fiber, or rotted leaf litter. Gravel or bark chippings are not suitable and will most certainly lead to problems, as the frogs will accidentally swallow pieces while feeding. The substrate should be damp but not wet and deep enough for the frog to burrow down completely until it is hidden from view. A few pieces of bark will give them something to shuffle down under and help to maintain some moisture. A water bowl is useful in providing local humidity.

Left: Juveniles are about the size and shape of a golf ball but grow quickly due to their prodigious appetites.

Cost		
Setup cost		
Running cost		

Size: C. ornata can grow to 5 in (12 cm); other species are slightly smaller than this

Distribution: South America

Life span: Many years; possibly to 10 years

Above and right: Large adults tend to spread sideways as they grow until they are as wide as they are long. Their legs are small, but they have no need to move fast.

WHAT environment?

Tropical. 77°F (25°C) in the day, 68°F (20°C) at night are ideal, but they will tolerate cooler conditions if they are healthy. Ventilation should be good.

HOW much time?

Five to ten minutes a day.

WHAT varieties?

There are many types, including the species and hybrids listed above, as well as albinos and other color forms.

WHAT care?

Daily spraying and general terrarium maintenance. Feeding is only necessary every other day for juveniles, and weekly for adults.

WHAT food?

Juveniles will require insects such as crickets and cockroaches, which should be dusted with a vitamin and mineral powder at each feed. Adults take much larger food items, including large earthworms, waxworms, and locusts. Some will accept dead mice that have been thoroughly thawed out, but these should be given only occasionally.

HOW easy are they to breed?

Difficult. Commercial breeders invariably use hormone injections to condition the adults and obtain eggs. A period of dry conditions followed by several days in a rain chamber sometimes stimulates them to breed. Care must be taken when introducing the male and the female.

WHAT drawbacks?

Some captive-bred strains are weak, especially the more unusual color forms, which are often inbred. Although most will tolerate some handling, a few will bite, which is not pleasant as they have powerful jaws; avoid dangling fingers in front of them as they may be mistaken for food.

Amietophrynus regularis

Square-marked toad

PROFILE

A large toad with smoother skin than many related species. It is generally grey, brown, or olive in color with a number of large, regular, darker markings on its back, arranged symmetrically on either side of a pale line that runs down the center. There is much variation in color and markings, and some toads going by this name may actually be different species. It lives in a range of habitats, including desert oases, grasslands, and forests. It is often common around towns and villages, and it sometimes goes under the name of African common toad.

WHAT temperament?
Nocturnal but will learn to feed during the evening. Very placid and responsive.

WHAT accommodation?
A terrarium with a floor area of about 24 × 18 in (60 × 45 cm) is the minimum for one or two adults, but larger cages are better. The substrate can be coconut fiber, leaf litter, or leaf litter mixed with sand. It should be several centimeters deep, and kept slightly moist in places by laying some flat pieces of bark or stone on the surface.

WHAT environment?
Tropical conditions are required: a temperature of 73–82°F (23–28°C) for at least part of each day, although it can become cooler at night. The terrarium should not be too humid; just some localized areas of damp substrate and perhaps a small water bowl will be sufficient.

HOW much time?
Five to ten minutes a day.

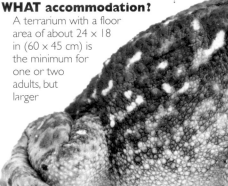

Cost	
Setup cost	
Running cost	

Size: 3.5–5 in (9–11 cm), females are larger than males

Distribution: West and Central Africa

Life span: Several years; exact information is unknown

WHAT varieties?
None, although there are several similar species.

WHAT care?
Daily feeding and light spraying.

WHAT food?
Small insects such as crickets. Some wild insects should be given to vary the diet.

HOW easy are they to breed?
Not bred in captivity.

WHAT drawbacks?
None, other than the lack of captive-bred young.

Left: This individual is lighter in color than some, and the species as a whole is highly variable, both in coloration and markings.

Anaxyrus cognatus

Plains toad

PROFILE

A large; chubby; pale brown, grey, or olive toad previously called *Bufo cognatus*. Its markings consist of large blotches of darker coloration arranged on either side of a central pale stripe, and there are two elongated poison glands above its eyes. It lives in the dry grasslands of the American prairies and breeds in temporary pools, ditches, and flooded fields after heavy summer rains.

WHAT temperament?

A placid and adaptable species. Naturally nocturnal but may become accustomed to emerging in the evening for food.

WHAT accommodation?

It requires a terrarium with a floor area of at least 24 × 18 in (60 × 45 cm) for one or two adults, but larger cages are better. The substrate can be leaf litter or coconut fiber mixed with sand. It should be several centimeters deep and kept slightly moist in places by occasional spraying and by laying some flat pieces of bark or stone on the surface.

WHAT environment?

It will be active with a temperature range of 59-73°F (15–23°C) and hibernates for long periods of time in parts of its range so it can tolerate much lower temperatures, provided it is well fed and in good condition.

Above: The plains toad is almost totally terrestrial in its habits, living under rocks and logs.

HOW much time?

Five to ten minutes a day.

WHAT varieties?

None. Several other toads from the region require similar care and conditions.

WHAT care?

Daily feeding and light spraying.

WHAT food?

Insects such as crickets. It will eat

Cost		
Setup cost		
Running cost		

Size: 2–4 in (5–11 cm)

Distribution: Central plains of North America, from Canada to Mexico

Life span: Many years; exact information is unknown

a variety of wild-caught insects, including woodlice.

HOW easy are they to breed?

Captive breeding has probably not been achieved.

WHAT drawbacks?

None apart from the lack of captive-bred young.

Left: Plains toads are heavily built, placid, and attractively marked.

Anaxyrus debilis

Western green toad

A small, dainty toad with a flattened body and attractive network of black markings on a green or yellowish-green background. It lives in dry regions of the American south and southwest, in desert scrub and dry grasslands—wherever there is a sandy soil into which it can burrow. It spends most of the year underground, emerging after heavy rains to breed in temporary pools and flooded desert flats.

WHAT temperament?
A lively toad that may not always adapt to captivity well, especially in the long term.

WHAT accommodation?
It requires a terrarium with a floor area of at least 24 × 18 in (60 × 45 cm) for two adults. Height is not important, but the cage should be covered. The substrate should be sandy soil, loose enough for the toad to burrow into and deep enough for it to cover itself completely. A few pieces of flat rock will help to keep parts of the substrate moist, and a water bowl should be available.

WHAT environment?
A temperature of 68–77°F (20–25°C) is ideal, but cooler conditions are tolerated. The substrate should be mostly dry, with only the lower layer holding some moisture. Occasional spraying in the evening may encourage the toads to be active; otherwise, they

Cost			
Setup cost			
Running cost			

Size: 1.5–3 in (4–8 cm)

Distribution: Southern and southwest North America, including Mexico

Life span: Unknown

Above: This toad lives in dry deserts and semi-desert habitats.

Right: This is one of the more colorful species in its family.

are inclined to burrow out of sight for long periods.

HOW much time?
Five to ten minutes a day.

WHAT varieties?
None. The Sonoran green toad has similar coloration but is larger and very rare.

WHAT care?
Daily feeding in the evening and light spraying.

WHAT food?
Insects such as crickets and small cockroaches.

HOW easy are they to breed?
Captive breeding has probably not been achieved. They would require a long, dry period, followed by several days in a rain chamber.

WHAT drawbacks?
This is a difficult species, and the lack of captive-bred young makes it a challenge; only for more experienced amphibian keepers.

Melanophryniscus stelzneri

Bumblebee toad

PROFILE

These startlingly colored little toads come from the southern half of South America, where they live in grasslands. Their coloration, consisting of a matte black dorsal surface spotted with yellow, is in contrast to their underside, which has areas of red toward the rear and on the palms of the hands and feet. This is warning coloration to indicate the poisonous nature of this toad's skin secretions, but they are not dangerous to humans provided normal precautions are taken.

WHAT temperament?

Diurnal and very active. Best kept in small groups so that their behavior can be observed.

WHAT accommodation?

Small terrariums are suitable, one measuring 18 × 12 × 12 in (45 × 30 × 30 cm) being suitable for four to six toads. Height is less important than floor space as they do not climb well, although a lid is essential. A substrate of compacted coconut fiber or broken-down leaf litter is ideal, and this should have some pieces of wood or bark scattered over it to provide different micro-habitats. Moss and small ferns can be grown directly in the substrate or left in small pots, and the terrarium should include a water dish containing no more than ¾ in (2 cm) of water.

WHAT environment?

A temperature of 68–77°F (20–25°C) is ideal, but they can tolerate much colder conditions, down to 45°F (7°C) at least. Humidity should be low, but the substrate needs to be slightly moist.

HOW much time?

Ten minutes a day.

WHAT varieties?

None, but there are several other species of *Melanophryniscus*, all similar in appearance.

WHAT care?

Daily feeding and light spraying.

WHAT food?

Small insects such as hatchling crickets, fruit flies, lesser waxworms. They have big appetites.

HOW easy are they to breed?

They have been bred in captivity —the females require a short, cold period to condition them, and heavy feeding. Raising the minuscule young is difficult.

WHAT drawbacks?

Captive-bred young are rarely available.

Cost		
Setup cost		
Running cost		

Size: 1–1.5 in (2.5–3.5 cm), females are larger than males

Distribution: South America

Life span: Unknown; probably several years

Left: It isn't difficult to see how the bumblebee toad got its name. It is also known as the "walking toadlet" as it rarely jumps.

Rhinella marinus

Marine or cane toad

PROFILE

This is one of the largest toads, originally from South and Central America but infamously introduced to Australia, where it gained the alternative name of "cane toad." It is normally brown in color, sometimes with darker markings on its back, and with a paler underside. The marine toad is an incredibly adaptable species and will live under a wide range of conditions, from rain forests to arid environments, but it is especially attracted to human dwellings, where it often waits under street lamps for the insects that are attracted there. In addition, it is one of the few amphibians that will take prey that is not moving, even stealing dog food from a bowl.

WHAT temperament?
Placid.

WHAT accommodation?
A large terrarium measuring at least 40 x 18 x 18 in (100 x 45 x 45 cm) is required for one or two adults. The substrate should be soil, leaf litter, coconut fiber, or a mixture of any of these. A hiding place such as a rock cave or a plant pot should be included, as should a water bowl.

WHAT environment?
A temperature of 68–77°F (20–25°C) is ideal but lower and higher temperatures are tolerated for short periods. Humidity should not be too high; a light

spraying daily and a well-ventilated terrarium will create suitable conditions.

HOW much time?
Five to ten minutes a day.

WHAT varieties?
None. A similar species, the Rococo toad, *Rhinella podocnemis*, has been available in the past.

WHAT care?
Daily spraying and feeding as required.

WHAT food?
Large insects such as locusts and cockroaches. Some individuals will learn to eat dog food, but this should not be given exclusively.

Cost			
Setup cost			
Running cost			

Size: 4–9 in (10–22 cm), females are much larger than males
Distribution: South and Central America
Life span: At least 25 years

HOW easy are they to breed?
Rarely, if ever, bred in captivity.

WHAT drawbacks?
None. Although they are not the most attractive toads, they do have their following. The poisons they sometimes secrete from their glands are potentially dangerous.

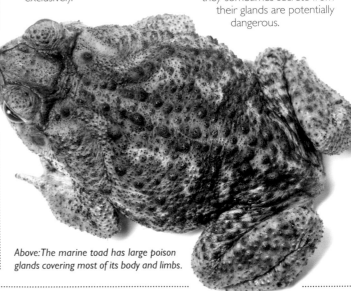

Above: The marine toad has large poison glands covering most of its body and limbs.

Dendrobates auratus

Green and gold poison dart frog

PROFILE

A small, attractive, and relatively tough poison dart frog that occurs in a number of different color forms. Typical examples are metallic green with brown or bronze spots and blotches, but there are also blue and brown forms as well as forms in which the dominant color is brown and the green areas are restricted to small spots.

WHAT temperament?
Active during the day and bold, displaying themselves well.

WHAT accommodation?
A tall terrarium measuring 24 × 24 × 24 in (60 × 60 × 60 cm) would be the minimum size for a small group. They need branches for climbing and plants, especially bromeliads, in which to hide and forage. A small artificial stream or an automatic misting system will provide the right amount of humidity. The terrarium should be well ventilated.

WHAT environment?
Tropical frogs requiring a temperature of 68–81°F (20–27°C) and high humidity.

HOW much time?
Ten to thirty minutes a day. Much longer for a major terrarium overhaul.

WHAT varieties?
Many geographic races are recognized, some from very small areas, and most are named after the places they are found. The typical green and black form is the most common and is probably the best choice for beginners.

WHAT care?
Feeding once or twice every day, and regular spraying

WHAT food?
Small insects, especially fruit flies and hatchling crickets, in large quantities. Every meal should be dusted with a vitamin and mineral powder.

HOW easy are they to breed?
Among the easiest poison dart frogs to keep and breed, although breeding requires special knowl-

Above: This is a very colorful and popular species of poison dart frog. Its skin has a metallic appearance.

Cost		
Setup cost		
Running cost		

Size: 1–1.5 in (2.5–4.2 cm), depending on origin; some forms larger than others

Distribution: Central America; introduced into Hawaii

Life span: 10 years or more

Above: Some regional forms of Dendrobates color have brown or bronze-colored spots.

edge and is time-consuming, as the tadpoles must be housed separately.

WHAT drawbacks?
One of the easiest species to keep, but you must have the time to care for them and an ample supply of food. Captive-bred young are frequently available.

Dendrobates leucomelas

Black and yellow poison dart frog

A stocky poison dart frog with a distinctive pattern of irregular bright yellow-orange bands on a jet-black background. The skin's texture is finely granulated, like orange peel. In young frogs the bands are quite broad, but as they grow they develop black spots within them. This is a lively and active species that is tougher than many other poison dart frogs. It comes from the rain forests of northern South America.

WHAT temperament?
Tame and lively. This is one of the least poisonous species, but precautions should still be taken after handling them.

WHAT accommodation?
A tall, spacious terrarium is required. One measuring 30 × 30 × 30 in (60 × 60 × 60 cm) would be the minimum for a

Above: All poison dart frogs climb well but also spend time foraging for food on the ground. They are active during the day.

small group. Include plenty of branches for climbing and plants, especially bromeliads. A small stream will provide the required humidity, or an automatic misting system can be included.

WHAT environment?
Tropical. A temperature of 68–81°F (20–27°C) and high humidity.

HOW much time?
Thirty minutes a day.

WHAT varieties?
None. There are no subspecies or similar species, but individuals vary in the amount and pattern of the black spots.

Left: This species is one of the most distinctively colored frogs and one of the best choices for beginners.

Cost			
Setup cost			
Running cost			

Size: 1–2 in (3–5 cm)

Distribution: Northern South America (Venezuela and neighboring countries)

Life span: Unknown, probably 5–10 years

WHAT care?
Daily feeding, preferably twice a day, and frequent spraying.

WHAT food?
Small insects, especially fruit flies and hatchling crickets, always dusted with a vitamin and mineral powder, and in large quantities.

HOW easy are they to breed?
One of the easier poison dart frogs to breed, but breeding is still very time-consuming. The eggs are laid on land and carried to water by one of the parents. The tadpoles are cannibalistic and must be kept separately.

WHAT drawbacks?
Time-consuming and require an elaborate setup, but otherwise these are one of the easiest poison dart frogs to keep. Captive-bred young are frequently available.

Dendrobates tinctorius azureus

Blue poison dart frog

PROFILE

This stunningly beautiful frog is a subspecies of the dyeing poison dart frog, *Dendrobates tinctorius*. Isolated colonies of the parent species have led to the evolution of many distinct color forms, of which the blue poison dart frog is but one. Other forms are also very popular, and their care is the same. These are fairly large species and quite robust. The blue poison dart frog is rich blue in color and adorned with large and small spots of black on its back and flanks. Its limbs are long and thin, and it has a hunched posture. It lives in the rain forests of the northern Amazon Basin, usually on rocks situated close to water.

WHAT temperament?

Bold and active during the day.

WHAT accommodation?

A tall, spacious terrarium is required. One measuring 40 × 24 × 40 in (100 × 60 × 100 cm) high would be the minimum for a small group. This should be furnished with plenty of branches for climbing, and living plants—especially bromeliads—and ground cover, such as mosses. A small artificial stream will provide the required humidity, or an automatic misting system can be included.

WHAT environment?

Tropical. A temperature of 68–81°F (20–27°C) and high humidity.

Above: The blue poison dart frog is one of the larger species of poison dart frogs.

HOW much time?

Fifteen minutes a day.

WHAT varieties?

There are many color forms of *D. tinctorius*, as mentioned, left.

WHAT care?

Daily feeding, preferably twice a day, and frequent spraying.

WHAT food?

Large quantities of small insects, especially fruit flies and hatchling crickets, always dusted with a vitamin and mineral powder.

Right: One of the most impressive of all frogs, the blue poison dart frog requires much more space than many of the other poison dart frogs.

Cost			
Setup cost			
Running cost			

Size: 1.5–1¾ in (4–4.5 cm)

Distribution: South America

Life span: 4–5 years

HOW easy are they to breed?

Fairly easy to breed, although rearing the tadpoles can be very time-consuming. The eggs are laid on land and carried to water by one of the parents. The tadpoles are cannibalistic and must be kept separately.

WHAT drawbacks?

They require an elaborate planted setup, but this can be regarded as an advantage. Otherwise, there are no obvious problems, and captive-bred young are frequently available (but expensive).

Epipedobates tricolor

Phantasmal poison dart frog

PROFILE

A cream and maroon-striped poison dart frog that is distinct from most other species. Small, plump, and very lively, this poison dart frog is not as brightly colored as some others but makes up for this by being one of the most adaptable species. It is endangered in the wild and may soon become extinct but there is a good supply of captive-bred young.

WHAT temperament?
Very active during the day.

WHAT accommodation?
A tall terrarium measuring 24 × 18 × 18 in (60 × 45 × 45 cm) would be the minimum size for a small group. They need plenty of plants, especially bromeliads, in which to hide, and they will lay their eggs there too. If an aquatic area is provided, they will use this for breeding.

WHAT environment?
68–81°F (20–27°C) in the day, although slightly lower temperatures are tolerated. A high humidity is required, but the terrarium should be well ventilated.

HOW much time?
Around fifteen to twenty minutes a day, for feeding and general maintenance. Much longer for a major terrarium overhaul.

Cost			
Setup cost			
Running cost			

Size: 1–1.5 in (2.5–4 cm)
Distribution: Central Ecuador
Life span: 10 years or more

WHAT varieties?
There is only slight variation in color and the width of the stripes. Some are redder than others, and some have a greenish or turquoise hue to their cream stripes. A separate species, *F. anthonyi*, is no longer valid.

WHAT care?
Daily or twice daily feeding and regular spraying.

WHAT food?
Fruit flies, hatchling crickets, and other very small insects in large quantities, always dusted with a vitamin and mineral powder.

Left: This small species adapts well to captivity. It is bred in large numbers.

Above: The phantasmal poison dart frog is easily recognized. The light stripes may be white, cream, or greenish in color.

HOW easy are they to breed?
The easiest of all poison dart frogs. They will lay their eggs on the leaves of bromeliad plants, and the parents will move the tadpoles to water when they hatch. They do not have to be raised separately. The young frogs are tiny and require springtails as a first food.

WHAT drawbacks?
None; this is probably the best species for beginners, and there are plenty of captive-bred young available.

Phyllobates terribilis

Yellow poison dart frog

PROFILE

A large species of poison dart frog, notable for the potency of its poison, which is among the most dangerous in the animal kingdom. Frogs reared in captivity, however, lose the ability to produce very strong toxins and are safe, although every precaution should be taken to handle them as little as possible, preferably not at all. It is uniform yellow in color, except for small areas of black on the tips of the toes and around the mouth and eyes. It occurs in Colombia and was a fairly recent discovery.

climbing, and, if possible, living plants, especially bromeliads and climbers. A small artificial stream will provide the required humidity or an automatic misting system can be included.

WHAT environment?
A temperature of 68–81°F (20–27°C) and high humidity. Lighting should be subdued, although if living plants are present this needs to be taken into account.

HOW much time?
Fifteen minutes per day.

WHAT varieties?
There are two color forms: the yellow form, as described above, and another, which is bronze-green in color.

Left: This frog is extremely poisonous.

WHAT care?
Daily or twice daily feeding and spraying (unless an automatic misting system or an artificial stream is installed).

WHAT food?
Fruit flies, hatchling crickets, small wax-worms, etc., always dusted with a vitamin and mineral powder.

Cost		
Setup cost		
Running cost		

Size: Around 2 in (5 cm)
Distribution: Colombia
Life span: At least 4–5 years

HOW easy are they to breed?
Fairly easy to breed. The eggs are laid on land and carried to water by one of the parents, and the tadpoles must be kept separately.

WHAT drawbacks?
These are potentially very toxic frogs, although captive individuals lose most of their potency. Even so, handling them is not recommended and, in particular, children should not be allowed anywhere near them.

Below: The color varies from bright yellow to greenish, but both forms are the same species and will breed with each other.

WHAT temperament?
Bold and active during the day.

WHAT accommodation?
A large terrarium measuring 40 x 40 x 24 in (100 x 100 x 60 cm) would be suitable for a small group. This should be furnished with plenty of branches for

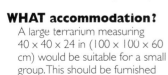

Tomato frog

PROFILE

Three species of tomato frogs come from Madagascar. One, *Dyscophus antongilii*, is endangered and rarely seen in captivity, but *D. guineti* is imported occasionally and is also bred in captivity in small numbers. They are stocky, pear-shaped when seen from above, and can inflate themselves when upset, making them even more rotund. They are yellowish-brown or orange-brown in color with fine black spots and a heart-shaped dark patch on their back. Females are more brightly colored than males. They live in rainforests and breed in stagnant pools.

Above: Female tomato frogs tend to be more brightly colored than males.

WHAT temperament?

Very placid and easy to handle, although their bright coloration suggests that their skin is toxic.

WHAT accommodation?

A terrarium measuring 24 x 6 x 6 in (60 x 15 x 15 cm) is sufficient for one or two adults, and it should have a substrate of leaf litter, sphagnum, or coconut fiber to a depth of at least 2 in (5 cm) so that the frogs can burrow down into it. Pieces of bark also provide hiding places and help to prevent the substrate from drying out. A water bowl is not essential as long as the substrate is always moist.

WHAT environment?

Warm and humid. A temperature of 74–77°F (18–25°C) is preferred and the substrate should be sprayed frequently to maintain a high humidity.

HOW much time?

Five to ten minutes a day.

WHAT varieties?

None. The other two species of tomato frog are *Dyscophus antongilii*, which is endangered, and *D. insularis*, which is smaller and duller in color.

WHAT care?

Feeding two or three times a week and regular spraying.

WHAT food?

Small insects such as crickets, which should be dusted with a

Cost					
Setup cost					
Running cost					

Size: 2.5–3.5 in (6–9.5 cm), females are larger than males

Distribution: Eastern Madagascar

Life span: Unknown

Above: Tomato frogs are large species belonging to the Microhylidae, or narrow-mouthed frogs, a widespread family that consists mainly of very small species.

vitamin and mineral supplement. They cannot take very large prey.

HOW easy are they to breed?

Breeding is possible but difficult. A rain chamber of some description is necessary.

WHAT drawbacks?

They are secretive and rarely seen. The toxic skin makes them unsuitable for children.

Kaloula pulchra

Asian bullfrog or Asian painted frog

PROFILE

Sometimes sold as "chubby frogs," this is a rotund species with distinctive markings of tan and brown with long toes ending in small pads for climbing, even though it lives mostly on the ground. It is very common around villages and on the outskirts of cities and is rarely seen in undisturbed habitats, indicating that it adapts well to a range of conditions. It breeds after heavy rain at any time of the year.

WHAT temperament?
Nocturnal but will learn to emerge in the evening to feed.

WHAT accommodation?
A terrarium measuring around 24 x 12 x 12 in (60 x 30 x 30 cm) is suitable for two or three frogs. A substrate of coconut fiber, sphagnum, or leaf litter is ideal, and this should be slightly moist but not wet. Some pieces of flat bark will give the frogs somewhere to hide and

Above: The rotund shape of this species can be clearly seen in this view. Despite its size, it prefers small prey.

create some local humidity underneath. A water bowl is not essential provided the substrate is not allowed to dry out.

WHAT environment?
Temperatures around 68–77°F (20–25°C) are suitable. Humidity should be fairly high but the terrarium must be well-ventilated.

Cost			
Setup cost			
Running cost			

Size: 2–3 in (5–7.5 cm), females are larger than males

Distribution: Southeast Asia

Life span: Unknown; likely to be 5 or more years

HOW much time?
Five to ten minutes a day.

WHAT varieties?
None. Occasionally other species of *Kaloula* come onto the market.

WHAT care?
Daily spraying and feeding; occasional cage maintenance.

WHAT food?
Insects such as crickets, which should be dusted with a vitamin and mineral powder. They cannot take large food items.

HOW easy are they to breed?
Not bred in captivity.

WHAT drawbacks?
None, other than the lack of captive-bred young.

Left: Asian bullfrogs do well in captivity, but they can be secretive and are rarely seen during the day.

Hyperolius puncticulatus

Spotted reed frog

A small reed frog from East Africa, sometimes confused with a similar species, Mitchell's reed frog (which may actually be a different form of the same species). Reed frogs (also known as sedge frogs) live around ponds and swamps, often resting on vegetation just above the water, hence their common names. This species is tan in color with a black-edged cream stripe running down each side of its back. This stripe stops at the eyes in some forms, and there are several other variations.

WHAT temperament?

Very active, agile frogs that make a good display if kept in small groups in planted terrariums, but not suitable for handling.

WHAT accommodation?

A tall terrarium, measuring about 18 x 18 x 24 in (45 x 45 x 60 cm) high is the minimum size for a small group, but they will do better in a larger terrarium. It should contain a large water bowl, and the bottom can be filled with 1–1.5 in (3–4 cm) of water. Tall plants are necessary for them to rest on.

WHAT environment?

They require a temperature of 68–77°F (20–25°C) and high humidity.

HOW much time?

Five to ten minutes a day.

WHAT varieties?

There are several color forms of this species and many other reed frogs, several of which may enter the pet trade from time to time. Some species are highly variable, and it is not always possible to know which is on offer. They all require similar care, although their breeding habits vary slightly.

WHAT care?

Daily feeding and spraying, unless an automatic spraying system is installed.

WHAT food?

Small insects such as crickets and flies.

HOW easy are they to breed?

They breed regularly under the

Left: All reed frogs are small, with large bulging eyes and adhesive pads on the tips of their toes.

Cost			
Setup cost			
Running cost			

Size: 1 in (2.5 cm)
Distribution: East Africa
Life span: Probably 1 to 2 years

Above: Despite its name, the spotted reed frog is distinguished by two broad stripes that run down its sides. Reed frogs are highly variable and often difficult to identify with certainty.

right conditions. They attach their eggs in clumps of 100 to 200 to branches or leaves overhanging water, and the tadpoles drip into the water when they hatch.

WHAT drawbacks?

Very good display species but not suitable for handling. Captive-bred stock are normally available.

Hyperolius tuberilinguis

Tinker reed frog

PROFILE

This is one of the larger reed frogs and comes from East and southern Africa. It is usually uniform green in color but yellow forms also exist. It serves as a representative of several other similar reed frogs that sometimes appear on the market. It lives in lowland grasslands, especially in flooded areas and the edges of shallow lakes. This species lays its eggs in water, in small clusters attached to submerged vegetation.

WHAT temperament?
Very lively and prone to erratic leaps but, provided they are not disturbed, they settle down well in captivity and are suitable for naturalistic terrariums.

WHAT accommodation?
A tall terrarium, measuring about 18 x 18 x 24 in (45 x 45 x 60 cm) high is suitable for a small group. It should include branches and living plants for the frogs to climb and rest on, and a water bowl if breeding is the aim.

WHAT environment?
Warm and humid. A temperature of 64–73°F (18–23°C) is suitable, and the humidity should be kept high by frequent spraying or an automatic misting system.

HOW much time?
Five to ten minutes a day.

WHAT varieties?
Green and yellow forms as noted above, and there are several similar species. Exact identification can sometimes be difficult.

WHAT care?
Daily feeding and spraying, unless an automatic system is installed.

Below: The tinker reed frog is one of several species that are predominantly green in color. Developing eggs can be seen through the skin of this female.

Cost			
Setup cost			
Running cost			

Size: 1–1.5 in (2.5–3.5 cm), females are larger than males
Distribution: Southern Africa, in the east
Life span: Probably 1 to 2 years

WHAT food?
Small insects such as crickets, flies, and sweepings (tiny insects gathered from the wild).

HOW easy are they to breed?
They often breed if they are well fed and the environment is suitable. Raising the tiny froglets is the hardest part.

WHAT drawbacks?
Not suitable for handling. Supply of captive-bred stock is erratic.

Ptychadena mascareniensis

Mascarene grass frog

PROFILE

This is an extremely lively terrestrial frog that can make huge leaps. It is brown in color, with some specimens having an orange stripe down the center of their back. There are a number of folds of skin running down the back, a characteristic of all members of the genus. Its snout is pointed, and its back legs are very long. This species lives in a range of habitats but is most often found in long grass in swamps, fields, and gardens.

WHAT temperament?
Nervous at first and very lively.

WHAT accommodation?
A large terrarium is needed, at least 24 × 18 × 18 in (60 × 45 × 45 cm), preferably larger. It should contain a land area of leaf litter, sphagnum, or coconut fiber and a separate area with a few centimeters of water. Plants in the land area will provide hiding places, which are important.

Right: This species occurs in two forms: this one has a broad orange stripe down the center of its back but it lives alongside plain-colored individuals. Both are extremely lively!

WHAT environment?
Tropical conditions are required: a temperature of 73–82°F (23–28°C) and high humidity, although the terrarium should be well ventilated.

HOW much time?
Five to ten minutes a day.

WHAT varieties?
None, apart from striped and plain individuals.

WHAT care?
Daily feeding and occasional cleaning of the water container or area.

WHAT food?
Insects, especially crickets and earthworms.

Cost				
Setup cost				
Running cost				

Size: 1¾–2 in (4.5–6 cm), females are larger than males

Distribution: Much of Central and southern Africa and all of Madagascar, where it was probably introduced

Life span: Unknown; probably 5 years or more

HOW easy are they to breed?
Not bred in captivity.

WHAT drawbacks?
Too lively to handle easily, and the lack of captive-bred stock makes them a species for the more experienced amphibian keeper.

Pyxicephalus adspersus and *P. edulis*

African bullfrog

PROFILE

Two species are commonly known as African bullfrogs and were formerly classified together as *Pyxicephalus adspersus*. Either species may appear in the pet trade, usually as juveniles, which are difficult to tell apart, although the "original" species, *P. adspersus*, eventually reaches a larger size. Both are large, heavy-bodied frogs with large mouths, and they are the African counterparts of the South American horned frogs. Juveniles are dappled green and yellowish-green, with a yellow stripe down their back. These markings change, and the adults are plain dark green above with yellow areas at the base of the limbs and on the flanks, which are brighter in males than females.

WHAT temperament?
Usually fairly placid, but some individuals can be aggressive.

WHAT accommodation?
Similar to that of the South American horned frogs (see pages 50–51), which they closely parallel.

WHAT environment?
They are tropical or sub-tropical depending on their origin and require warm conditions, 68–82°F (20–28°C) being ideal, and high humidity.

HOW much time?
Five to ten minutes a day.

Above: Adult African bullfrogs are mostly green and breed in shallow water.

WHAT varieties?
Just the two species, as listed. *P. edulis* is smaller and lacks the folds of skin that run along the back of *P. adspersus*. Juveniles are indistinguishable.

WHAT care?
Daily spraying. Feeding once or twice weekly; juveniles need feeding more often than adults.

Cost			
Setup cost			
Running cost			

Size: *P. adspersus* to 9 in (23 cm), *P. edulis* to 4 ¾ in (12 cm). Males are larger than females

Distribution: Southern Africa

Life span: Over 20 years, the record being 45 (*P. adspersus*)

WHAT food?
Large insects, such as crickets and locusts. Adults will eat small vertebrates, such as mice, and they will also eat other frogs, so they must be kept individually.

HOW easy are they to breed?
Difficult to breed, requiring a long dry spell followed by a period in a rain chamber. Commercial breeders make use of hormone injections.

WHAT drawbacks?
Easy and satisfactory captives but occasionally belligerent. Always start with a captive-bred juvenile as it will adapt to captive conditions more readily. Can only be kept individually.

Left: Juvenile African bullfrogs are more colorful than adults, have hearty appetites, and grow rapidly.

Boophis rappiodes

Bright-eyed frog

Over 70 species in the genus *Boophis* are known as bright-eyed frogs. This species is one of the smaller ones and is bright green in color with red and yellow markings. Females tend to have more red on them than males, and both sexes have characteristic silver pupils with bright blue rims. There are several similar species, and it is possible that they are sometimes mislabeled when they are imported. These small frogs live at the edges of rain forests in eastern Madagascar, often near streams, and males call from leaves overhanging the water.

WHAT temperament?

Very lively and agile, but they normally settle down well provided they are not disturbed.

WHAT accommodation?

A tall terrarium measuring about 18 × 18 × 24 in (45 × 45 × 60 cm) is suitable for a pair or a small group. It needs plenty of branches and, if possible, living plants, for the frogs to climb on. A water bowl is not essential, except for breeding.

WHAT environment?

Warm and humid. A temperature of about 64–77°F (18–25°C) suits them, and the humidity should be raised by frequent spraying or, better yet, an automatic misting system or a small stream. Lighting is necessary if living plants are included, but the frogs are mainly nocturnal.

HOW much time?

Five to fifteen minutes a day, depending on the complexity of the set-up.

Cost			
Setup cost			
Running cost			

Size: 1–1.5 in (2–3.5 cm), females are larger than males

Distribution: Eastern Madagascar

Life span: Unknown; probably several years

WHAT varieties?

None, but as mentioned above, there are several very similar species.

WHAT care?

Daily feeding and spraying as necessary.

WHAT food?

Small insects such as crickets and sweepings (tiny insects gathered from the wild). All meals should be dusted with a vitamin and mineral supplement. They should be fed in the evening.

HOW easy are they to breed?

Not bred in captivity, although there is no reason why this could not be achieved. A rain chamber would probably be helpful.

WHAT drawbacks?

Lack of captive-bred stock. Not suitable for regular handling.

Above: Several bright-eyed frogs are green with translucent skin.

African grey tree frog

PROFILE

This is a large, rough-skinned tree frog from East and southern Africa. Unusually for a tree frog, they live in lightly wooded grassland, often near water holes. They have several mechanisms for preventing themselves from drying out during very hot, dry weather, including the excretion of uric acid, which is a white, paste-like substance that contains very little water; birds and reptiles use the same system, but it is rarely found among amphibians. They often bask on branches in full sun, where their mottled grey coloration keeps them well camouflaged, and they lay their eggs in a foam nest that they attach to branches overhanging pools of water.

WHAT temperament?
Nocturnal, spending the daytime resting on branches, often in full view.

WHAT accommodation?
They need a tall terrarium, measuring 18 × 18 × 24 in (45 × 45 × 60 cm) high as a minimum requirement. This will accommodate two or three frogs.

WHAT environment?
A temperature of 68–82°F (20–28°C) is suitable during the day, and it can fall slightly at night. They should be sprayed every day as long as their cage is well ventilated so that it dries out quickly. A bowl of water will provide local humidity.

HOW much time?
Five to ten minutes a day.

WHAT varieties?
There are two other species of *Chiromantis* from Africa, both rarely available.

WHAT care?
Daily feeding and spraying. Missing a day or two is allowed provided they are in good condition.

WHAT food?
Insects such as crickets, flies, and moths.

HOW easy are they to breed?
They are rarely bred in captivity, although this should be relatively easy by giving them a spell of dry conditions followed by a thorough spraying.

WHAT drawbacks?
None, except the lack of captive-bred young.

Above and left: African grey tree frogs are well adapted to hot, dry conditions and often live in arid places.

Cost			
Setup cost			
Running cost			

Size: 2–3 in (5–8 cm), females are larger than males
Distribution: East and southern Africa
Life span: Unknown; certainly several years

Mantella aurantiaca

Golden mantella

This is a beautiful little frog, being completely bright orange apart from its eyes, which are black. It lives in Madagascar, where it is restricted to a few swamps, and is considered to be critically endangered. It prefers sunny, open habitats. Males have a chirping call. There are sixteen species of mantellas, some of them highly variable, and they are all brightly colored and diurnal, presumably because their skin contains substances that are distasteful to predators, giving them immunity from attack. In this respect they parallel the poison dart frogs from Central and South America.

Above: Small but perfectly formed, the golden mantella is one of the most distinctively colored frogs. Its skin has the color and texture of an orange peel.

Below: Mantellas lay their eggs on land, in damp places, and the tadpoles wriggle into water when they hatch.

WHAT temperament?

Lively and bold. It hides under leaves and pieces of wood but frequently appears during the day in search of food.

WHAT accommodation?

Although small, this species requires plenty of space as they are very territorial. Height is not so important, but the floor space should be at least 24 × 18 in (60 × 30 cm) for a pair or small group. The substrate can be leaf litter, sphagnum, or orchid bark, and there should be pieces of bark for the frogs to hide under. Living plants often do well in this sort of setup. The substrate should be changed regularly to prevent the buildup of toxins in the terrarium.

WHAT environment?

Mantellas prefer cool conditions, ideally 64–68°F (18–20°C)

during the day and slightly cooler at night. Humidity should be high, but the terrarium must be well ventilated. An automatic misting system is the easiest way to maintain these conditions.

HOW much time?

Ten to fifteen minutes a day for feeding and spraying; longer periods—up to one hour—for changing part of the substrate every two to four weeks.

WHAT varieties?

There is a similar species, *Mantella milotympanum*, sometimes regarded as a subspecies, that differs from the golden mantella because it has a black tympanum (eardrum) and a small area of black around its nostrils. Other species that are sometimes available include the painted mantella, *M. baroni*, and the yellow mantella, *M. crocea*. The care of these, and others, is similar to that of the golden mantella, but they can be kept slightly warmer (although none of them likes very warm conditions).

WHAT care?

Daily feeding and spraying and occasional partial changing of the substrate. If a small water bowl is included, this should be replenished every day.

WHAT food?

Small insects such as crickets, lesser waxworms, and sweepings (tiny insects gathered from the wild). Make sure that insects from the previous day's feeding have been eaten before introducing more as they can accumulate in the substrate. Meals should be dusted with vitamin and mineral powder.

HOW easy are they to breed?

Relatively easily. In the wild they lay their eggs on damp substrate and they hatch when the water level rises to inundate them. In captivity, they will lay clutches of eggs under pieces of bark on damp moss or leaf litter. The eggs have to be removed to develop in a separate container away from the adults' terrarium. The newly metamorphosed young are very small and require fruit flies and hatchling crickets.

Left: The internal organs can be seen clearly in this unusual ventral view.

Cost			
Setup cost			
Running cost			

Size: ¾–1 in (2–2.5 cm), females are slightly longer than males

Distribution: Northeastern Madagascar

Life span: At least 10 years

WHAT drawbacks?

This is an endangered species. Only captive-bred animals should be considered, and every effort should be made to breed them. In other respects, these little frogs make ideal terrarium subjects as they display themselves well and will often breed given the correct conditions.

Polypedates leucomystax

Asian foam-nest tree frog

This is a very common tree frog in parts of Southeast Asia, where it goes by a number of different names. It is brown, tan, or golden-brown in color and some forms have four darker lines running down their back. It has large toe-pads and is highly arboreal and very agile. It lays its eggs in a nest of foam about the size of a tennis ball, either attached to an overhanging branch or on the bank of a small pool or ditch. As the tadpoles hatch, the foam disintegrates and they are released into the water.

WHAT temperament?
Nocturnal and very lively.

WHAT accommodation?
A large terrarium measuring about 24 x 24 x 40 in (60 x 60 x 100 cm) high is necessary. It should contain plenty of branches and, if possible, living plants, for the frogs to climb on. A pool of water should be included.

WHAT environment?
They are tropical frogs and need a temperature of 68–77°F (20–25°C) day and night. They also require high humidity, although their cage must be well ventilated.

HOW much time?
Five to ten minutes a day.

WHAT varieties?
There are several other species of *Polypedates* that sometimes enter

Above: The Asian foam-nest tree frog is common over much of Southeast Asia and is very adaptable.

the pet trade, and the related *Rhacophorus* species, some of which are "flying frogs," also occur from time to time. The care of these is similar to that of the more common species described, although larger species require larger terrariums.

WHAT care?
Daily feeding and spraying. An automatic spray or misting system is useful.

Cost			
Setup cost			
Running cost			

Size: 2–3 in (5–8 cm)

Distribution: Widespread in Southeast Asia

Life span: Unknown; probably several years

WHAT food?
Insects such as crickets and cockroaches. They have large mouths and can handle relatively large insects.

HOW easy are they to breed?
Captive breeding is rarely attempted but should not be difficult. A rain chamber would probably be useful.

WHAT drawbacks?
They can be lively and difficult to handle; captive-bred young are rarely available.

The slender shape is distinctive, but coloration is variable.

Theloderma corticale

Mossy frog

PROFILE

A strange but interesting-looking frog whose coloration and texture resembles moss, hence its name. It is a climbing species with expanded toe discs, and it belongs to the same family as many other Asian tree frogs and flying frogs. It is tolerant of a wide range of conditions and will breed in captivity, laying small clumps of eggs attached to rocks or wood above the water line. When the eggs hatch, the tadpoles drop into the water below and develop in the normal way.

Cost				
Setup cost				
Running cost				

Size: To about 3 in (7.5 cm)

Distribution: Vietnam

Life span: Several years

Above: The mossy frog makes an excellent terrarium subject and breeds readily in captivity in suitable conditions.

WHAT temperament?
Nocturnal. Placid but may play dead if picked up.

WHAT accommodation?
A large glass terrarium, ideally at least 24 in (60 cm) long and 24 in (60 cm) high, is required for a pair of adults or a small group of juveniles. This should have about 2–4 in (5–10 cm) of water, with emergent piles of rocks or branches for the frogs to climb and rest on. A platform of cork bark or a flat rock is useful for adding the food.

WHAT environment?
They are very undemanding and will tolerate temperatures as low as 59°F (15°C) and as high as 77°F (25°C). Room temperature is often adequate.

HOW much time?
Five to ten minutes a day. Occasional longer periods for cleaning and changing the water.

WHAT care?
Feeding every day, with small amounts: too much food placed

Below: The color and texture give excellent camouflage.

in their cage will simply drown and contaminate the water. Regular water changes are necessary.

WHAT food?
Insects such as crickets and cockroaches. They have large appetites but only feed at night. Insects should be dusted with a vitamin and mineral supplement and placed in the cage after dark so that the frogs eat them while they still have powder on them.

HOW easy are they to breed?
Easy if a pair is available, but sex determination is only possible with adults. Raising the tadpoles and young is straightforward.

WHAT drawbacks?
The males call at night. This is not an unpleasant sound, but some people find it annoying.

Theloderma aspera

Pied mossy frog

PROFILE

This is a smaller species than the more common mossy frog and is very different in appearance. It is marked with patches of cream, brown, and tan, which makes it hard to see when resting on mottled bark; there is also a theory that this coloration disguises the frogs as bird droppings. Its toes end in well-developed pads for climbing, and its eyes are large and dark red. It lives and breeds in holes in rotting trees and stumps and attaches its eggs to the sides of the holes, above a small volume of water.

WHAT temperament?

Nocturnal. They will often rest in full view during the day, relying on their camouflage, and are not especially nervous. Plays dead if picked up.

WHAT accommodation?

A small terrarium is suitable, one measuring 18 × 12 × 18 in (45 × 30 × 45 cm) high can accommodate a small group of adults. There should be 1–1.5 in (3–4 cm) of water in the bottom, and pieces of bogwood, branches, and potted plants can be stood in the water. A platform of cork bark provides a surface for live insects to be added.

WHAT environment?

They require cool temperatures, 64–73°F (18–23°C) being suitable, although short spells at slightly cooler or warmer temperatures will not harm them.

HOW much time?

Five to ten minutes a day.

WHAT varieties?

None.

WHAT care?

Feeding every one or two days.

WHAT food?

Small crickets, moths, etc.

HOW easy are they to breed?

A small group containing both sexes will usually breed without any special arrangements. Females lay three to six eggs every two to three weeks, attaching them to wood or stone just above the water surface. The tadpoles drop into the water when they hatch and can be removed or allowed to stay where they are to develop. They eat fish flake and grow slowly.

WHAT drawbacks?

None, but not often available.

Below: Like the mossy frog, this species also relies heavily on camouflage.

Cost				
Setup cost				
Running cost				

Size: 1–1.5 in (3–4 cm)

Distribution: Southern China and Southeast Asia

Life span: At least 5 years

Occidozyga lima

Spotted puddle frog

PROFILE

Spotted puddle frogs are sometimes known as Asian floating frogs—both names sum them up quite well. They are small, plump species that spend their time in shallow bodies of water such as puddles, flooded fields, and seepages. They are brown or olive green in color, with small dark spots over their backs. Some also have a pale yellow or cream stripe down their back. They occur in Southeast Asia, where there are several other species in the genus, all very similar.

WHAT temperament?

Shy at first, but they soon become used to captivity provided they are not disturbed too much.

WHAT accommodation?

A semi-aquatic terrarium of about 18 × 12 × 12 in (45 × 30 × 30 cm) is required, containing a few centimeters of water and a land area for them to climb onto. This can be a flat rock placed in the water or a piece of floating cork bark. Floating plants such as *Salvinia* can be included.

WHAT environment?

Warm conditions of about 73–77°F (23–25°C) seem to suit them best. Humidity needs to be high, as it will be anyway if they are kept semi-aquatically, but the terrarium needs to be well ventilated.

HOW much time?

Five to ten minutes a day. Longer periods for water changes.

WHAT varieties?

Striped and plain, as mentioned above. In addition, there are other species, sometimes known as rice-paddy frogs, in the genus, and their care is likely to be similar.

Cost		
Setup cost		
Running cost		

Size: 1–1.5 in (3–4 cm)
Distribution: Southeast Asia
Life span: Unknown

Above: Puddle frogs are easy to house.

WHAT care?

Daily feeding and occasional water changes as filters are not practical in shallow water.

WHAT food?

Small insects such as crickets. They may also eat aquatic invertebrates such as bloodworms and insect larvae.

HOW easy are they to breed?

Unknown. There do not appear to have been any serious attempts to breed them, although this is probably quite easy to achieve.

WHAT drawbacks?

Lack of captive-bred stock. In other respects they are easy.

Lithobates pipiens

Northern leopard frog

PROFILE

The northern leopard frog has the widest distribution of all the species commonly known as "leopard frogs." It occurs from Canada to the northern half of the United States. It is a handsome species that may be green or tan with large rounded blotches of dark brown. It is an aquatic species, rarely found away from water, and lives within a variety of habitats. It is very tolerant of cold and hibernates for long periods in the north.

WHAT temperament?
Nervous and active, often making long jumps if disturbed.

WHAT accommodation?
Large terraria are required, ideally at least 40 × 18 × 18 in (100 × 45 × 45 cm). The terrarium should include a large area of water, either by including a large bowl or by dividing it into two parts with a strip of glass. The land area should have plenty of cover in the form of plants, bark, moss, etc., and the water section should also be planted. Without these precautions the frogs will continually crash into the sides of the terrarium and damage themselves.

Right: Leopard frogs are among the most common frogs in North America.

WHAT environment?
A temperature of 59–64°F (15–23°C) is suitable but they will tolerate much cooler conditions if required and do not need supplementary heating. Provided they have water, humidity will not be a problem.

HOW much time?
Five to ten minutes a day.

WHAT varieties?
This is a variable species, and there are several naturally occurring color variants.

WHAT care?
Feeding daily and general cage maintenance.

WHAT food?
Insects such as crickets.

HOW easy are they to breed?
Not bred in captivity. In areas where they occur

Cost		
Setup cost		
Running cost		

Size: 3–4 in (8–10 cm)

Distribution: North America, from Canada to the central states

Life span: Unknown; probably over 10 years

Above: Leopard frogs are lively and inclined to take large, erratic leaps, sometimes damaging their snouts.

naturally they can be kept outdoors and will breed without any special arrangements.

WHAT drawbacks?
Their nervous nature often leads to injuries, and they are difficult to handle. Captive-bred young are not available.

Rana temporaria

European common frog

PROFILE

A common and widespread frog, this species is native to much of northern Europe, including the British Isles. Trade in native species is prohibited, but this species can easily be kept in outdoor ponds, either enclosed or in the open. Most are brown or olive in color. The black "mask" is characteristic of this variable species, although some related frogs have similar markings. It hibernates over the winter, either at the bottom of ponds or on land, deep underground, and it can tolerate temperatures down to freezing.

Cost*		
Setup cost		
Running cost		

Just build a pond and the frogs will come!

Size: To about 4 in (10 cm), females are slightly larger than males

Distribution: Central and northern Europe

Life span: 10 years or more

HOW much time?
None!

WHAT varieties?
There is variation in coloration, with yellowish and reddish individuals occurring in the wild.

WHAT temperament?
Active and lively, making it unsuitable for small terrariums.

WHAT accommodation?
Outdoor ponds are easily the best place to keep this species, where it will quickly establish itself and breed. If the surrounding area can be left fairly untidy with log piles and overgrown vegetation, it will remain in the vicinity throughout the year. Advice on building suitable ponds is freely available.

WHAT environment?
A pond for breeding and somewhere to hunt for food and hibernate outside of the breeding season is all that is required.

WHAT care?
None, other than general pond maintenance.

WHAT food?
It will find its own food, consisting of flies and insects, many of which are garden pests.

HOW easy are they to breed?
Provided a suitable pond is available, they will breed every spring.

WHAT drawbacks?
A garden pond is necessary, and this may be a drawback for those with small children or no garden.

Common frogs are variable in color. Females (left) tend to be more heavily built than males.

Turtles and tortoises

■ Turtles and tortoises are reptiles and all possess, to a greater or lesser extent, a shell into which they can pull their heads and limbs in order to protect themselves from predators. Species that live on land, usually known as tortoises, normally have high domed shells, whereas those that live in the water, variously known as turtles or terrapins (or, perversely, "pond tortoises") tend to have flatter, more streamlined shells. Regardless of its shape, the upper shell is called the carapace and the lower one is the plastron. The carapace and plastron are made up of a number of separate plates or "scutes" that are fused together to form a continuous shell. One group of turtles, the highly aquatic soft-shelled turtles, have a leathery covering to their shells.

■ At present, 327 species of turtles and tortoises are recognized and they are found in a variety of habitats, from hot, dry conditions favored by the desert tortoises to the completely aquatic conditions favored by marine turtles and soft-shelled turtles. Even aquatic turtles need to come ashore to lay their eggs, however, and there are no live-bearing species. Their closest relatives are the crocodilians (25 species) and the tuataras (2 species), none of which are included in this book.

■ Accommodation for turtles and tortoises ranges from aquariums with a small basking area, such as an emergent rock or branch positioned under a heat lamp, to open pens or enclosures with a substrate of dry straw or wood shavings. A few species can be kept in outdoor enclosures in northern Europe, but even then they need indoor accommodation to extend their active period in the early spring and late autumn. All species need to bask, and if they do not have access to natural sunlight, they need to be given an artificial source of ultraviolet radiation in the form of ultraviolet B, or UV-B. There are a number of products on the market that cater for this, but the main choice is between pure UV-B lamps and natural sunlight lamps that give off a wide spectrum of light including some UV-B. There are many variables, such as the power of the lamp, the distance of the basking site from the lamp, and the age of the lamp, and advice needs to be sought at the point of sale, or researched on the Internet, for example.

■ UV-B is essential to allowing turtles to synthesize Vitamin D3, and without D3 they cannot absorb calcium into their systems. Calcium is important in bone-building and the transmission of nerve impulses. Calcium deficiency shows itself by poor muscle tone and a weak skeleton and is sometimes known as metabolic bone disease (MBD). Conversely, too much calcium, especially if accompanied by a high-protein diet, results in the creation of excess bone, and, in land tortoises especially, this results in thickening of the plates until they become pyramid-shaped. Tortoise diet, therefore, should consist of low-protein foods and plenty of fiber, accompanied by UV-B and calcium given in moderation. Aquatic and semi-aquatic turtles, on the other hand, are often carnivorous, although they will sometimes eat vegetation too. Their diet can consist of insects, aquatic plants if they will eat them, and a balanced artificial diet such as turtle sticks.

■ Turtles are rarely bred in captivity, but the few captive-bred species are always recommended over wild-caught specimens. Some tortoises are bred in fair numbers, but many species have restrictions placed on their sale, even if captive-bred. Buyers must ensure that any tortoise they buy is being sold legally.

Chelydra serpentina

Common snapping turtle

PROFILE

Fascinating rather than attractive, the snapping turtle has a huge head, sharp beak, and small shell into which its limbs will not fit. Its back is black and rough and has three distinct keels; the plastron is very much reduced and the tail proportionally long. It is common in many types of aquatic habitat, including ponds, streams, swamps, and ditches. A thoroughly aquatic turtle that only rarely leaves the water (although I once found one trying to cross a three-lane highway in South Texas).

WHAT temperament?
Snappy!

WHAT accommodation?
Juveniles will live in small aquariums with a gravel substrate and filter, but adults require very large containers. They should be able to extend their heads above the surface while resting on the bottom. The terrarium should be covered, as much to prevent potential victims from falling in as to prevent the turtle from climbing out.

WHAT environment?
Individuals from the north of their range can be very hardy, but captives require a temperature of 64–77°F (18–25°C) to be on the safe side. A basking light can be installed but they rarely bask. An ultraviolet source, however, is advisable.

HOW much time?
Juveniles require five to ten minutes a day for feeding, but as they grow, so do their demands on time.

WHAT varieties?
None, but there is another species, the alligator snapping turtle, even larger than the common snapper.

WHAT care?
Juveniles simply require feeding daily or every other day; adults require frequent cleaning as well.

Cost		
Setup cost		
Running cost		

Size: 8–12 in (20–30 cm), occasionally much larger

Distribution: Eastern North America, from southern Canada to the Gulf of Mexico

Life span: To 50 years or more

WHAT food?
Anything. Hatchlings eat small insects, turtle sticks, aquatic larvae, small worms, etc. Adults eat plants and fruit but mainly fish, rodents, raw chicken, etc.

HOW easy are they to breed?
Not bred in captivity.

WHAT drawbacks?
Not for the faint-hearted. Adult snapping turtles can inflict serious harm; although most become tame, they can never be trusted. Remember that juveniles eventually grow into adults that can weigh up to 44 pounds (20 kg) in captivity.

Left and top: Hatchling common snappers have more appeal than adult specimens.

Clemmys guttata

Spotted turtle

PROFILE

This is a very small turtle with an unmistakable pattern of round yellow spots on a black background. Young individuals have one spot per plate, but as they grow these may divide into several spots, or they may fade away. The limbs and head are also spotted, sometimes with orange spots. They live in shallow water in swamps and ditches, basking around the edges and burying themselves in the mud on the bottom if they are disturbed.

WHAT temperament?
They adapt well to captivity and soon lose their initial nervousness.

WHAT accommodation?
They need a large terrarium measuring a minimum of 40 x 20 in (100 x 50 cm). Height is not important, although they can climb surprisingly well. The terrarium should be divided into roughly equal land and aquatic sections but the water should be shallow, no more than 6 in (15 cm) for adults, less for juveniles. Alternatively, juveniles can be kept in an aquatic setup with about 2 in (5 cm) of water and a couple of flat rocks for them to climb out on. There must be a basking lamp and a UV lamp above the basking spot.

WHAT environment?
A water temperature of about 68°F (20°C) is sufficient, with access to a warmer basking spot during the day.

HOW much time?
Fifteen minutes a day.

WHAT varieties?
There are no varieties and no similar species.

WHAT care?
Daily feeding and regular cleaning; filters are usually impractical in shallow water.

Above and below: Spotted turtles are attractive and make good pets, but only captive-bred young should be acquired.

Cost			
Setup cost			
Running cost			

Size: 3.5–5 in (9–12 cm) (shell)

Distribution: Eastern North America from Canada to northern Florida

Life span: Unknown; probably more than 25 years

WHAT food?
Juveniles eat small insects and worms, whereas adults will take some vegetable matter. Turtle sticks can also be used but not exclusively.

HOW easy are they to breed?
They are not difficult, but quite a large terrarium with somewhere for the female to lay her eggs is necessary.

WHAT drawbacks?
Poor supply. They are protected where they live, and captive bred young are hard to come by.

Emys orbicularis

European pond turtle

PROFILE

Sometimes known as the European pond tortoise, or terrapin, this is a hardy species that occurs over a large part of Europe, living in ponds, canals, rivers, and ditches. It climbs out to bask and dives into the water at the slightest disturbance. It is predominantly black or dark brown with indistinct yellow markings that radiate out from the center of each plate.

WHAT temperament?

Very adaptable and becomes quite tame in captivity.

WHAT accommodation?

Adults are best kept outside in a pond with an enclosed land area around it. This can include a rock garden or log pile, which will encourage the invertebrate prey that the turtle eats, although they feed mainly in the water. Juveniles can be kept in a small unheated aquarium with about 4 in (10 cm) of water, and a UV lamp.

WHAT environment?

A European climate is suitable. In cooler parts extra warmth can be gained by siting its pond in an open, sunny spot.

HOW much time?

Hardly any if kept outdoors, other than the usual pond maintenance.

WHAT care?

General pond maintenance. It might be necessary to catch the turtle in the autumn and move it to a warm place indoors, but most will hibernate outside if the enclosure is suitable.

Cost			
Setup cost*			
Running cost			

* Nothing to set up outside

Size: About 8 in (20 cm) (shell)
Distribution: Europe
Life span: 30–40 years; possibly up to 50

WHAT varieties?

None.

WHAT food?

Earthworms put into the water. They also eat fish and tadpoles, so they are unsuitable for ponds containing these.

HOW easy are they to breed?

If a large enough pond is available, they may breed naturally. The female will require an area of warm soil in which to dig a burrow for her eggs.

WHAT drawbacks?

None, but captive-bred young are rarely available.

Left: European pond turtles are among the few species that thrive in outdoor ponds in the UK.

Glyptemys insculpta

Wood turtle

PROFILE

The wood turtle is a semi-aquatic species that lives in and around cool streams and rivers. It also wanders across fields and woods eating a variety of vegetable and animal material. It has a low shell, and the individual plates are roughly sculptured and rich brown in color. Its neck and front legs are orange or red. The young lack this orange coloration, and their shells are almost circular. They are not widely available, but captive-hatched young are occasionally available.

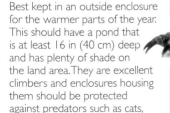

WHAT temperament?
A seemingly intelligent turtle, recognizing its owner and approaching for food. Can be restless at times, trying to escape.

WHAT accommodation?
Best kept in an outside enclosure for the warmer parts of the year. This should have a pond that is at least 16 in (40 cm) deep and has plenty of shade on the land area. They are excellent climbers and enclosures housing them should be protected against predators such as cats, dogs, and large birds. Indoors they need large terraria, at least 22 ft² (2 m²), with access to a large pool and a basking area. Hatchlings are more easily accommodated in smaller terrariums with a land and water area. When kept indoors they require access to UV-B.

WHAT environment?
They prefer cool conditions, and can be kept outside or in a cold frame that is protected from frost and they will hibernate underwater.

HOW much time?
Fifteen to thirty minutes a day.

WHAT varieties?
None, but the related Central America wood turtle, *Rhinoclemmys pulcherrima*, is sometimes offered. It is similar but requires much warmer conditions.

WHAT care?
Daily feeding and general maintenance of their enclosure or terrarium.

Cost				
Setup cost				
Running cost				

Size: 6–7.5 in (15–19 cm) (shell)

Distribution: Northeastern North America

Life span: At least 50 years

WHAT food?
Insects such as crickets, earthworms, fruit and leafy vegetables, and weeds such as dandelion.

HOW easy are they to breed?
Not easy; they require large enclosures and ideal conditions.

WHAT drawbacks?
Lack of a good supply of captive-bred young and the large amount of space required by adults.

Left and below: Wood turtles are attractive, active, and intelligent, but they require large areas in which to live and forage.

Graptemys geographica

Common map turtle

PROFILE

Map turtles get their name from the map-like markings on their shells, which are more obvious in the young than in adults. This species has a light yellow marking behind each eye, in addition to the many pale lines on its face and neck. It lives in large rivers and lakes, basking on logs and on the river bank. In the wild it feeds mainly on water snails and crayfish,

WHAT temperament?
Adaptable but usually remaining shy.

WHAT accommodation?
A large terrarium with a large aquatic section and a smaller land section, for basking.

WHAT environment?
Very hardy; although it prefers temperatures of 64–73°F (18–23°C) and will be most active when warm, it can tolerate very low temperatures if necessary.

Above: Wild map turtles often acquire a dense covering of algae by the time that they are fully grown.

A basking light is essential, as is access to ultraviolet. It is also possible to keep them in enclosed outdoor ponds.

HOW much time?
Adults require frequent cleaning; juveniles can be kept in an aquarium with a filter, cutting down on the amount of time needed.

WHAT varieties?
None. There are a number of other map turtles, including the Mississippi map turtle (page 85).

Cost		
Setup cost		
Running cost		

Size: 4–10 in (10–25 cm), females are much larger

Distribution: North America, from the Great Lakes to northern Louisiana

Life span: Many years; probably 25 or more

WHAT care?
Daily feeding and regular cleaning, as necessary.

WHAT food?
Juveniles will eat freeze-dried shrimp and similar diets but should be given fresh food in the form of aquatic plants and insects. Adults will also eat plants but prefer water snails, earthworms, and other natural foods.

HOW easy are they to breed?
Not bred in captivity.

WHAT drawbacks?
They require large amounts of space, food, and time. Large females can be aggressive toward smaller individuals, including males.

Left: The markings on the shell are more easily seen in captive map turtles.

Graptemys pseudogeographica kohni

Mississippi map turtle

PROFILE

Mississippi map turtles have the typical map turtle pattern of squiggly lines on their carapace but are easily distinguished from other species by the prominent orange crescent just behind their eyes. In addition, they have a knob on each of the central dorsal plates, forming a serrated ridge. This is present in juveniles but becomes larger in adults. Several other map turtles have this feature. Their behavior is similar to that of the common map turtle.

WHAT temperament?
Juveniles (which are usually the only ones available) will adapt to captivity quite easily.

WHAT accommodation?
A large terrarium with a large aquatic section and a smaller land section for basking.

WHAT environment?
A temperature of about 64–73°F (18–23°C) is necessary as this is not as hardy as some other map turtles. A basking light is essential, creating a hot-spot of at least 77–86°F (25–30°C). Access to ultraviolet is also essential. This species is not suitable for housing outdoors in Northern Europe.

HOW much time?
Ten to fifteen minutes a day for feeding and aquarium maintenance. Adults need more time.

WHAT varieties?
None.

WHAT care?
Daily feeding (juveniles), filter maintenance, and water changes as necessary.

WHAT food?
Live food such as crickets, earthworms, aquarium snails, and aquatic insect larvae, and commercial turtle sticks.

HOW easy are they to breed?
Not bred in captivity.

Cost			
Setup cost			
Running cost			

Size: 4–10 in (10–25 cm) (shell length), females about twice as large as males

Distribution: Southeastern United States

Life span: Many years; probably 25 or more

WHAT drawbacks?
Adults, especially females, become very large and require a spacious terrarium. They may also be aggressive toward each other. Buying juveniles avoids this drawback, but only temporarily.

Below: Hatchling Mississippi map turtles have lots of character, but accommodating adults can be demanding on both space and time.

Trachemys scripta

Yellow-bellied turtle

PROFILE

This is a colorful turtle that occurs in a number of forms, or subspecies. It is typically dark green above, with lighter green or yellow markings on each plate. Its lower shell (plastron) is predominantly yellow with intricate dark blotches, and the legs, neck, and head are green with yellow spots and streaks. The distinctive red-eared slider, *Trachemys scripta elegans*, has an additional orange or red stripe behind its eye. Other related forms include members of the genera *Pseudemys*, sometimes known as sliders, and the painted turtle, *Chrysemys picta*. All these turtles have similar lifestyles and can be cared for in more or less the same way, only making allowances for variation in size.

They live in quiet bodies of water, including ditches, swamps, ponds, and slow-moving rivers and streams, preferring places where there is plenty of aquatic vegetation.

Above: Wild yellow-bellied turtles often float just beneath the surface.

They also need somewhere to bask, and this may be a log, rock, or a sloping portion of the river bank. They tend to be nervous and disappear into the water at the slightest disturbance, hence the name "sliders" that is sometimes used. The young eat mainly aquatic insects, but as they grow they gradually include more vegetation in their diet.

WHAT temperament?

Given the right conditions, they adapt well to captivity and overcome their initial nervousness, especially when food is on offer.

WHAT accommodation?

Adults require a large semi-aquatic terrarium, measuring at least 40 × 20 in (100 × 50 cm). Height is not important as long as they cannot climb out. At least half of this area should be water, to a depth of 12 in (30 cm) or more, and the rest can be land or a platform of bark, rock, or wood. This area needs a spotlight installed above it so that the turtles can bask. The water will need to be changed frequently, and it may be an advantage to fit a plug if this is feasible. Depending on their origins, it

Above and lower left: Striped heads and necks are characteristic of many turtles in this family and they retain the markings throughout their lives.

Cost			
Setup cost			
Running cost			

Size: 5–8 in (12–20 cm) (shell length); females are much larger than males

Distribution: Eastern North America; the painted turtle ranges as far north as Canada

Life span: Many years; probably 25 or more

might be possible to keep some species outside for at least part for the year. Hatchling turtles require less spacious terrariums but they will grow in time!

WHAT environment?
They are not especially delicate, and a background temperature of about 64–73°F (18–23°C) is suitable, but the temperature under the basking light needs to be higher than this. Ultraviolet light must also be provided unless the turtles are kept outside.

HOW much time?
Large turtles are labor-intensive and require frequent cleaning as well as regular feeding.

WHAT varieties?
Apart from the yellow-bellied turtle, several similar species are occasionally available, including the red-eared turtle.

WHAT care?
Daily feeding and cleaning as necessary.

WHAT food?
Young turtles will eat commercially available turtle sticks, but this should be supplemented with crickets, earthworms, bloodworms, and other natural food as often as possible. Calcium and vitamin supplements are important, as is ultraviolet light. As they grow, their diet can be switched to a more herbivorous one, using pond plants such as *Elodea*, starwort and duckweed, watercress, and, in an emergency, romaine lettuce.

HOW easy are they to breed?
Very rarely bred in captivity unless a large outdoor pond is provided. The eggs will not hatch unless they are moved to a warmer place.

WHAT drawbacks?
They require large amounts of space, food, and time but can be attractive and rewarding pets for a dedicated keeper.

Above: Hatchling red-eared turtles are among the most colorful and easily identified turtles. They make good pets, but they eventually outgrow their housing and need larger terrariums.

Cuora flavomarginata

Yellow-margined box turtle

PROFILE

The yellow-margined box turtle is a dark brown species with a high-domed carapace that has a central keel, often picked out with orange or yellow streaks. The edges of the shell are turned up slightly and these are yellow, hence the common and scientific names. The plastron is hinged and can be closed up tightly, protecting the turtle's head and limbs. The head is olive green with a prominent yellow stripe on each side, reaching from the neck to the eye. This species lives along the edges of flowing bodies of water and is mainly terrestrial, although it can swim well.

WHAT temperament?
Shy at first, retreating into its shell, but eventually it will become tame.

WHAT accommodation?
A large terrarium, measuring at least 40 × 20 in (100 × 50 cm), is required, divided into land and water areas. The land area should have plenty of shady hiding places as well as a basking area with a UV lamp.

WHAT environment?
A background temperature of 77–82°F (25–28°C) is recommended with a basking area that reaches 86–95°F (30–35°C) in the day.

HOW much time?
Ten to fifteen minutes a day; more for thorough cleaning.

WHAT varieties?
None, although other species of *Cuora* are sometimes imported.

Cost			
Setup cost			
Running cost			

Size: 4–5 in (10–12 cm)
Distribution: Asia
Life span: Unknown; probably at least 20 years

Above and far left: The yellow-margined box turtle is rare in captivity; related species are sometimes seen, and they have similar requirements.

WHAT care?
Daily feeding, regular cleaning, and general maintenance.

WHAT food?
A wide variety, including dead mice, insects, snails, trout pellets, root vegetables and fruit in moderation, always dusted with a vitamin and mineral powder. Calcium should also be available separately, as cuttlefish bone, for instance.

HOW easy are they to breed?
Rarely bred in captivity.

WHAT drawbacks?
Lack of captive-bred young. Imported animals are often parasitized and in poor condition. Best left to experienced turtle keepers.

Agrionemys horsfieldii

Horsfield's tortoise

PROFILE

Horsfield's tortoise is a small species from Central Asia with a more rounded shell than most other species of tortoise. It is predominantly yellowish-brown with a darker area in the center of each plate, or scute. It lives on the dry steppes and is naturally a burrowing species, spending up to nine months underground each year to avoid extremes of weather.

WHAT temperament?
Can be quite restless, constantly trying to escape from its enclosure.

WHAT accommodation?
As for Hermann's tortoise (see pages 94–95). An escape-proof and predator-proof outdoor enclosure on dry, well-drained land is suitable for the warmer parts of the year, but they will also need a more protected enclosure,

such as a greenhouse or cold frame, for times when the weather is cold and damp: they are very susceptible to damp.

WHAT environment?
Warm and dry, as for Hermann's tortoise. They can hibernate in the winter provided they are in good condition.

HOW much time?
Twenty minutes a day for feeding, unless they have a large outdoor enclosure with a variety of plant species.

WHAT varieties?
None

WHAT care?
Daily feeding and checking for parasites and general condition.

WHAT food?
The same as Hermann's tortoise.

Cost			
Setup cost			
Running cost			

Size: To 8 in (20 cm) (shell length). Females are slightly larger than males

Distribution: Central Asia

Life span: Many years; perhaps more than 50

Left and above: Horsfield's tortoise is often available, but its specialized needs have to be taken into account.

HOW easy are they to breed?
Horsfield's tortoises are more reluctant to breed in captivity than the Mediterranean species, for instance, but the reasons for this are unclear.

WHAT drawbacks?
Horsfield's tortoises require extensive outdoor facilities if they are to be healthy and live long. Obtaining a good diet and preparing it for them can be time-consuming.

Chelonoides carbonaria

Red-footed tortoise

PROFILE

The red-footed tortoise is a large species that comes from the forests of South America. Its shell is dark brown or black with lighter centers of yellow or pale orange. Their feet and heads have orange or red scales, hence their name. Adults have elongated shells, especially the males, in which the shell may become shaped like an hour-glass, with a distinct "waist" about halfway along. Males also have concave plastrons, in common with most other terrestrial tortoises.

Above and below: Adult and juvenile red-footed tortoises are tropical and need constant heat and high humidity if they are to thrive.

Cost					
Setup cost					
Running cost					

Size: 10–14 in (25–35 cm) (shell)

Distribution: Northern South America and some Caribbean islands

Life span: Many years; possibly 50 or more

HOW much time?
Fifteen to thirty minutes per day.

WHAT varieties?
No varieties. The yellow-footed tortoise is similar but rarely available.

WHAT care?
Daily feeding and spraying. Cleaning as necessary.

WHAT temperament?
Active and responsive. Red-footed tortoises tame easily, although they sometimes take a long time to get used to new surroundings.

WHAT accommodation?
They need large enclosures as adults, at least 21.5 ft² (2 m²) for a small group. This should have a substrate of bark chippings or similar so that it will retain some moisture for a while after spraying. They also require a powerful heat lamp as well as a UV lamp, and a shallow bowl of clean water in which they can soak. Juveniles can be kept in smaller terrariums appropriate for their size.

WHAT environment?
A background temperature of 79–86°F (26–30°C) is required, and the temperature under the heat lamp should be at least 95°F (35°C). They require a higher humidity than European or African tortoises and should be sprayed regularly, although the substrate must not be allowed to become waterlogged.

WHAT food?
This species is omnivorous and will not thrive on a diet of greens; it also needs fruit in its diet, and this should be fed with skins (banana, etc.). Low-fat cat food can be used in moderation.

HOW easy are they to breed?
Breeding has been achieved, but only in extensive facilities.

WHAT drawbacks?
The large amount of space and time required.

Geochelone sulcata

African spurred tortoise

PROFILE

The African spurred tortoise is the largest mainland species, sometimes reaching a weight of 220 pounds (100 kg) (making them too heavy for one person to lift!). Their shell is pale yellowish-brown as adults, with a narrow dark border to each plate: juveniles' shells are more heavily marked. They live in desert and semi-desert habitats.

WHAT temperament?
They become very tame, but because of their size they can be destructive. Their enclosure must be substantial if it is to remain intact.

WHAT accommodation?
Very large indoor enclosures are essential for adults, measuring at least 13 × 6.5 ft (4 × 2 m). Juveniles can be kept in smaller, open-topped pens. They require powerful heaters creating one or more hot-spots for basking, a "hutch" to retreat into, and a shallow tray of water for soaking in. They can be put outside on warm, sunny days and will benefit from feeding on growing grasses.

WHAT environment?
A temperature of 73–86°F (23–30°C) is necessary throughout the year. African spurred tortoises do not hibernate. They must be kept dry and a substrate of hay is ideal.

HOW much time?
Up to one hour a day for food preparation and cleaning.

WHAT varieties?
None.

WHAT care?
Daily feeding and cleaning.

WHAT food?
Same as the leopard tortoise (page 92). Incorrect feeding of either of these species, especially too much protein and/or not enough calcium and Vitamin D3, leads to shell deformities.

This page: The African spurred tortoise is the largest mainland species and has an appetite to match.

Cost				
Setup cost				
Running cost				

Size: To 31 in (80 cm) (shell)

Distribution: Northern half of Africa (Sahara Desert and the Sahel)

Life span: Probably in excess of 100 years

HOW easy are they to breed?
They are bred regularly in captivity by dedicated tortoise specialists, but this is a serious undertaking.

WHAT drawbacks?
A large space is required for accommodation, and they are time-consuming and expensive to maintain properly.

Leopard tortoise

PROFILE

A tortoise from the southern half of Africa, with a high-domed shell, attractively marked in black and yellow. Hatchlings are more brightly marked than adults. Leopard tortoises are among the largest mainland species and can grow to nearly 88 lbs (40 kg) in weight. They live in a variety of habitats in their native southern Africa, including semi-desert scrub, rocky hillsides, and dry grasslands.

Above and below: Leopard tortoises are arguably the most attractive of the commonly available tortoise species. They need large enclosures.

Cost		
Setup cost		
Running cost		

Size: Can reach 24 in (60 cm) (shell length), usually smaller

Distribution: Southern Africa

Life span: Many years; perhaps up to 100

WHAT temperament?

Very responsive and can become very tame.

WHAT accommodation?

They require very large indoor enclosures, with a powerful heater and ultraviolet light. They can be moved outdoors on warm, sunny days but should be kept in a dry environment to avoid respiratory problems. A large water bowl or tray for soaking is needed. Juveniles can be kept in smaller indoor terrariums but they grow very quickly.

WHAT environment?

A temperature of 73–82°F (23–28°C) is ideal, and they will seek out slightly higher temperatures if given a basking spot. Humidity should be low at all times. Leopard tortoises do not hibernate and need a constantly high temperature throughout the year.

HOW much time?

Up to one hour per day for food preparation and cleaning.

WHAT varieties?

None, although the spurred tortoise *Geochelone sulcata* (page 91) requires similar care (and is even larger).

WHAT care?

Daily feeding and cleaning.

WHAT food?

A high-fiber diet is essential. When they are outdoors they will graze on grasses and garden plants, but in indoor enclosures they require hay and leafy greens such as watercress and carrot tops. Avoid root vegetables, fruit, and leaves with a high water content, such as lettuce. All meals must be dusted with a calcium and vitamin D3 supplement.

HOW easy are they to breed?

They are bred regularly in captivity, but maintaining a breeding colony is a big commitment.

WHAT drawbacks?

Very time-consuming and expensive to house and feed properly, especially in the winter.

Pelodiscus sinensis 📷🏛

Chinese soft-shell turtle

PROFILE

The Chinese soft-shell turtle is an unusual species with a leathery covering to its shell. It has a long neck and a snorkel-like snout so that it can breathe at the surface while its body remains hidden under water. Its feet are webbed and flipper-like. It lives in shallow water with sandy or muddy substrates, and is widely farmed for food in Southeast Asia.

WHAT temperament?
Bad-tempered. Chinese soft-shelled turtles have long necks and can reach around to the back of their shells. Adults can give a nasty bite if they are handled carelessly.

WHAT accommodation?
They need large aquatic terrariums with a water depth equivalent to the length of their neck so that they can breathe while resting on the bottom.

They need a substrate of sand, or no substrate at all – gravel and rocks should be avoided. A shelf across one end will give them a hiding place while in the water, and a place to come out to bask if they want to. All surfaces should be smooth so that the turtle does not damage its shell, which is quite delicate. A UV lamp is recommended.

WHAT environment?
A daytime temperature of 73–86°F (25–30°C) but cooler temperatures are tolerated for short periods.

HOW much time?
Fifteen to thirty minutes a day.

WHAT varieties?
Other soft-shelled turtles are occasionally available, including those from North America, the *Apalone* species.

Cost			
Setup cost			
Running cost			

Size: To 18 in (30 cm) (shell)

Distribution: Asia

Life span: Unknown; probably 25–50 years

WHAT care?
Daily feeding and cleaning. They produce a lot of waste, and frequent water changes are necessary. Filters are only effective with very small turtles.

WHAT food?
Whole fish, shellfish, prawns, watersnails, etc. They will also eat strips of meat, and some will eat vegetation such as water plants, and fruit such as melon. Juveniles will eat insects such as crickets, dusted with a vitamin and mineral supplement.

HOW easy are they to breed?
Not bred in captivity.

WHAT drawbacks?
They require large aquariums and considerable amounts of time. And they bite.

Left: Soft-shelled turtles are unmistakable.

Testudo hermanni

Hermann's tortoise

Hermann's tortoise is a Mediterranean species that used to be more common in captivity than it is nowadays, due to protective legislation, although captive-bred specimens are often available. It is yellowish-brown or bone colored with dark areas in every plate, or scute. These vary in size according to the origins of the tortoise, and several subspecies are recognized. They can be distinguished from the similar spur-thighed or Greek tortoise by the large scale on the tip of their tail and the paired plates immediately above the tail: the spur-thighed tortoise lacks the large scale and has a single scute over the tail.

They live in fields, meadows, and scrub-covered hillsides, grazing on low plants, especially members of the pea family (legumes). Males have concave shells, which makes it easier for them to mount the female during mating. Females lay three to twelve eggs, which are rounded and look like ping-pong balls, and which hatch after two to three months.

Above: Hermann's tortoises are the most familiar of the commonly available "garden" tortoise species.

WHAT temperament?

An easygoing species that tends to do better in captivity than other tortoises. Males are inclined to wander off during the breeding season unless their enclosure is well built and has a high wall.

WHAT accommodation?

An escape-proof and predator-proof outdoor enclosure measuring at least 265 ft ^{2} (2 m²) is best, but it must be situated on dry, well-drained land, otherwise the tortoise will suffer respiratory problems. The height of the walls of the enclosure, which can be of bricks or timber, should be twice the largest tortoise's shell length, and an overhang is also advised. It might be necessary to cover the enclosure with wire mesh if predators (including domestic dogs and cats) are present. The enclosure should be planted with a variety of wild flowers, especially vetches, clovers, dandelions, and hawkweeds, all of which grow quickly and form a good diet for the tortoise.

Depending on the climate, they will also need a more protected enclosure, such as a greenhouse, for times when the weather is cold and damp; they can tolerate cold, but not damp. Provided they are in good condition, they can be allowed to hibernate in a frost-free place in the winter.

Left: A young adult with a well-marked shell.

WHAT environment?

Warm and dry. Summer temperatures in northern areas are adequate if the tortoises are kept in an open, south-facing situation, but higher temperatures will be required in the early spring and autumn.

HOW much time?

Thirty minutes a day for preparing food, unless their enclosure contains enough growing plants.

WHAT varieties?

The spur-thighed or Greek tortoise, *Testudo graeca*, is similar and requires similar care.

WHAT care?

Daily feeding and checking for parasites and general condition.

WHAT food?

Tortoises require high-fiber diets consisting of plants such as clover, dandelions, and other weeds, preferably eaten while growing in their enclosure. Artificially formulated diets are too high in protein and often lack sufficient calcium, leading to rapid growth and shell deformities. Root vegetables are best avoided, as is lettuce, which contains very little vitamins or minerals.

Calcium can be added to the diet in the form of powdered cuttlefish bone or a proprietary calcium food supplement. If the tortoises are kept outside, they will receive enough sunlight to enable them to assimilate calcium, but if they are kept indoors they will need an ultraviolet light to take the place of sunlight. In summary, tortoise nutrition is a very complicated subject, and anybody keeping tortoises should make sure they are fully aware of the relevant information.

HOW easy are they to breed?

They are regularly bred in captivity.

WHAT drawbacks?

They require a large area for their enclosure and accommodation indoors during cold weather.

Cost			
Setup cost			
Running cost			

Size: 8 in (20 cm) (shell length)

Distribution: Mediterranean region

Life span: Many years; reputedly over 100

Below: Hermann's tortoises become very tame and are among the most rewarding to keep. They will breed in captivity given the right conditions.

Sternotherus carinatus

Razorback musk turtle

PROFILE

This musk turtle is distinguished by the single keel running the length of its carapace, giving the shell a tent-like shape. Other species are keeled but not to the same extent. It is yellowish-brown or gray in color with a pattern of dark streaks on its shell and many small brown spots on its head and neck. It has the hooked beak found in all the members of this family. It lives in streams and large swampy areas, and spends a lot of time basking.

WHAT temperament?
Although wild individuals can be belligerent, captives soon calm down and make very responsive pets.

WHAT accommodation?
Identical to that of the common musk turtle (page 97).

WHAT environment?
A water temperature of at least 73°F (23°C) is recommended, and they must have an opportunity to bask under a spotlight supplemented with a UV lamp. Juveniles bask less than adults and can be set up with a small aquarium heater and thermostat, and a mechanical aquarium filter.

HOW much time?
Ten minutes a day for feeding; longer periods occasionally for cleaning.

Cost			
Setup cost			
Running cost			

Size: 3–4 in (8–10 cm)

Distribution: Southeastern United States

Life span: Probably 25 years or more

WHAT varieties?
None, although other musk and the related mud turtles are available occasionally.

WHAT care?
Daily feeding and occasional filter maintenance or water changing.

WHAT food?
Turtle sticks are useful as a standby, but they should be supplemented with earthworms and aquatic live foods such as bloodworms as often as possible.

Above: The prominent ridge along its carapace gives this species its common name.

HOW easy are they to breed?
Breeding should be possible, although it seems to be rarely attempted.

WHAT drawbacks?
None, save the lack of captive-bred young. A good choice if space is limited.

Above: Hatchling musk turtles are among the smallest, but they have good appetites and grow quickly.

Sternotherus odoratus

Common musk turtle or stinkpot

PROFILE

Common musk turtles have smooth, domed shells, elongated when seen from above. In this species the shell is uniform dark brown or black, and the head and limbs are equally dark, except for a pair of cream stripes that run above and below the eyes. In the wild, old individuals are often covered with a carpet of filamentous algae, which enhances their camouflage. These turtles prefer still water and spend their time walking along the bottom or climbing onto sloping tree trunks to bask.

WHAT temperament?
Sometimes bad tempered and large ones can give a painful bite, but they soon adapt to captivity.

WHAT accommodation?
A terrarium consisting of mainly water, and a branch or platform for basking is ideal. Its size will depend on the age and quantity of the turtles but, being small, this species is not as demanding of space as some other species.

A spotlight should be directed onto the basking place.

WHAT environment?
They need a water temperature of 68–73°F (20–23°C) and a basking spot that reaches at least 86°F (30°C) for part of each day. Juveniles can be heated by a small aquarium heater and thermostat. Ultraviolet light should be available to the basking turtles.

HOW much time?
Ten minutes a day for feeding; longer periods occasionally for cleaning.

WHAT varieties?
None. Other musk turtles are available occasionally, including the razorback (page 96).

WHAT care?
Daily feeding and occasional filter maintenance or water changing.

Below: Though not particularly colorful, common musk turtles have plenty of character and make good pets.

Cost		
Setup cost		
Running cost		

Size: 3–5 in (8–12 cm)	
Distribution: The eastern half of North America	
Life span: Up to 25 years or more	

Above: An old musk turtle whose shell has become worn over time.

WHAT food?
Turtle sticks, but not exclusively; they should be supplemented with earthworms and aquatic live foods such as bloodworms.

HOW easy are they to breed?
Breeding has been achieved but is not a regular occurrence.

WHAT drawbacks?
This is one of the best turtle species to keep. Despite its rather alarming name, this turtle does not deploy its musk glands in captivity.

Chelus fimbriatus

Matamata

The matamata (sometimes spelled mata mata) is a bizarre and interesting side-neck turtle from South America. Its reddish-brown shell is rough and has three keels running down it, but its head and neck are its most arresting features. These are flattened, with fleshy frills and flaps, while its snout is long and pointed with nostrils at the tip, allowing it to breathe while submerged. It is highly aquatic, living on the muddy bottom of quiet waters, where it ambushes fish.

WHAT temperament?
Sluggish except when feeding.

WHAT accommodation?
A large aquatic terrarium, i.e., an aquarium, with 2–12 in (5–30 cm) of water, depending on the size of the turtle. A soft substrate of sand or dead leaves is required, with some pieces of driftwood to provide cover. A filter can be used to keep the water clean, but it should not create too much turbulence; matamatas prefer still or slowly moving water.

WHAT environment?
A constant temperature of 77–82°F (25–28°C) is needed, and the air above the water should be the same temperature. The water should be acidic (pH 5 to 5.5 is recommended) and contain tannins so that it looks like weak tea. A UV lamp is recommended but may not be essential.

Below: With its frilly neck and triangular head, the South American matamata is among the strangest species.

Cost			
Setup cost			
Running cost			

Size: 12–16 in (30–40 cm)

Distribution: South America

Life span: Unknown

HOW much time?
Ten to twenty minutes a day.

WHAT varieties?
None. This is a one-of-a-kind turtle!

WHAT care?
Daily monitoring of the water temperature and conditions. A filter may help but manual cleaning is inevitable occasionally.

WHAT food?
Fish, which must be alive or made to appear so. The young will sometimes eat earthworms and aquatic invertebrates.

HOW easy are they to breed?
Bred only on very rare occasions.

WHAT drawbacks?
Expensive when available, and difficult to provide the right conditions. They need a constant supply of live fish. Best left to the experts.

Emydura subglobosa

Pink-bellied shortneck turtle

PROFILE

This species, which is also known as the pink-bellied side-neck turtle, comes from Australia and New Guinea, although those in the pet trade will be of the New Guinea subspecies. It belongs to a group of turtles that withdraw their heads by turning them to the side, rather than pulling them straight back into their shell, as most species do. Hatchlings are very colorful, with orange markings on the head and shell, but they lose these bright colors as they grow.

WHAT temperament?
They adapt well to captivity and become bolder as they grow.

WHAT accommodation?
Same as the yellow-bellied slider (pages 86–87), although this species requires constant heat. A basking area beneath a heat lamp and a UV source is very important.

WHAT environment?
A constant water temperature of about 77°F (25°C) is necessary and the spot under the basking lamp should rise to at least 86°F (30°C) during the day.

HOW much time?
Five to ten minutes a day for feeding; longer periods for tank maintenance.

WHAT varieties?
None. Other side-neck turtles are occasionally offered for sale, and their care is similar.

WHAT care?
Daily feeding. A filter will keep the water in the tank clean, although as the turtle grows it will require frequent water changes.

Left: As this species grows, its bright colors gradually fade.

Cost				
Setup cost				
Running cost				

Size: To 10 in (25 cm)
Distribution: Australia and New Guinea
Life span: Many years; probably over 25

WHAT food?
Juveniles are mostly insectivorous and will also eat turtle sticks. Adults also eat some leafy greens and a small amount of fruit. Vitamins and minerals, especially calcium, should be added to their food.

HOW easy are they to breed?
Breeding is possible but a large setup is required.

WHAT drawbacks?
Adults require large terrariums and are not as colorful as the young.

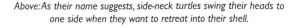

Above: As their name suggests, side-neck turtles swing their heads to one side when they want to retreat into their shell.

Lizards

■ Lizards are reptiles and are closely related to snakes. At present there are 5,634 recognized species but they vary so much in size, shape, and color that it is difficult to generalize them. Most have four limbs, but some have only two; others have none. Their scales may be rough or smooth, large or small, and almost every imaginable color is found within the group. The smallest species will sit on the head of a match, whereas the largest can grow to 10 ft (3 m) in length and weigh 150 lbs (70 kg).

■ Captive lizards are equally diverse, meaning that there should be something to interest everyone. Species such as bearded dragons and leopard geckos have almost become domesticated, with many different color forms available, while others are very specialized and kept only by dedicated followers. Geckos are very popular, as are chameleons, but the latter should be left to the experts, apart from one or two species that adapt well and are widely bred in captivity.

■ Terrariums for lizards can consist of, in their most simple form, small plastic boxes with ventilation holes and a substrate of sand or paper towels; terrariums of this type are useful for raising young lizards or for quarantining new acquisitions. Large species, on the other hand, need very large enclosures, up to the size of greenhouses or walk-in cages indoors. Most species, however, can be kept in moderate-sized glass or wooden terrariums fitted out in a suitable way.

■ Lizards may be active in the day or in the night; many diurnal species require specialized UV-B equipment to provide them with Vitamin D3 (please see the section on turtles and tortoises for more about this important topic). Nearly all species require supplementary heating, and desert species, in particular, require very high temperatures and powerful heat lamps. As a general rule, all heating should be

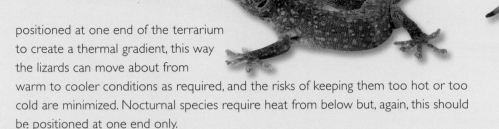

positioned at one end of the terrarium
to create a thermal gradient, this way
the lizards can move about from
warm to cooler conditions as required, and the risks of keeping them too hot or too
cold are minimized. Nocturnal species require heat from below but, again, this should
be positioned at one end only.

■ Similarly, a choice of humidity is important to many species, and even those from
deserts often burrow down to a level where the sand or soil retains some moisture.
A convenient way to arrange this is to give desert species a humid hide box containing
a layer of moss or vermiculite that is kept slightly moist, and a narrow opening so that
it does not dry out. They will use this if necessary, such as when they are about to
shed their skin (and also for egg laying). The rest of the cage can then be kept dry.
Other species need high humidity throughout the cage and require frequent spraying
or an automatic misting system that raises the humidity for an hour or more once or
twice each day. Chameleons in particular benefit from this type of arrangement but
other species, such as forest dragons and anoles, also require humid environments.

■ Lizards may be carnivorous, herbivorous, or omnivorous. Dietary requirements are
given under the species' accounts. Live foods such as crickets should be kept in well-
ventilated boxes and fed on nutritious food until they are required for feeding. They
should then be dusted with a vitamin and mineral supplement specially formulated
for reptiles, of which there are a number on the market. Herbivorous species should
be given a good variety of leafy plants, including plenty of garden weeds such as
dandelions. Lettuce contains very little of anything except water and is best avoided,
or given in small quantities. Again, a vitamin and mineral supplement is essential.

Acanthosaura crucigera

Mountain horned dragon

| **Size:** To 12 in (30 cm) |
| **Distribution:** Southeast Asia |
| **Life span:** Not known; probably 5–10 years |

PROFILE

Horned dragons, also known as forest dragons, rely heavily on camouflage and are not as active as some other members of their family. They have a row of spines starting behind their head and running down their back and are sometimes known as pricklenape lizards. Males also have short spines over each eye. This species is predominantly green or olive-brown, and has a brilliant orange eye. They are arboreal forest lizards, living on vertical tree trunks and branches, and rarely descend to the ground in the wild.

WHAT temperament?
Calm when they feel secure, in a well-planted terrarium, but easily stressed if kept in a more open setup.

WHAT accommodation?
Large, tall terrariums are necessary, at least 3 ft (1 m) high, and well filled with vertical or steeply-sloping branches and plenty of leafy plants for cover. Artificial plants may be used. The substrate can be bark chippings, and they should have a large water bowl in which to soak. A basking light is necessary, as is a UV lamp.

WHAT environment?
Not too warm; a temperature of 64–72°F (18–22°C) suits them during the day, and it can be lower during the night. A

basking light will give them an opportunity to raise their body temperature if necessary. Regular spraying is essential to raise the humidity, but ventilation should be good.

HOW much time?
Ten to twenty minutes a day.

WHAT varieties?
None. Other species of *Acanthosaura* are sometimes available, and their care is similar.

WHAT care?
Daily feeding, spraying, and general monitoring of the lizards and their environment.

WHAT food?
Insects such as locusts and crickets. Meals should be dusted with a vitamin and mineral supplement.

HOW easy are they to breed?
Very rarely bred in captivity.

WHAT drawbacks?
Lack of captive-bred stock and the large amount of vertical space they require.

Left and above: The mountain horned dragon is a typical forest species that requires a tall terrarium and branches to cling to.

Chlamydosaurus kingii

Frilled lizard

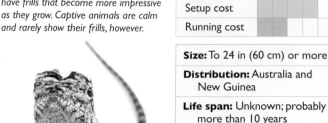

PROFILE

A large and spectacular lizard from Australia and New Guinea that is famous for the large throat fan that it erects when it is frightened, and for its ability to raise itself up onto its hind legs when running quickly (bipedal locomotion). Mainly mottled grey in color; some strains have orange or red markings on their frills, but captive individuals rarely reveal their frills.

WHAT temperament?

Very adaptable and soon become tame, approaching their owner for food.

WHAT accommodation?

Very large terrariums are required, measuring 6 x 3 x 4.5 ft (2 x 1 x 1.5 m) high as a minimum. This should be fitted with stout branches and plenty of opportunities to climb. A substrate of dust-free bark chippings, mixed with sand if desired, will hold sufficient moisture to maintain the right humidity, and a large water bowl should be present. A powerful basking light will be required, as will an ultraviolet lamp.

WHAT environment?

A background temperature of 68–77°F (20–25°C) is necessary, rising to at least 95°F (35°C) under the basking lamp. The humidity should be raised for at least part of each day, although the cage must be well ventilated.

Both below: Even juvenile frilled lizards have frills that become more impressive as they grow. Captive animals are calm and rarely show their frills, however.

HOW much time?

Fifteen to thirty minutes per day.

WHAT varieties?

None. Most of the colonies in captivity originated in New Guinea, but they are similar to those from Australia and have the same requirements.

WHAT care?

Daily feeding, spraying, and replenishing the water bowl.

WHAT food?

Insects such as crickets and locusts, dusted with a vitamin

Cost			
Setup cost			
Running cost			

Size: To 24 in (60 cm) or more

Distribution: Australia and New Guinea

Life span: Unknown; probably more than 10 years

and mineral supplement. Larger frilled lizards will eat mice that have been thawed.

HOW easy are they to breed?

They breed regularly in captivity, but only if given enough room.

WHAT drawbacks?

They require a large amount of space and time.

Calotes versicolor

Common garden lizard

Size: To 14 in (35 cm), most of which is tail

Distribution: South Asia

Life span: Unknown; at least 5 years

PROFILE

This is a common lizard over much of South Asia, where it can be seen on fence posts, trees, and buildings. It has the alternative name of "blood-sucker," owing to the patch of red scales on the throats of males when they are in breeding condition. It has a long tail and long legs. Its head is angular with a crest of spiny scales on its neck, and the scales covering the rest of its body are strongly keeled, giving a rough or prickly appearance.

WHAT temperament?

Nervous and quick-moving but adaptable; calms down in captivity if it is given a large enough area.

Above and below: Male garden lizards have bright red throats (above) in the breeding season, whereas females and juveniles lack this feature and have smaller heads.

WHAT accommodation?

A large, tall terrarium measuring at least 40 × 24 × 40 in (100 × 60 × 100 cm) high is required. This should be lined with cork and furnished with several pieces of rough-barked branches so that the lizard has places to rest vertically. The substrate can be orchid or reptile bark, sand, or a mixture, and plastic or living plants will provide hiding places. A basking light, UV lamp, and a water bowl are essential.

WHAT environment?

A temperature of 68–77°F (20–25°C) suits them during the day, and it can be lower during the night. A basking light will allow them to raise their body temperature if necessary. Regular spraying is essential to raise the humidity, but ventilation should be good.

HOW much time?

Ten to fifteen minutes per day.

WHAT varieties?

None. There are other species of *Calotes*, but they are rarely imported.

WHAT care?

Daily feeding and spraying. Cleaning as necessary.

WHAT food?

Large insects such as crickets and locusts, waxworms, and small mice. Vitamin and mineral supplements are required.

HOW easy are they to breed?

Unlikely to breed in captivity.

WHAT drawbacks?

They require a large amount of space, and captive-bred young are rarely available.

Physignathus cocincinus

Thai water dragon

PROFILE

The Thai water dragon is a large, green dragon lizard that is widely kept in captivity. They lead a semi-aquatic, semi-arboreal life along river courses in Southeast Asia, quickly diving into the water if they feel under threat. Their accommodation needs to reflect this lifestyle. Males are larger than females, have a raised crest on their necks, and tend to be more colorful.

WHAT temperament?

Captive-bred animals are calm and tame down quickly, but wild ones are nervous, frequently bashing their snouts on the side of the terrarium in their efforts to escape.

WHAT accommodation?

Large terrariums are required, measuring a minimum of 3 x 3 x 3 ft (1 x 1 x 1 m) for one or two adults, and ideally 3 x 6 x 4.5 ft (1 x 2 x 1.5 m). The floor should be divided into aquatic and terrestrial sections, and there should be strong branches extending over the water for the lizards to bask on. A powerful heat lamp is necessary, as is a UV lamp.

WHAT environment?

A background temperature of 77–86°F (25–30°C) is required, and the area under the heat lamp should reach 95°F (35°C) at least. Humidity is important but should be adequate if a large water area is provided.

HOW much time?

Fifteen to thirty minutes a day; longer periods for thorough cage cleaning.

WHAT varieties?

None.

WHAT care?

Daily feeding, and cleaning as necessary. The water must be kept clean, and some form of drainage will facilitate this.

Cost			
Setup cost			
Running cost			

Size: 24–35 in (60–90 cm), mostly tail. Males are much larger than females

Distribution: Southeast Asia

Life span: At least 10 years in captivity

WHAT food?

Insects such as crickets and locusts, dusted with vitamin and mineral powder.

HOW easy are they to breed?

They will breed readily if they have a large enough cage. Males are territorial, so breeding groups can consist of a pair or a male and two to four females.

WHAT drawbacks?

They require a lot of space and an elaborate cage setup.

Left: Thai water dragons are large, colorful, and impressive lizards that will thrive in captivity if given a large enough cage.

Physignathus lesueurii

Eastern water dragon

PROFILE

This water dragon is not as colorful as the Thai species, but adult males develop reddish patches on their throats and chests. Otherwise, this species is olive-brown with a dark stripe across its face and additional dark markings on its back. It has a crest of small, pointed scales, and its body and tail are flattened from side to side for swimming. It lives along bodies of water in Australia, where it is quick to drop into the water to escape from predators.

WHAT temperament?

Can be nervous and prone to rush around its cage if disturbed, but will become tame if given plenty of cover and regular handling.

WHAT accommodation?

Similar to that of the Thai water dragon (see page 105), but this species can be put outside on warm days in the summer, like in a greenhouse, for instance.

WHAT environment?

Similar to the Thai water dragon, but this species is more tolerant of cold and adults can be allowed to hibernate. Juveniles should be kept in smaller, warmer cages throughout the year.

WHAT varieties?

There are two subspecies of which only one, the eastern water dragon, *Physignathus lesueurii lesueurii,* is available. This is the more colorful subspecies.

WHAT care?

Daily feeding, and cleaning as necessary. The water must be kept clean, and some form of drainage will help to make this easier.

Cost			
Setup cost			
Running cost			

Size: 30–40 in (75–100 cm), males are larger than females

Distribution: Australia

Life span: Unknown; probably 10–20 years

Above: The eastern water dragon is a large and impressive species.

Above: Male eastern water dragons have pink-flushed throats. This species is tolerant of a wide range of conditions but requires a large cage with plenty of perches and hiding places.

HOW much time?

Fifteen to thirty minutes a day, more for cage cleaning.

WHAT food?

Mostly insects such as crickets, but adults will sometimes eat fruit and vegetables and, occasionally, canned dog or cat food.

HOW easy are they to breed?

They are bred in captivity, but this is not easy.

WHAT drawbacks?

Like the Thai water dragon, they require large amounts of space and an elaborate cage setup.

106

Pogona henrylawsonl

Rankin's bearded dragon

PROFILE

This species is smaller than the inland bearded dragon (see pages 108–109), and its beard is not as well developed, nor is the row of spiny scales along its flanks. Its head is proportionately smaller and more rounded. Its overall coloration is pale yellowish-brown and its throat and underside are paler, almost white. It lives in desert regions of central Australia, inhabiting treeless plains. It is less frequently seen than its more popular relative, and there are no color forms. Having said that, this is an easier species to accommodate, as it is smaller, and it makes a good pet.

Above and below: Rankin's dragon is smaller and more delicately built than the inland bearded dragon.

Cost			
Setup cost			
Running cost			

Size: To 9.5 in (24 cm)

Distribution: Central Australia

Life span Many years; probably 10 or more

WHAT temperament?
Very calm and easily tamed. Diurnal and active. Individuals are less competitive toward each other than the inland bearded dragon, and small groups consisting of one male and several females will live harmoniously

WHAT accommodation?
Similar to that of the inland bearded dragon, but its terrarium can be smaller.

WHAT environment?
The same as for the inland bearded dragon.

HOW much time?
Fifteen to thirty minutes each day for feeding, spraying, and cleaning. Time spent getting the lizards used to being handled will be well spent, and they become very tame.

WHAT varieties?
None.

WHAT care?
Daily feeding and spot cleaning. Longer periods occasionally for a complete clean.

WHAT food?
Insects such as crickets when young, with the introduction of vegetable material as they grow larger. A vitamin and mineral supplement is essential.

HOW easy are they to breed?
Not as easy as inland bearded dragons, for reasons that are not clear, and not as prolific, but careful attention to diet and the light/temperature cycle should bring success.

WHAT drawbacks?
None, although they are not as readily available as inland bearded dragons.

Pogona vitticeps

Inland bearded dragon

The inland bearded dragon is one of the most popular reptiles and is familiar to everyone who has an interest in reptile keeping. In the wild, inland bearded dragons are light brown or yellowish-brown, with an indistinct pattern of darker markings, which are better defined in juveniles. They have a row of pointed scales around their flanks, marking the edge of the dorsal surface, and another row around the back of their head. The characteristic that gives them their name, however, is their throats, which can be inflated when the lizard is stressed, making the scales stand on end to form the "beard." Captive individuals rarely display this, however.

Bearded dragons live in dry, lightly wooded habitats and often use fence posts and tree stumps as lookout posts from which to monitor their surroundings and from where they will dash if they see a potential meal. When basking they flatten their body and angle it toward the sun to warm up more quickly. Individuals communicate to each other through a series of movements such as head bobbing and arm waving, making them one of the more interesting species to keep and observe.

WHAT temperament?

The inland bearded dragon has proved to be very adaptable and is easy to keep and breed in captivity. It can be safely handled, with care, even by beginners. Individuals become very tame and will approach their owner to be fed.

WHAT accommodation?

A terrarium measuring 47 × 20 × 20 in (120 × 60 × 60 cm) is the minimum requirement for a pair or small group of adult bearded dragons; if it can be made larger, it is even better. Juveniles, however, should be kept in proportionately smaller terrariums so that they can find food more easily, and then moved on gradually to larger terrariums. The cage needs to be furnished with a substrate such as reptile sand, some rocks, and driftwood so that the lizards can bask and behave naturally. A powerful heat lamp is essential, as is a UV lamp.

WHAT environment?

Hot and dry conditions are required. A minimum background temperature of 68–77°F (20–25°C) is required with a temperature of 86–104°F (30–40°C) directly beneath a spotlight during the day. A shallow water bowl will provide sufficient humidity, and the terrarium should be well ventilated.

Above: An attractive reddish form of the inland bearded dragon.

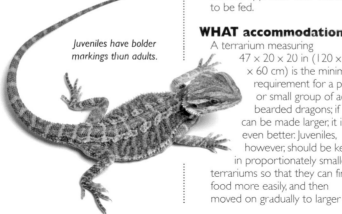

Juveniles have bolder markings than adults.

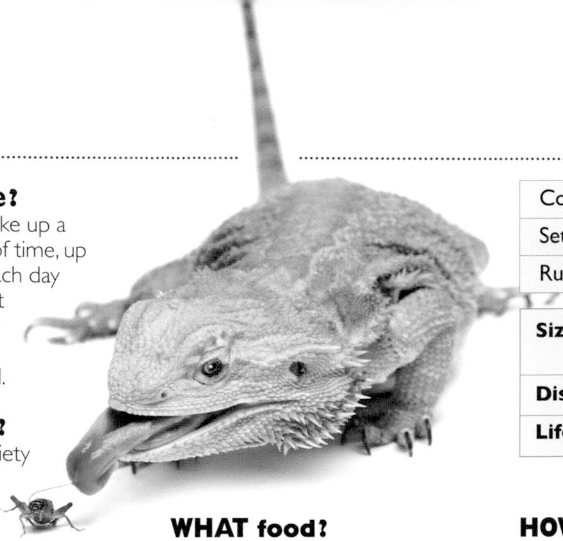

HOW much time?

Bearded dragons take up a significant amount of time, up to thirty minutes each day for feeding and spot cleaning, and longer for thorough cage cleaning as required.

WHAT varieties?

There is a great variety of color forms, or "morphs" as they are known by hobbyists. These are given descriptive names by breeders, and new forms are appearing all the time through selective breeding.

WHAT care?

Daily feeding, general health check, changing the water in the dish, and monitoring temperature. Cleaning as necessary.

Above top: A bearded dragon snaps up a cricket. They will also eat some vegetable material.

Right: Bearded dragons flatten their bodies when they are basking under a heat lamp.

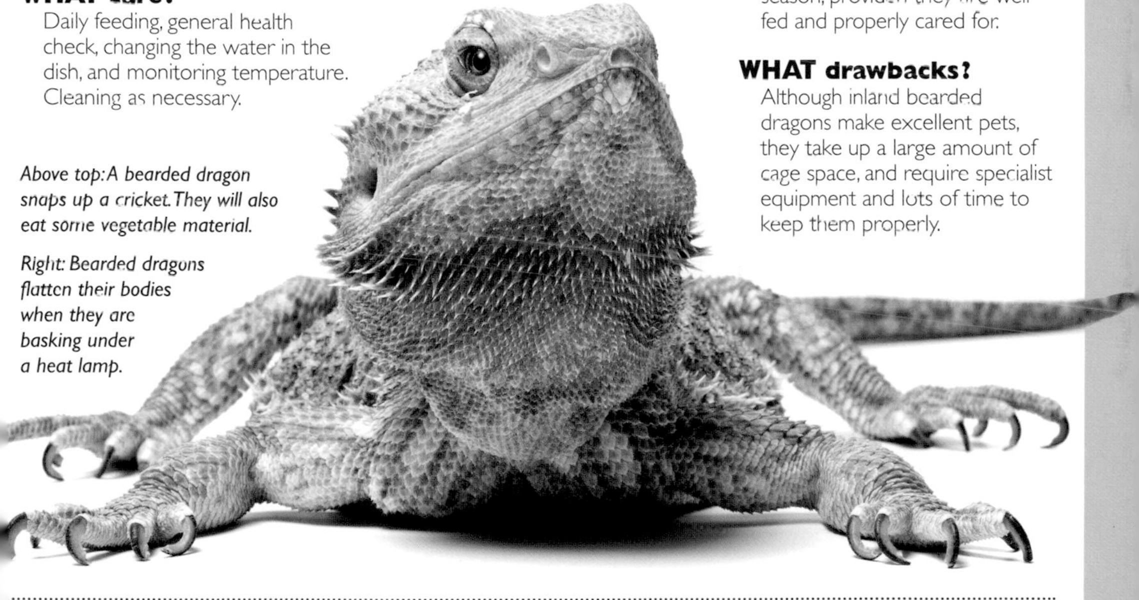

WHAT food?

Juveniles feed mostly on small insects such as crickets, whereas adults include some vegetation in their diet. All meals should be dusted with a good vitamin and mineral preparation.

HOW easy are they to breed?

They breed readily in captivity, providing a constant supply of captive-bred young. Females can lay sets of twenty or more eggs several times in a single breeding season, provided they are well fed and properly cared for.

WHAT drawbacks?

Although inland bearded dragons make excellent pets, they take up a large amount of cage space, and require specialist equipment and lots of time to keep them properly.

Cost			
Setup cost			
Running cost			

Size: 12–20 in (30–50 cm), about half is tail

Distribution: Australia

Life span: To 10 years

Red Niger Uromastyx, or mastigure

PROFILE

A number of different dab lizards are imported occasionally, of which this is one of the most common. In any case, all can be treated in the same way as captives. They have short heads and are snub-nosed, making them very tortoise-like. They are pale brown or yellowish-brown in color to blend in with their natural surroundings. Some species are more colorful. Their bodies are broad and stocky and their tails are heavily armored with rings of spiny scales running around them. Dab lizards are members of the agama family but lead a very specialized life style, feeding entirely on vegetation and living in colonies. They build large underground burrow systems that contain chambers: they use their tails to block their tunnels and to lash out at enemies. They live in areas of North Africa and the Middle East that experience very hot summers and very cold winters, and they hibernate for long periods to avoid extremes of cold.

Above: Saharan or Red Niger Uromastyx, Uromastyx geyri.

WHAT temperament?

Shy by nature, but they will adapt to captivity if the conditions are correct.

WHAT accommodation?

Very large terrariums are required, measuring at least 6.5 x 3 ft (2 x 1 m) floor area. The substrate should be gravel, with piles of sturdy rocks for basking: a heat lamp should be directed onto at least

Spiny-tailed dab lizard, U. acanthinurus.

one of these rock piles, and UV light should also be available. Some means of simulating their natural tendency to retreat into burrows at night is necessary, and this can be a cave made of pieces of rock or large sections of earthenware drainpipe, or something similar.

WHAT environment?

A daytime background temperature of 77–86°F (25–30°C) is necessary, and a hot spot under the heat lamp of 104–122°F (40–50°C). They need these high temperatures to digest their food and will not thrive in the long term at lower temperatures. The heat lamps must be placed at one end of the terrarium so that the lizards can retreat to a cooler place if they want to. The humidity must be low, although a shallow bowl of water must be present so that the lizards can soak.

HOW much time?

Fifteen to thrity minutes a day for feeding and monitoring the environment.

WHAT varieties?

Red Niger Uromastyx may be reddish in color in addition to the normal yellow form. Apart from Red Niger Uromastyx, other species that are occasionally for sale include the spiny-tailed dab lizard, U. acanthinura, the ornate dab lizard, U. ornata, and the similar eyed dab lizard, U. ocellata.

WHAT care?

Daily feeding, changing the water in their bowl, and spot cleaning. Occasional major overhaul of the cage may be necessary.

WHAT food?

Green leafy vegetables, including kale, watercress, dandelions, and clover, and legumes such as peas and beans (fed with their pods). Yellow flowers, especially dandelions, are greatly relished. Young animals may take some insects, but these should be given sparingly. All meals need to be liberally dusted with a vitamin and mineral supplement.

Cost			
Setup cost			
Running cost			

Size: 14–16 in (35–40 cm)

Distribution: North Africa

Life span: Many years; possibly up to 25

Above: The spiny-tailed dab lizard is well named and is one of the largest and more colorful species. Adults may be yellow or red.

The eyed dab lizard, U. ocellata, is an attractive small species.

HOW easy are they to breed?

Much time and dedication is required to breed them, although it is achieved regularly, resulting in a trickle of captive-bred young.

WHAT drawbacks?

The huge amount of space and time required to care for them properly. Captive-bred young are occasionally available but are expensive. Wild-caught animals are often heavily parasitized and many die after a few weeks or months.

Leiolepis reevesii

Chinese butterfly lizard

PROFILE

The Chinese butterfly lizard is one of seven species in the genus that have similar habits. They live in hot, dry habitats and dig burrows to shelter from the sun. This species is variously marked but is usually brown with lighter spots and streaks on its head and body. Other species have brightly colored flanks that they show off by flattening their body, hence the name "butterfly" lizards.

WHAT temperament?

Usually calm but inclined to be nervous at first.

WHAT accommodation?

A large terrarium of around 24 x 18 x 12 in (60 x 45 x 30 cm) is the minimum size for a pair. It should have a sandy substrate and ample hiding places, otherwise the lizards will panic when anyone approaches. A powerful heat lamp and a UV lamp are essential.

Above: Chinese (upper picture) and a pair of red-sided butterfly lizards.

WHAT environment?

A background temperature of 68–77°F (20–25°C) and a hot spot under the basking lamp of at least 95°F (35°C) is ideal. Humidity should be low but a water bowl should be present at all times.

HOW much time?

Ten to fifteen minutes a day.

WHAT varieties?

The other six species may appear at irregular intervals. *L. belliana*, is possibly the most colorful, and *L. guttata* is the largest species. Little is known about them, but their care should all be similar.

WHAT care?

Daily feeding and cage maintenance

WHAT food?

Mainly insects such as crickets, but some will also take vegetation, especially yellow flowers such as dandelions.

HOW easy are they to breed?

Not bred in captivity as far as we know.

WHAT drawbacks?

The lack of captive-bred stock is a problem because imported animals are often parasitised and require treatment from a vet before they can be expected to thrive.

Cost				
Setup cost				
Running cost				

Size: To 18 in (45 cm), ⅔ is tail

Distribution: Eastern Asia; mostly China

Life span: Unknown

Trioceros hoehnelii

Helmeted chameleon

PROFILE

The helmeted chameleon is a small species from the mountains of Kenya and Tanzania in East Africa, with a large bony "helmet" on its head (called a casque – this species is also called the high-casqued chameleon) and a rudimentary nose horn in the form of a raised knob. It is green, greenish-yellow, or blue-green in color, the males usually being more brightly colored and having a higher casque than the females. It is a live-bearing species that lives in highland forests.

Above: Helmeted chameleons have a bony nose horn that varies in size according to sex and the locality in which they live, and elongated scales on their chin and throat.

Cost			
Setup cost			
Running cost			

Size: 8 in, almost half is tail

Distribution: East Africa

Life span: Unknown; probably 2–3 years at most

Above: Rotund chameleons such as this are usually females, whereas males are usually more colorful.

WHAT temperament?

Usually adapts well to captivity, at least in the short term, and, like all chameleons, feeds readily. Males will not tolerate each other and may also attack females.

WHAT accommodation?

A large mesh terrarium of at least 3 × 3 × 3 ft (1 × 1 × 1 m) is called for, thickly furnished with branches and, if possible, living, leafy plants. A basking light and a UV lamp are essential.

WHAT environment?

Tolerant of cool conditions, therefore a temperature of 59–77°F (15–25°C) will be suitable, but the basking area should reach 86°F (30°C) for part of each day. The humidity should be raised through frequent spraying and the chameleons will drink drops of water from leaves.

HOW much time?

All chameleons are labor-intensive. At least fifteen minutes a day should be set aside for feeding, spraying, and general maintenance, but feeding and spraying two or three times each day will be better.

WHAT varieties?

There are two subspecies, but identifying them is difficult without locality information.

WHAT care?

Feeding and spraying at least once each day, preferably more often.

WHAT food?

Insects such as crickets.

HOW easy are they to breed?

Not known. Imported females are often pregnant and give birth to small litters of young, which are small and difficult to rear.

WHAT drawbacks?

Lack of availability of captive-bred stock. Some imported animals are collected illegally.

Chamaeleo calyptratus

Veiled, or Yemen, chameleon

The veiled chameleon is a large and impressive species that adapts well to captivity. Males have tall bony structures on the top of their heads, looking like helmets and known as casques. These grow enormous in older individuals. Juveniles lack these structures, and they are greatly reduced in females. They are green or blue-green in color with two or three broad diagonal stripes of yellowish-tan, and white stripes on their faces and flanks. Like most chameleons, however, these colors are subject to change. Pregnant females become much darker green, almost black, with blue and yellow spots.

This species occurs in the southern parts of the Arabian Peninsula, mainly in Yemen. It lives on dry hillsides among acacia shrubs and bushes, mostly along bodies of water. Its tolerance of harsh conditions is probably the reason why this species does so well in captivity. It is also very prolific, and females can lay three or more clutches in a single season, each consisting of 30–50 eggs, although clutches of more than 90 have been recorded.

This has resulted in captive breeding on a large scale, and captive-bred young are usually available in the summer.

WHAT temperament?

They tame down well, although like all chameleons, they prefer not to be picked up and physically restrained. Allowing them to climb onto your hand or arm is the best way of moving them. Males will not tolerate each other and must be kept separately, preferably out of sight of each other. Males are also very violent toward females during the breeding season and will sometimes kill them, so they should be supervised during mating.

WHAT accommodation?

Large mesh cages of at least 3 x 3 x 3 in (1 x 1 x 1 m) in volume, preferably larger. Only one adult can be kept in each cage, which should contain plenty of branches of various diameters and some living or artificial plants. A powerful heat lamp should be directed onto a branch at the top of the cage, alongside a UV lamp.

WHAT environment?

A background temperature of about 68–77°F (20–25°C) is required, and the heat lamp should provide a warmer spot, up to 86°F (30°C), or even more, during the day. Daily

Above: The helmet-like casque indicates that this is a male.

Right: Bugs-eye view of a prowling veiled chameleon.

Cost			
Setup cost			
Running cost			

Size: About 12 in, but males occasionally reach 18 in

Distribution: Arabian Peninsula

Life span: Males can live for many years, probably up to 10; breeding females are short-lived—only 3 or 4 years

spraying will be necessary as they are reluctant to drink from a bowl, preferring to lap drops of water from leaves. This is best done first thing in the morning to simulate the morning mists that they experience in their natural habitat.

HOW much time?
Thirty minutes to one hour a day.

WHAT varieties?
There are no varieties.

WHAT care?
They require daily attention and need to be fed at least once every day. Feeding and spraying is best done in the morning, and, if possible, a second feed should be given later in the day.

WHAT food?
Insects such as crickets, locusts, cockroaches, waxworms (in moderation), and wild collected insects and spiders. They have huge appetites. All meals should be dusted with a vitamin and mineral supplement. Breeding females require large amounts of calcium in addition. They are one of the few chameleons that will

also eat vegetation but rarely do so in captivity (but there is no harm in trying).

HOW easy are they to breed?
They breed readily, but providing the correct conditions for egg laying, incubation,

and raising young is quite a commitment. Separate cages will be required for the male and female, as well as for the juveniles.

Above: A healthy young juvenile with good color, bright eyes, and an alert disposition.

WHAT drawbacks?
Large amounts of space and time are needed to care for them properly, but if you are determined to keep a chameleon, this is the best choice.

Furcifer pardalis

Panther chameleon

PROFILE

This chameleon is highly variable, depending on which part of Madagascar it originates from, but all forms are colorful and attractive. Individuals from the north of the island, around Diego Suarez, are mostly green with orange stripes, whereas those from some of the small islands, such as Nosy Be and Nosy Faly, are often predominantly blue or bluish-green. Males are usually somewhat brighter in color and larger than the females.

They are very territorial, and males cannot be kept together under any circumstances. Females should only be introduced to males when they are in good condition, and the pair must be watched to ensure that the male does not injure the female. Females lay large clutches of eggs and will breed several times in a single breeding season if they are well fed and healthy. The eggs take several months to hatch, with the exact period depending on temperature. The young require very small food at first, supplemented with vitamins and minerals, but they grow quickly. Panther chameleons are bred in fairly large numbers, and captive-bred young are readily available, but because rearing them is expensive and time-consuming, they are always likely to be a high-value species.

Below and right: A red form (below) and a blue form (right) of the panther chameleon from the Ambilobe region of Madagascar.

WHAT temperament?

Like all chameleons, they are aggressive toward each other, and individuals must be housed separately. Interactions with humans vary and they occasionally bite, so handling is best kept to a minimum. If possible, let the chameleon climb onto your hand rather than trying to grab it.

Cost			
Setup cost			
Running cost			

Size: Males to 20 in; females to 15 in total length

Distribution: Northern Madagascar

Life span: Several years

Right: A spectacular bright blue panther chameleon from the island of Nosy Faly.

WHAT accommodation?

Large, tall cages, at least 3 x 3 x 3 ft (1 x 1 x 1 m), preferably larger, are required. Cages must be well ventilated and at least one side should be fine mesh. The cage should contain plenty of branches for climbing and leaves for hiding among; these can be natural or artificial. The substrate can be orchid bark or dead leaves, but something that will retain some moisture works best. The cage should be thoroughly sprayed every day, as some individuals are reluctant to drink from a bowl but will lap water from a leaf. A heat lamp for basking and a UV lamp are essential.

WHAT environment?

Temperatures under the heat lamp should be 86–95°F (30–35°C) during the day, and back-ground temperatures of 68–77°F (20–25°C) should be maintained at all times. Humidity will fluctuate throughout the day, becoming high immediately after spraying and falling as the cage dries out.

HOW much time?

Thirty minutes to one hour per day for feeding and spraying. All chameleons require daily attention and a considerable investment in time and resources.

WHAT varieties?

Several regional varieties are available, some of them spectacularly marked in bright red, green, and blue. The most colorful strains command a premium price.

WHAT care?

Spraying and feeding at least once every day, preferably twice.

WHAT food?

Insects such as crickets and locusts, depending on size. They have large appetites and require plenty of food.

HOW easy are they to breed?

Breeding is not difficult, but large cages and an intensive feeding regimen is essential.

WHAT drawbacks?

Chameleons require large amounts of space, special lighting, vitamin and mineral supplements, and lots of food.

Rieppeleon brevicaudatus

Short-tailed leaf chameleon

PROFILE

This is a small chameleon that lives on the forest floor among dead leaves, where its shape and coloration make it hard to see. As it doesn't climb much, its tail is reduced to a short stump. It is brown or olive in color and has only a limited ability to change color. There is a small tuft of scales under the chin. Males and females are similar in size, but males have a relatively longer tail.

WHAT temperament?

Shy, relying on its camouflage to escape detection. Slow and deliberate in its movements.

WHAT accommodation?

A terrarium measuring about 24 × 12 in (60 × 30 cm) and about 18 in (45 cm) high is ideal for a pair or small group. At least one side, and the top, should be mesh. A layer of dead leaves on the bottom and a few twigs and perhaps a small plant makes a suitable setup.

WHAT environment?

Not too hot. A background temperature of 64–73°F (18–23°C) seems to suit them, and a basking light is not strictly necessary. Similarly, UV is optional but may be beneficial. A relatively high humidity should be created by spraying once or twice each day.

Cost			
Setup cost			
Running cost			

Size: About 3.5 in (9 cm)

Distribution: East Africa (Tanzania and southern Kenya)

Life span: Probably not long-lived

HOW much time?

Fifteen minutes a day.

WHAT varieties?

None. Other leaf chameleons are occasionally offered, and their care is similar. Madagascan species, *Brookesia,* should not be purchased as they are endangered.

WHAT care?

Daily or twice daily feeding and spraying.

WHAT food?

Small insects such as crickets. Vitamin and mineral supplements are required.

HOW easy are they to breed?

Probably not easy.

WHAT drawbacks?

Lack of captive-bred young. Wild individuals may be parasitized and their age is unknown. Interesting but not showy.

Above: The small, brown leaf chameleons are interesting but not particularly showy. They can be difficult to maintain.

Anolis carolinensis

Green anole

PROFILE

Anoles are widespread lizards in North and South America, and more than 100 species are known. The green anole is from North America and is one of the more colorful species. It is slender, with a long narrow head, long limbs, and a long tail. It is agile and alert and has the ability to change color from green to brown. Males have a pink throat fan, which they flick out to attract the attention of females and rival males.

WHAT temperament?
Very lively and alert.

WHAT accommodation?
A tall terrarium measuring about 18 x 18 x 24 in (45 x 45 x 60 cm) is suitable for one or two anoles. The substrate can be leaf litter or orchid bark, and it needs some branches for them to climb on. Including one or two living plants gives them an opportunity to drink drops of water from the leaves. A basking light is needed, as is a UV lamp.

WHAT environment?
A background temperature of 68–77°F (20–25°C) is sufficient,

Above: Green anoles are agile, always active, and make an interesting display.

and the area under the heat lamp should reach 86–95°F (30–35°C) during the day. They should be sprayed regularly to increase the humidity, but the terrarium should be well ventilated.

HOW much time?
Five to ten minutes a day.

WHAT care?
Daily feeding and spraying.

WHAT varieties?
None.

Cost			
Setup cost			
Running cost			

Size: ¾–1 in (20–30 mm)

Distribution: Madagascar

Life span: Average 3–5 years

WHAT food?
Small insects such as crickets and lesser waxworms, dusted with a vitamin and mineral supplement. They are agile and lively hunters.

HOW easy are they to breed?
If a pair are present they may breed spontaneously. One egg is laid at a time, often at the base of a plant.

WHAT drawbacks?
Not easy to handle. Captive-bred stock is not available.

Right: "Green" anoles may also be brown and can change color in a matter of minutes.

119

Anolis sagrei

Brown anole

PROFILE

Slender (but slightly stockier than the green anole) with a relatively large head. Brown in color, but they can change from light to dark brown, and indistinct darker markings may be present on the back. Females have a cream line down the center of their back. An adaptable and opportunistic lizard that is very numerous in suitable places and can often be seen around human dwellings, on tree trunks, fences, outbuildings, etc. Males display from a head-down position, flicking out their orange throat fan.

WHAT temperament?
Lively and active; always alert.

WHAT accommodation?
A tall planted terrarium as described for the green anole (page 119). The two species

Above: Female brown anoles have a cream stripe down their back.

Above: A male brown anole flicks out its throat fan to stake a claim to its territory and attract a mate.

can be kept together, although the brown anole may become more dominant and take most of the food. Males cannot be kept together, but a number of females can be kept with a single male.

WHAT environment?
Same as the green anole.

HOW much time?
Five to ten minutes a day.

Cost			
Setup cost			
Running cost			

Size: 6–8 in (15–20 cm), of which half is tail

Distribution: West Indies, but introduced into Florida and other Caribbean localities

Life span: 2–4 years

WHAT varieties?
None, although other similar anoles are sometimes available, including the large-headed anole, *Anolis cybotes*, and a variety of small West Indian species. The knight anole, *A. equestris*, is a much larger species that requires a larger terrarium, and it cannot be kept with any of the small species.

WHAT care?
Daily feeding and spraying.

WHAT food?
Small insects such as crickets, dusted with a vitamin and mineral powder.

HOW easy are they to breed?
Rarely attempted although they may breed spontaneously in a well-planted terrarium.

WHAT drawbacks?
Difficult to handle, and there is no supply of captive-bred young.

Crotaphytus collaris

Collared lizard

PROFILE

The collared lizard is a North American member of the iguana family, living in dry, rocky habitats in the southern United States and northern Mexico. It varies in color from green to brown but it always has a broad black-and-white "collar" marking. Its head is large, its limbs are long, and it has a long, whip-like tail. Collared lizards are powerful, fast-moving predators that run down their prey. They are very aware of their surroundings and often take up a position on a prominent rock or stump.

WHAT temperament?
Active, alert lizards that like to be able to see what's going on. Very lively but easily tamed.

WHAT accommodation?
A large terrarium is essential, at least 40 × 20 in (100 × 50 cm) floor space; height is not important, but it should be covered. A substrate of sand or gravel works equally well, and there should be several large rocks or rock piles

for the lizards to use. A powerful heat lamp should be directed onto one of these, and a UV lamp must also be available.

WHAT environment?
Very hot conditions are necessary. A background temperature of 68–77°F (20–25°C) in the day, although they will tolerate quite cool conditions at night. Importantly, a heat lamp should create a basking spot that reaches at least 86°F (30°C) and preferably more; 104°F (40°C) is not too hot provided they can retreat to a cooler part of the cage. Spraying is unnecessary provided there is a water bowl present.

Cost		
Setup cost		
Running cost		

Size: To 12 in (30 cm), over half is tail. Males larger than females

Distribution: North America

Life span: Unknown; probably 5 years or more

HOW much time?
Ten to fifteen minutes a day.

WHAT varieties?
No varieties, although there are several similar species, including other collared lizards and the leopard lizard, *Gambelia wislizenii*.

WHAT care?
Daily feeding.

WHAT food?
Insects, liberally dusted with a vitamin and mineral preparation.

HOW easy are they to breed?
They are bred in captivity but require plenty of space. Males are territorial, but a single male can be kept with two or three females.

WHAT drawbacks?
They need a lot of space, and there is an unfortunate lack of captive-bred young.

Left: A large head and a black and white collar are characteristic.

Iguana iguana

Green iguana

PROFILE

The green iguana is a common lizard that lives in the forests of Central and South America, and on some West Indian islands. It is highly arboreal, normally found in trees growing along rivers or at the edge of clearings, and rarely lives in dense, closed-canopy forest. Males are territorial and often perch high on a prominent branch in the canopy. There is some variation in coloration. At hatching, all green iguanas are green. Some of them stay bright green throughout their lives, but others become greyish-blue or orange. Adult males are most likely to change color, and it depends to some extent on their place of origin.

Their hind limbs are long, as are their toes, which end in sharp claws. Their tails are also long and have a series of dark bands along their length. All individuals have a crest of thin, pointed scales that run along their backs, and these are larger in mature males than females. Males also develop large folded dewlaps and they use these to display by "head bobbing."

Above: A typical "green" green iguana male.

WHAT temperament?

Most iguanas adapt well to captivity and become tame, but a few remain nervous and never settle down. They may bite or, more likely, use their tail as a whip. Their claws can give painful scratches.

Below: The red form of the green iguana. This is simply a color variant, not a different species.

WHAT accommodation?

Green iguanas need very large cages. One measuring 6 x 6 x 6 ft (2 x 2 x 2 m) is a minimum for one or two adults, and twice this size is preferable; in other words, a walk-in enclosure. Juveniles can be kept in smaller terrariums but they will eventually need to be moved on. The terrarium will need several strong branches firmly attached to the structure. A wooden shelf near the top will be used for basking. This should be positioned beneath a heat lamp and UV lamp. A large water bowl—at least the size of a washing-up bowl—will be needed, and this should be fixed in some way to prevent it from being spilled.

WHAT environment?

A background temperature of 73–82°F (23–28°C) is needed, with a hot spot of at least 104°F (40°C) beneath the heat lamp. Humidity should be kept high for juvenile green iguanas, by frequent spraying, but adults are more tolerant of

dry conditions. Nevertheless, they should be sprayed occasionally and given an opportunity to soak in a large water bowl. Problems in shedding their skin are an indication that conditions are too dry.

HOW much time?

Thirty minutes a day.

WHAT varieties?

There are several natural color variations, and several closely related species, such as spiny-tailed iguanas and basilisks, are occasionally available. Some of these are carnivorous or omni-vorous, and their care differs from that of the green iguana.

WHAT care?

Daily feeding and cleaning. The water bowl should be washed out and replenished

Above and below: Although smaller, the brown basilisk (below) is a close relative of the green iguana (above), and also prefers to live near bodies of water.

every day, and the behavior of the iguana needs careful monitoring to make sure everything is well.

Cost				
Setup cost				
Running cost				

Size: 69–80 in (150–200 cm), males significantly larger than females

Distribution: Central and South America as well as the West Indies; introduced into Florida

Life span: 15–20 years

WHAT food?

Green iguanas are herbivores and eat green leafy vegetables, chopped root vegetables, and occasional fruit (including the skins). Juveniles will need their food chopped into appropriate sizes. All meals must be liberally dusted with a vitamin and mineral supplement, and calcium is especially important for rapidly growing iguanas.

HOW easy are they to breed?

Rarely attempted due to the amount of space required.

WHAT drawbacks?

Huge amounts of time and space are required. Although they usually become tame, some can be difficult to handle and they are not suitable for children to keep.

Phrynosoma platyrhinos

Desert horned lizard

PROFILE

There are about fifteen species of horned lizard, all from the drier parts of North America. They are strange and interesting lizards, with wide, flattened bodies that they tilt toward the sun in order to warm up in the morning. The desert horned lizard is one of the largest and most colorful species, with a row of spiny scales along its flanks and a series of "horns" around the back of its head. It lives in sandy deserts, among cactus plants and desert shrubs.

Above and below: Horned lizards have an unmistakable shape. There are sixteen species of Phrynosoma *altogether.*

Cost		
Setup cost		
Running cost		

Size: 2.5–3.5 in (6.5–9 cm)

Distribution: Southwest North America

Life span: Unknown; probably up to 5 years

WHAT temperament?
Active by day, and easily handled.

WHAT accommodation?
A terrarium with a floor area of 24 x 18 in (60 x 45 cm) is the minimum for one or two horned lizards. It needs a substrate of sand or gravelly sand, some rock, and a shallow water bowl. A powerful heat lamp and a UV lamp must be provided at one end, above a basking rock.

WHAT environment?
Very hot conditions are needed. A background temperature of 68–77°F (20–25°C) is sufficient but the area under the basking lamp should reach 104°F (40°C) or more. However, the lizard must be able to retreat to a cooler part of the cage.

HOW much time?
Five to ten minutes a day.

WHAT varieties?
None, although other species of horned lizards may be available occasionally.

WHAT care?
Daily feeding and light spraying. They often prefer to drink from drops of water rather than visiting a water bowl. The cage must be well ventilated, however, to keep the humidity low.

WHAT food?
Small insects. In the wild they eat large quantities of ants, so a

steady supply of ant-sized crickets would be a good substitute, always dusted with a vitamin and mineral supplement.

HOW easy are they to breed?
Rarely attempted, unfortunately.

WHAT drawbacks?
Their requirements are poorly understood, and they are not always easy to keep alive in the long term. There is a lack of captive-bred young. For the specialist only.

Sceloporus occidentalis

Western fence lizard

PROFILE

The western fence lizard is a common species of the North American west and belongs to a group of similar fence lizards, spiny lizards, and swifts that occur throughout North America. It is brown or grey in color with an indistinct pattern of blotches on its back and patches of bright blue scales on its throat and chest—these are brighter and more extensive in males. Its scales are pointed and heavily keeled, giving it a rough, spiny appearance. It lives in dry grassland, forest clearings, and farmland and often perches on prominent posts and stumps.

WHAT temperament?
Nervous and fast-moving at first but calming down in time.

WHAT accommodation?
A terrarium measuring about 40 × 12 in (100 × 30 cm) floor space is adequate for one or two

fence lizards. A heat lamp should be placed at one end, directed onto a basking place, and a UV lamp should also be provided. It should have a substrate of gravel or sand.

WHAT environment?
A background temperature of 68–77°F (20–25°C) in the day, cooler at night. The basking spot should reach at least 95°F (35°C). Spraying is unnecessary provided there is a water bowl present.

HOW much time?
Ten minutes a day.

Cost			
Setup cost			
Running cost			

Size: About 6 in (15 cm)

Distribution: Western North America

Life span: Unknown; probably several years

WHAT food?
Insects such as crickets, dusted with a vitamin and mineral supplement.

The western fence lizard is one of several small North American spiny lizards.

WHAT varieties?
There are several other fence lizards and related lizards, the care of which is similar.

WHAT care?
Daily feeding. They can be lightly sprayed, but humidity should be low.

HOW easy are they to breed?
Probably easy but rarely attempted.

WHAT drawbacks?
Lack of captive-bred stock.

Above: A lizard displaying in Yosemite National Park.

Gekko gecko

Tokay gecko

PROFILE

The tokay gecko is a large, colorful species from Southeast Asia. It is typically grey or blue-grey in color with many orange spots scattered over its entire head and body. Its eyes are huge and have intricate black reticulations on a cream or pale yellow background. The pupil is vertical and closes down to a narrow line joining four small pinpoints in bright light. Its name is derived from its vocalizations, which are interpreted as a loud and raucous "Toe – Kay!" Like many geckos, the tokay communicates by sounds, establishing territories and attracting mates. It is nocturnal, emerging from its hiding place in the evening to look for food. In nature it often takes a position near a light, where insects such as moths and cockroaches are attracted. It has a large mouth and a hearty appetite and will also eat smaller geckos. Tokays have large feet with very effective adhesive toe pads, enabling them to walk on vertical surfaces and even to cling upside down to ceilings. They rarely move around on the ground. Although they live in forests and other natural habitats, they are closely associated with human dwellings, attracted by the insects that live around houses and restaurants.

WHAT temperament?

Tokays can be aggressive and will often try to bite if they are restrained. They prefer to be left in peace and, in a large setup, will establish a territory and a feeding routine and should not be handled unless there is a very good reason to do so.

WHAT accommodation?

A large terrarium measuring at least 40 × 20 × 40 in (100 × 50 × 100 cm) high. Its inner back and side surfaces should be covered with cork bark or a similar rough material, and additional slabs of cork should be laid up against them to provide vertical cracks in which the geckos can hide. A water bowl is necessary, but other cage furnishings are up to the owner. Any plants need to be tough varieties, or artificial ones.

WHAT environment?

Geckos need tropical conditions, with a temperature of 68–77°F (20–25°C), and a relatively high humidity. Background heating is best provided by under-cage heat pads, which can also be attached to the back, but lighting and UV are unnecessary.

HOW much time?

Five to ten minutes a day.

Right and above: Juvenile (upper) and adult tokay geckos. This is a large and colorful tropical species.

Cost			
Setup cost			
Running cost			

Size: 12–16 in (30–40 cm), males are larger than females

Distribution: Southeast Asia

Life span: Unknown, but at least 10 years in captivity

Left: Gekko smithii *is known as the green-eyed gecko.*

WHAT varieties?
The genus *Gekko* also includes several other species that might be considered for captivity, all relatively large and all quite hardy captives. They include the marbled gecko, *G. grossmanni*, the lined gecko, *G. vittatus*, and the green-eyed gecko, *G. smithii*, all from the same part of the world and all requiring similar treatment.

WHAT care?
Daily feeding and lightly spraying. Occasional cage cleaning and maintenance.

Above: The marbled gecko, G. grossmanni, *is another large species that is easy to keep in captivity.*

WHAT food?
Large insects such as adult crickets, locusts, and cockroaches. They are especially fond of the latter. All meals should be dusted with a vitamin and mineral supplement, and breeding females require extra calcium.

HOW easy are they to breed?
They will breed in captivity but need plenty of space and suitable places to lay their eggs, such as a crack between two vertical surfaces. The eggs are stuck on and can be left in place to incubate, or the material to which they are attached can be removed together with the eggs to be incubated separately.

WHAT drawbacks?
Not suitable for handling. Very fast-moving and nocturnal, so not often seen. Escaped tokays are difficult to recapture.

Hemidactylus turcicus

Turkish gecko

PROFILE

A small gecko with a translucent, pinkish skin marked with small dark spots and raised tubercles, some of which are white. The toes have adhesive pads and long claws so that the gecko can climb smooth and rough surfaces. It is very agile and easily climbs up glass and will even run upside down across ceilings. It lives in rocky places, including stone walls, but is most likely to be seen on and around human buildings, where it ambushes insects that are attracted to lights.

Above: A Turkish gecko in the wild, clinging to a rock. This is a common Mediterranean species.

Below: Turkish gecko, Hemidactylus turcicus.

Cost		
Setup cost		
Running cost		

Size: To 4 in (10 cm)

Distribution: Mediterranean region, including many islands*

Life span: Unknown; probably about 5 years

* *Introduced accidentally elsewhere as stowaways in goods and produce. Geckos that turn up in supermarkets and grocery shops usually belong to this, or a related, species.*

WHAT temperament?
Nocturnal. Very fast-moving and agile and almost impossible to handle.

WHAT accommodation?
A small terrarium measuring 20 × 12 × 12 in (50 × 30 × 30 cm) is adequate for an adult pair. Males are territorial and will not tolerate each other. The substrate can be sand or grit, and stones or pieces of wood can be arranged to add interest. A small water bowl is the only other essential.

WHAT environment?
They prefer hot, dry conditions but will tolerate a wide range of environments. The temperature should be 73–82°F (23–28°C), most easily provided by an under-cage heat mat. Lighting and UV are unnecessary.

HOW much time?
Five to ten minutes a day.

WHAT varieties?
None, although there are other species of *Hemidactylus*, often called "house geckos."

WHAT care?
Daily feeding. Occasional light spraying.

WHAT food?
Small insects such as crickets and young cockroaches, dusted with a vitamin and mineral supplement. Females require extra calcium to help with egg formation.

HOW easy are they to breed?
Very.

WHAT drawbacks?
They are quick and agile and, given an opportunity, inclined to escape. Once this problem is solved they are trouble-free and interesting. This is an under-rated species.

Teratolepis fasciata (Hemidactylus imbricatus)

Viper gecko

PROFILE

The viper gecko is a small desert species with a distinctive swollen tail, giving it the alternative name of turnip-tailed gecko. It has recently been reclassified as *Hemidactylus imbricatus*, but this name is not widely accepted at the moment. It is a plump species, brown in color with alternating dark and light brown lines down its back and pale spots arranged in the form of bands across its body.

WHAT temperament?
Quick-moving but usually calm and easily handled (with care).

WHAT accommodation?
A small terrarium, measuring 18 x 10 in (45 x 25 cm) floor area, is suitable for a pair or small group of viper geckos. They cannot climb up smooth surfaces but their terrarium should be covered. The substrate may be sand or paper towels, and a small water dish and two hide boxes complete the setup. Driftwood or rocks can be added according to taste, but the setup should be kept simple.

WHAT environment?
A thermal gradient covering about 68–90°F (20–32°C) is suitable with a hide box at each end. Lightly spraying the area in or under the hide box will create some local humidity.

HOW much time?
Five to ten minutes a day.

WHAT varieties?
None.

WHAT care?
Daily feeding and light spraying.

WHAT food?
Small insects such as crickets and lesser waxworms. All meals should be sprinkled with a vitamin and mineral supplement, and an additional small bowl of calcium should be kept in the terrarium all the time.

HOW easy are they to breed?
They breed readily if kept in small groups.

Cost				
Setup cost				
Running cost				

Size: 3 in (8 cm)

Distribution: Pakistan

Life span: Unknown; probably several years

Above and below: Viper geckos have thick, carrot-shaped tails that they use to store fat.

WHAT drawbacks?
The newly hatched young are very small and somewhat delicate, but otherwise they are easily cared for.

Lepidodactylus lugubris

Mourning gecko

PROFILE

This is a very interesting little gecko; its life cycle makes up for its rather nondescript appearance. The mourning gecko is parthenogenic, a female-only species in which fertile eggs can be laid without the necessity of mating. All the hatchlings are females – they are clones of their mother. This has helped it to spread to many small tropical islands. It is pale brown in color with roughly chevron-shaped darker markings along its back. Its tail has a yellow or orange tinge.

WHAT temperament?
Strictly nocturnal. A very quick and agile gecko that cannot be handled easily but adapts well to captivity.

WHAT accommodation?
Small terrariums measuring about 12 x 12 x 12 in (30 x 30 x 30 cm) are sufficient. They do not require a light, and under-cage heating is sufficient. A substrate of sand or gravel, some pieces of driftwood, and one or two small potted plants are all it requires.

WHAT environment?
A temperature of about 77°F (25°C) and moderately high humidity, achieved by spraying the terrarium once a day. A potted plant will increase the humidity locally.

HOW much time?
Five to ten minutes a day.

WHAT varieties?
None.

WHAT care?
Daily feeding and spraying. This should be done in the evening when the gecko becomes active.

WHAT food?
Small insects such as crickets and flies. Every meal should be dusted with a vitamin and mineral supplement and should be offered in the evening, so that the gecko has a chance to eat before the insects clean off the supplement. A small dish of extra calcium, in the form of powdered cuttlefish shell, should be available all the time.

HOW easy are they to breed?
Very! Feed them and they will breed. The eggs are very small and are best left where they are laid.

WHAT drawbacks?
Difficult to handle and not seen very often, but very easy to keep and breed.

Cost				
Setup cost				
Running cost				

Size: 5 in (10 cm)

Distribution: Southeast Asia, introduced to many other regions

Life span: At least 3 years; possibly longer

Above: The mourning gecko is a female-only species that breeds readily.

Lygodactylus williamsii 🦎🏔️☢️

Electric blue day gecko

PROFILE

The African day geckos, *Lygodactylus*, are not closely related to the Madagascan day geckos belonging to the genus *Phelsuma*, but their care is similar. There is a number of species, all very small, that occasionally enter the pet trade, but the electric blue day gecko is far and away the most colorful. Males are brilliant blue in color with just a few black lines on their head, and yellow below. Females are less colorful and are brown with a blue or green tint. They come from a very small area of rain forest in Tanzania and are endangered.

WHAT temperament?
Diurnal, fast, and agile.

WHAT accommodation?
Similar to that of the neon day gecko (see page 133), a well-planted cage with plenty of opportunities to climb and bask. Living plants will help to keep the humidity at the correct level and also provide egg-laying places. Males are territorial, and only one can be kept in a cage.

WHAT environment?
Similar to that of the neon day gecko. Natural daylight lamps containing UV-B are recommended.

HOW much time?
Five to ten minutes a day.

WHAT varieties?
There are several other species of *Lygodactylus*, but none is as colorful.

WHAT care?
Daily or twice-daily feeding and spraying.

WHAT food?
Small insects, especially young crickets and lesser waxworms, always dusted with a vitamin and mineral supplement.

Cost			
Setup cost			
Running cost			

Size: To 3 in (8 cm)	
Distribution: East Africa (Tanzania)	
Life span: Unknown; probably 3 to 5 years	

HOW easy are they to breed?
They breed regularly in captivity but are not prolific. Females require extra calcium and plenty of food.

WHAT drawbacks?
They are difficult to handle. Young males look like females, so buying a true pair can be difficult. Captive-bred stock is hard to source, and wild-caught stock should not be purchased because it is endangered.

Above: Electric blue day geckos are stunningly colorful. This one is most definitely a male, but less colorful individuals may be females or immature males, making it difficult to establish a true pair.

Paroedura pictus

Painted big-headed gecko

PROFILE

A mid-sized gecko with a large head and rough-scaled body. It is rich brown in color with markings of cream or white. Their toe pads are small and they do not climb

WHAT environment?
A temperature of 68–77°F (20–25°C) is probably ideal, although they will tolerate cooler conditions for short periods. Humidity should be low, although they can be lightly sprayed occasionally. Lighting is unnecessary.

HOW much time?
Five to ten minutes a day.

Cost			
Setup cost			
Running cost			

Size: To 6 in (15 cm), males usually larger than females

Distribution: Southern Madagascar

Life span: Several years; possibly up to 10

Above: Big-headed geckos are ground-dwelling species.

smooth surfaces, an adaptation to living on the ground. They live in dry forests with sandy soil, and move about among dead leaves at night.

WHAT temperament?
They adapt well to captivity and tolerate a certain amount of handling. Males are aggressive toward each other, though, and cannot be kept together.

WHAT accommodation?
A terrarium measuring about 24 x 12 x 12 in (60 x 30 x 30 cm) is adequate for a pair. It needs a sandy substrate and some rocks or dead wood for the geckos to hide among.

WHAT varieties?
There are two forms: about half have a broad stripe down the back, whereas the others lack this. There are several other species in the genus that probably require similar care.

WHAT care?
Daily feeding, preferably at night when they are active. Light spraying occasionally.

WHAT food?
Insects such as crickets and cockroaches, but they will take larger prey. All meals should be dusted with a supplement, and females require extra calcium.

HOW easy are they to breed?
Very easy. Females will lay several sets of one or two eggs after a single mating. It is best to separate them once they have mated, otherwise the female will deplete her system of calcium, exhaust herself, and die.

WHAT drawbacks?
None. They are ideal lizards to keep, requiring a minimum of equipment and time, and captive-bred young are readily available. They are nocturnal, however, so they often hide in their terrariums.

Phelsuma klemmeri

Neon day gecko

PROFILE

This is a small day gecko with almost unbelievable colors. It has a lime-green head, a yellow ring around its eyes, and a blue body. There are dark stripes along its flanks and on its back. It is rare in the wild, living only in bamboo thickets in a small area of northern Madagascar, but it is widely bred in captivity.

WHAT temperament?

Lively and agile, making it difficult to handle. It shows itself off well, however, and adapts well to captivity.

WHAT accommodation?

A tall terrarium is called for, and one measuring around 12 x 12 x 18 in (30 x 30 x 45 cm) is adequate for one or two individuals. They will do even better in larger cages, however, and there will then be an opportunity to plant them out and incorporate more natural features. A heat lamp will be required as will a UV source.

WHAT environment?

A background temperature of 68–77°F (20–25°C) with a heat lamp creating a hot spot of 86°F (30°C) at the top of the terrarium. There are mixed opinions on the necessity for UV, but it is a good idea to use at least a low-power UV lamp or a natural daylight lamp. Humidity should be high, so the cage will need to be sprayed once or twice each day or an automatic system should be installed and set to run at least twice each day.

HOW much time?

Five to ten minutes a day.

WHAT varieties?

None.

WHAT care?

Daily or twice-daily feeding and spraying, and general cage maintenance.

Cost			
Setup cost			
Running cost			

Size: To 3.5 in (9 cm)

Distribution: Northern Madagascar

Life span: At least 5 years; probably more

WHAT food?

Small insects such as crickets, lesser waxworms, small cockroaches, etc. A good variety of food is important. Every meal should be dusted with a vitamin and mineral supplement, and breeding females need extra calcium in order to produce the shells of their eggs.

HOW easy are they to breed?

They breed readily given the right conditions, plenty of food, and extra calcium.

WHAT drawbacks?

Not easy to handle.

Above: The aptly named neon day gecko differs in color and size from all other species, which are mostly green.

Phelsuma madagascariensis

Giant day gecko

As its name suggests, this is the largest day gecko, about twice as big as the next largest species. It is spectacularly colored in bright green, with red bars across its back and a red line from its nostril to its eye on each side. There is some variation between individuals, and there are at least four subspecies, of which *P. m. grandis* is the one most often seen. It occurs in northern Madagascar and is very common around villages, on tree trunks and the walls of buildings, often visiting outside lights to hunt for insects that have been attracted to them. Day geckos differ from most other species by being active during the day. Because of this, they are brightly colored so that they can communicate visually to each other. Most other geckos communicate by sound.

WHAT temperament?
Agile, but a calm disposition.

WHAT accommodation?
A tall terrarium measuring 24 x 24 x 40 in (60 x 60 x 100 cm) high is the minimum size for an adult pair or group of youngsters and it should be furnished with plenty of branches, bamboo poles, and living or artificial plants. Smaller species require smaller accommodation, but generally speaking their terrariums need to be tall.

Right: A typical giant day gecko.

Below: Like most geckos, day geckos lack eyelids and use their tongues to wipe dust and liquids from the surface of their eyes.

Day geckos lend themselves to large planted terrariums with running water. Not only does this look attractive but it also provides the geckos with the security of plentiful hiding places and areas of high humidity. UV lighting is necessary for the geckos and, if plants are included, additional lights may be necessary to keep them healthy.

WHAT environment?
A background temperature of 68–77°F (20–25°C), with a basking spot of 86°F (30°C) or more. Humidity can be raised temporarily by spraying, but the terrarium should be well ventilated. A UV lamp is essential.

HOW much time?
Ten to twenty minutes a day.

Cost			
Setup cost			
Running cost			

Size: 8–11 in (20–28 cm)

Distribution: Northern Madagascar (*subsp. grandis*)

Life span: At least 5 years; probably 10 or more

WHAT varieties?

Four subspecies as noted before. In addition, there are many other species that may be available occasionally, some of them widely bred in captivity. The peacock day gecko, *Phelsuma quadriocellata*, is intermediate in size and is bright green with a few scattered red markings on its back and a blue eyespot on each flank. The gold-dust day gecko, *P. laticauda*, is also green but has a flattened, yellowish tail and yellow flecks over its back, like gold dust.

WHAT care?

Daily feeding and spraying. Cleaning as necessary.

WHAT food?

Insects such as crickets, liberally dusted with vitamins and minerals. Females require extra calcium, which they store in pouches in their throats. They will also lick honey and soft fruit such as bananas, and this is a good way of getting extra vitamins into them.

HOW easy are they to breed?

Fairly easy. Males are highly territorial and so are females of some species, but this can be overcome to a certain extent by giving them large cages with plenty of hiding places. Two eggs at a time are laid in hidden places, especially in sections of hollow bamboo, which can be removed if necessary and moved to a separate cage for incubation.

WHAT drawbacks?

Not easily handled but otherwise a good choice.

Above and top: The giant day gecko (upper) and the peacock day gecko (below) are among the most attractive and readily available species, both of which are regularly bred in captivity.

135

Uroplatus fimbriatus

Madagascan leaf-tailed gecko

PROFILE

This is an unusual and spectacular gecko from the rain forests of western Madagascar that has a very specialized lifestyle, making it difficult to keep in captivity for any length of time. It rests on tree trunks during the day, where it is almost impossible to see due to its camouflage. Its tail and body are fringed with flaps of skin, and its coloration matches the bark on which it rests. It has a large triangular head and huge bulbous eyes.

WHAT temperament?
Very high-strung and easily stressed.

WHAT accommodation?
They require very large cages, at least 3 ft (1 m) high, with large branches on which to climb. Running water or an automatic misting system is required to maintain the correct humidity. Lighting should be subdued.

Right: Leaf-tailed gecko, Uroplatus fimbriatus.

Above: A well camouflaged gecko on a tree trunk in Madagascar.

WHAT environment?
A constant temperature of about 77°F (25°C) is required. There is no need for a basking light or UV but the humidity should be maintained at as close to 100 percent as possible.

HOW much time?
Ten to twenty minutes a day.

Cost			
Setup cost			
Running cost			

Size: To 12 in (30 cm)

Distribution: Western Madagascar

Life span: Unknown

WHAT varieties?
There are several other *Uroplatus* species from Madagascar, including some smaller ones, but they are all very specialized lizards requiring equally specialized care.

WHAT care?
Daily feeding. Close monitoring of the conditions is vital, but the lizard should be disturbed as little as possible as they are easily stressed.

WHAT food?
Large insects, dusted with a vitamin and mineral supplement.

HOW easy are they to breed?
They have been bred, but this is a serious undertaking requiring large amounts of time and excellent facilities.

WHAT drawbacks?
Captive-bred stock is hardly ever available, and wild-caught animals are difficult to acclimatize (apart from being legally protected). They will only survive in very large, elaborate setups.

Strophurus williamsi

Eastern spiny-tailed gecko

PROFILE

A slender, pale, silvery-grey gecko with two rows of small spines running down its tail and onto its back. Its eyes are orange. They are partially arboreal and rely on their excellent camouflage to remain hidden during the day, typically clinging head-down to thin twigs, which are often the same color as the geckos. At night they descend to the ground to feed and move around.

WHAT temperament?
Adaptable and hardy. Like all small lizards, they dislike being handled.

WHAT accommodation?
A tall terrarium is called for and one measuring about 12 × 12 × 18 in (30 × 30 × 45 cm) is suitable for a pair or trio of adults. It should have a substrate of dry sand or leaf litter, furnished with several thin branches resting diagonally against the side.

WHAT environment?
Warm and dry conditions are best, although they will tolerate humid conditions

for short periods. A daytime temperature of about 68–77°F (20–25°C) is ideal, and this can be allowed to fall at night. The cage can be lightly sprayed in the morning, and lighting with some element of UV, such as a natural daylight lamp, is usually recommended, although whether this is essential is uncertain.

HOW much time?
Five to ten minutes a day.

WHAT varieties?
Some variation in markings. Related species, including the very beautiful golden-tailed gecko, *Strophurus taenicauda*, are sometimes available.

WHAT care?
Daily feeding in the evening and light spraying in the morning.

WHAT food?
Small insects such as crickets. They are not able to take large prey.

HOW easy are they to breed?
Breeding takes place regularly, although they are not very prolific.

WHAT drawbacks?
Expensive and in short supply.

Cost			
Setup cost			
Running cost			

Size: 4–4¼ in (with tail)

Distribution: Eastern half of Australia

Life span: Unknown, probably 10 years or more

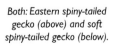

Both: Eastern spiny-tailed gecko (above) and soft spiny-tailed gecko (below).

Rhacodactylus ciliatus

Crested gecko

PROFILE

The crested gecko is one of the success stories of the more recently introduced lizards because it adapts so well to captivity. It comes from the remote island of New Caledonia, where it inhabits humid forests, moving around among twigs and leaves at night. This species has adhesive toe pads and an additional pad on the tip of its tail, making it especially "sticky." Its feet are large and webbed, and the toes have prominent claws as well as the pads. Its name comes from the fringe of pointed scales above its eyes, and this crest continues down the neck and onto the body, where it gradually tapers away. It is highly variable in color and markings, making it even more popular, and breeds readily. It ranges in color from plain tan or golden-brown to intricately marked forms that may be dark chocolate-brown with cream or orange markings, or any other combinations of these colors. Several forms have been given names by breeders ("flame," "harlequin," "brindle," etc.), none of which has any taxonomic value. There are several related species, all of which seem to thrive in captivity.

WHAT temperament?

Very calm and easy to tame. It prefers to climb onto a hand than to be picked up, and rough treatment may result in the loss of its tail, which will regrow but not as completely as the original.

Left and below: Crested geckos are attractive and easily tamed lizards that occur in a variety of patterns and colors.

WHAT accommodation?

Large cages are called for, at least 40 × 20 × 40 in (100 × 50 × 100 cm) and preferably bigger. The cage should have a substrate of leaf litter or coconut fiber mixed with sphagnum. Branches should be arranged diagonally for the gecko to climb on, and, if possible, include some living plants. An automatic misting system can be installed or the cage can be misted by hand.

WHAT environment?

This species prefers relatively low temperatures, 68–77°F (20–25°C) being about right, dropping to the cooler end of the range at night. In winter they can be kept even cooler, and it seems that this is useful in encouraging them to breed. The terrarium should be misted every evening.

HOW much time?

Ten to twenty minutes a day.

WHAT varieties?

Many color forms as noted above. In addition, other species, such as the gargoyle gecko, *R. auriculatus,* the mossy gecko, *R. chahoua,* and the very large New Caledonia giant gecko, *R. leachianus,* are bred in captivity, although not in such large numbers as *R. ciliatus*. Their care is much the same, although they should not be kept together. *Rhacodactylus leachianus* can grow to 18 in (45 cm) or more in length and is probably the world's largest gecko, so its terrarium should be larger than what is recommended for the crested gecko.

WHAT care?

Daily feeding and spraying, unless a misting system is installed. General cleaning as necessary.

WHAT food?

Insects such as crickets and cockroaches, and fruit. They are fond of bananas, which can be fed mashed up, or canned banana puree (or baby food) can be used. This is a good way of introducing vitamins and minerals to their diet, and females will also eat cuttlefish shavings as an additional source of calcium, which is especially important if they are breeding.

HOW easy are they to breed?

Very easy provided they are given plenty of food and are relatively undisturbed. Several sets of two eggs are laid throughout the breeding season, hence the need for additional calcium. The young are quite large and easy to rear.

Cost			
Setup cost			
Running cost			

Size: 8 in (20 cm) (with tail)
Distribution: New Caledonia
Life span: At least 10 years; probably more

Above: This species has very large eyes, intricately patterned irises, and no eyelids.

Right: The gargoyle gecko, R. auriculatus, has a pattern of irregular stripes that may be in a variety of colors. It is less common in captivity than the crested gecko.

WHAT drawbacks?

None. These are excellent lizards for beginners and more advanced enthusiasts, and there is a ready supply of captive-bred animals.

Eublepharus macularius

Leopard gecko

PROFILE

The leopard gecko is one of the most often kept reptiles; only the bearded dragon is as popular as this species. This is due to its adaptability under captive conditions, the ease with which it can be tamed, and its attractive coloration in all its forms. It provides plenty of scope for selective breeding, and a plethora of color forms or "morphs" have been created through selective breeding. Their attractiveness, otherwise, is very much in the eye of the beholder, and many enthusiasts, myself included, prefer the wild type. This is colored yellow or tan with spots of dark brown randomly scattered over its body. Juveniles, however, are banded in brown and cream, and as they grow the bands gradually fade and are replaced by spots. The tail is ringed in black and white and is thick, like a turnip, in well-fed individuals. Unlike most geckos, the leopard gecko and its close relatives have eyelids (and are sometimes known collectively as "eyelid geckos") and, as they are ground-dwellers, they

lack the adhesive toe pads that some other geckos have. They live in the rocky deserts of Asia, where they form large colonies.

WHAT temperament?

Very placid and easily tamed. They rarely, if ever, bite.

WHAT accommodation?

A terrarium with a floor area measuring 24 × 12 in (60 × 30 cm) is the minimum size for a single adult or a pair. Height is not important, although it should have a cover. They can be kept in a clinical setup or a naturalistic way. Sand is not recommended as a substrate as they are inclined to swallow it, but gravel or pebbles can be used. They can also be kept on a paper substrate, although this is obviously not as attractive. They require somewhere to hide, which, again, can be natural, such as a curled piece of bark or a hollow branch, or it can be an artificial hide made from plastic

Above: A normal "wild" type leopard gecko.

Left: A patternless form of the leopard gecko – the "blizzard" form.

Cost				
Setup cost				
Running cost				

Size: 8–10 in (20–25 cm), occasionally bigger

Distribution: South-central Asia

Life span: At least 15 years; occasionally to 30

or terra-cotta. The only other essential furnishing is a water bowl, but desert plants can be added to make the terrarium more attractive. Heating can be by under-cage pads installed at one end only, so there will be a thermal gradient, allowing the gecko to choose its preferred temperature. Lighting is not necessary, unless living plants are included.

WHAT environment?
A temperature of 68–82°F (20–28°C) is required (bearing in mind the remarks above regarding a thermal gradient). They tolerate much colder conditions, however, and can be cooled off during the winter. They need to be dry, and there is no need to spray their cage unless they are having trouble shedding their skin, in which case the substrate in or under the hide should be lightly sprayed every day until shedding has taken place.

HOW much time?
Five to ten minutes a day,

but extra time spent handling the gecko will be worthwhile.

WHAT varieties?
There are many color forms, including some in which various colors are missing (albinos, hypomelanistic, etc.), and others in which the markings are different from wild individuals, such as striped and mottled forms. These all have names, which are not always constant from one breeder to another, including "jungle," "high-yellow" (or "hi-yellow"), "lavender," "chocolate," and so on.

WHAT care?
Daily feeding and checking general health.

WHAT food?
Insects such as crickets, always dusted with a vitamin and mineral supplement. Breeding females require extra calcium.

HOW easy are they to breed?
Extremely. There is a constant supply of captive-bred leopard geckos of all colors and sizes.

WHAT drawbacks?
None; perhaps the ideal reptilian pet.

Below: This form lacks most of the dark pigment (termed hypomelanistic).

Hemitheconyx caudicinctus

Fat-tailed gecko

Size: 6–8 in (15–20 cm), males occasionally larger

Distribution: West Africa

Life span: 10 years or more

PROFILE

The fat-tailed gecko is an African relative of the leopard gecko, although it is not as popular in captivity, nor as easy to breed. It is a stocky species with broad alternating bands of tan and chocolate-brown and, as its name suggests, a thick tail. Some individuals have a bright cream line running down their back, whereas others lack this marking. They occur in dry grasslands and hillsides in West Africa, where they live in burrows.

WHAT temperament?

Placid but slightly more nervous than the leopard gecko.

WHAT accommodation?

Similar to the leopard gecko (pages 140–141). Hiding places are especially important for this species, as it becomes stressed if it is forced into the open. Several are recommended, at different ends of the terrarium so that it can choose whether to be warm or cool while still feeling safe.

WHAT environment?

This species has temperature requirements that are similar to the leopard gecko, but it seems to do better in a slightly more humid environment. Spraying the substrate underneath one of its hiding places will create a localized damp environment that they can use if they want to.

HOW much time?

Five to ten minutes a day.

WHAT varieties?

Apart from the striped and unstriped forms mentioned above, there is a form in which most of the dark pigment is missing (hypomelanistic), and these have bright orange stripes; they sometimes go under the name of "tangerine" geckos. There is also another species, Taylor's fat-tailed gecko, *H. taylori*, from northeast Africa, but it is rarely available.

WHAT care?

Daily feeding and light spraying. Cleaning as necessary.

WHAT food?

Insects such as crickets, dusted with a vitamin and mineral supplement.

Above: This is a striped hypomelanistic form of the fat-tailed gecko.

HOW easy are they to breed?

Not as easy as leopard geckos, but a number are bred in captivity.

WHAT drawbacks?

Poor supply of captive-bred stock. Rather shy compared with the leopard gecko.

Teratoscincus scincus

Frog-eyed gecko

PROFILE

Frog-eyed geckos occur in the deserts of Central Asia, where they live on gravel plains. They have thick bodies, large heads, huge eyes, and long limbs, holding themselves clear of the ground when they stand or move. Their scales are large, and they can produce a hissing sound by moving their tail from side to side, causing the scales' edges to rub together. Their toes do not have pads, but they have a fringe of serrated scales that help them to move quickly across loose sand.

WHAT temperament?

They become used to human disturbance but should not be handled more than necessary, as their skin is very delicate and easily torn.

WHAT accommodation?

A terrarium measuring 24 × 18 in (60 × 45 cm) is suitable for a pair; height is not important. The substrate should be sand, and there should be somewhere for each individual to hide, either an artificial hide box or a cave of flat rocks. Only one male can be kept in each terrarium.

Above: Keyserling's frog-eyed gecko is sometimes thought to be a separate species.

Cost			
Setup cost			
Running cost			

Size: 6–8 in (15–20 cm)

Distribution: Central Asia (southern China to Iran)

Life span: 5–10 years

WHAT environment?

They need a daytime temperature of 77–86°F (25–30°C), which can be allowed to fall at night. They can also be kept cooler during the winter.

HOW much time?

Ten minutes a day.

WHAT varieties?

There are two subspecies, *T. scincus scincus* and *T. scincus keyserlingii*, which are sometimes considered separate species. The latter are larger and more brightly colored.

WHAT care?

Daily feeding and light spraying.

WHAT food?

Insects such as crickets, waxworms, and sweepings (tiny insects gathered from the wild). All insects should be dusted with a vitamin and mineral supplement, and females require extra calcium.

HOW easy are they to breed?

Possible but not easy. The females require extra calcium, and the eggs are thin-shelled and easily broken.

WHAT drawbacks?

Rather delicate and only rarely available as captive-bred.

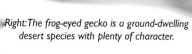

Right: The frog-eyed gecko is a ground-dwelling desert species with plenty of character.

Cordylus rhodesianus

Zimbabwe girdle-tailed lizard

The girdle-tailed lizards, of which there are twenty species, all have similar requirements, and several species may be for sale. *Cordylus rhodesianus* is a medium-sized species with yellow or cream markings on a dark brown or black background. Girdle-tailed lizards are associated with rocky outcrops, living in cracks and emerging to bask in the sun. They use their spiny tails to block the entrance to the cracks.

WHAT temperament?
Often shy at first but usually becoming tame after a while.

WHAT accommodation?
They are best kept in groups, requiring a terrarium of 40 × 18 × 18 in (100 × 45 × 45 cm) with a substrate of gravel and one or two piles of rocks on which they can climb. There should be plenty of crevices for them to retreat into and flat areas for them to bask on. A powerful heat lamp should be directed onto one of these basking spots, and a UV lamp is essential.

WHAT environment?
A background temperature of 68–77°F (20–25°C) and a spot under the heat lamp that reaches 95–104°F (35–40°C) during the day. They must have opportunities to retreat to cooler parts of the cage. Different species may have slightly different temperature preferences depending on their origin.

HOW much time?
Ten to fifteen minutes a day.

WHAT varieties?
Several similar species, not always accurately identified by importers. Lizards labeled as *C. rhodesianus* may actually be *C. tropidosternum*.

WHAT care?
Daily feeding. A light spray in the morning will allow them to drink drops of water from the rocks.

WHAT food?
Small insects such as crickets, and some plant material, such as dandelion leaves and flowers. Not all individuals will eat plants.

HOW easy are they to breed?
Rarely bred in captivity. They are live-bearers and have small litters of one to six young.

WHAT drawbacks?
Lack of captive-bred young.

Cost			
Setup cost			
Running cost			

Size: 3.5–4¾ in (9–12 cm)

Distribution: East Africa

Life span: Many years, perhaps up to 25

Above: The Zimbabwe girdle-tailed lizard belongs to a complex of species from southern Africa that are superficially very similar to each other.

Hemisphaeriodon gerrardii

Pink-tongued skink

PROFILE

The pink-tongued skink is an Australian species that resembles a small, more slender blue-tongued skink. It is pinkish-buff in color with wide bands of a darker shade, sometimes black, running across its body. This species lives in thick vegetation in eastern Australia, and feeds almost exclusively on snails. It is also listed under the names of *Tiliqua gerrardii* and *Cyclodomorphus gerrardii* in some publications.

WHAT environment?

A background temperature of 68–77°F (20–25°C) is about right, with a basking light raising this to 86–95°F (30–35°C) at one end of the terrarium. UV is also recommended. Humidity should be moderate, and spraying the cool end of the terrarium on a daily basis will help to maintain a humidity gradient, which is ideal.

Cost		
Setup cost		
Running cost		

Size: To 14 in (35 cm), occasionally longer

Distribution: Australia

Life span: 10–15 years; possibly longer

Above: An attractively marked pink-tongued skink, one of the easier skinks to keep and breed.

WHAT temperament?

Agile but not especially nervous and quite easy to manage.

WHAT accommodation?

A terrarium measuring about 40 × 12 × 18 in (100 × 30 × 45 cm) is suitable for a pair or small group. They like to climb so they should be given some stout branches and living plants if possible. The substrate can be coconut fiber or orchid bark. They also need a water bowl and somewhere, such as a piece of curved bark, to hide.

HOW much time?

Ten to fifteen minutes a day.

WHAT varieties?

None.

WHAT care?

Daily feeding and spraying. Occasional cleaning.

WHAT food?

Snails are the preferred food, and some will not take other types of nutrition. If you do not live in a place where snails are plentiful, this can be a problem. Some will eat minced meat mixed with raw egg yolk, although this should only be used occasionally.

HOW easy are they to breed?

They breed readily in captivity and are live-bearers.

WHAT drawbacks?

Obtaining enough snails on which to feed them.

Above: A pink-tongued skink showing the tongue that gives it its name.

Lepidothyris fernandi

Fire skink

PROFILE

This is a colorful and well-named skink from West Africa. Its flanks have large areas of bright red scales, and there is more red on its upper jaw. It has areas of black on its neck, and its back is golden-brown. It has the smooth, shiny scales common to most skinks and a long, cylindrical body and short limbs. It moves by wriggling rapidly from side to side and can be difficult to catch. Their natural history is poorly known, but they are thought to live on forest floors, among leaf litter.

WHAT temperament?
Nervous and fast-moving. They usually calm down in captivity but dislike being handled.

WHAT accommodation?
A terrarium measuring about 40 x 18 x 18 in (100 x 45 x 45 cm) is suitable for a pair. It needs a deep substrate of leaf litter or coconut fiber (or a mixture of the two) into which the skink can burrow. Pieces of dead wood can be sunk into the substrate, and living plants can be used to decorate the terrarium. A water bowl is important, and heating should be provided by a heat mat and an overhead heat lamp. A UV lamp should be included.

WHAT environment?
A background temperature of 73–82°F (23–28°C) with a warmer area under the heat lamp, which should be on during the day only. They require moderately humid conditions, and the substrate should be slightly moist, but not waterlogged.

HOW much time?
Five to ten minutes a day.

WHAT varieties?
None.

Cost		
Setup cost		
Running cost		

Size: To 12 in (30 cm), males are slightly larger than females

Distribution: West Africa

Life span: Unknown; several years at least

WHAT care?
Daily feeding and spraying. The cage should be disturbed as little as possible.

WHAT food?
Insects such as crickets, waxworms and cockroaches, all dusted with a vitamin and mineral powder.

HOW easy are they to breed?
Rarely attempted.

WHAT drawbacks?
Lack of captive-bred stock. Not suitable for people who like to handle their reptiles

Right: This is a beautiful skink, but it is not easy to handle.

Scincus scincus

Sandfish

PROFILE

The sandfish is an interesting member of the skink family that lives entirely in loose, wind-blown sand, where it "swims" beneath the surface by pressing its limbs to its sides and wriggling its body rapidly, like a fish. Its scales are smooth and shiny, and its head is pointed, with an underslung lower jaw, so that it can push through the sand. Coloration varies, but they are usually grey with about ten broad bands of yellow or tan across their body.

WHAT temperament?

Fast-moving and rarely seen, but very interesting.

WHAT accommodation?

A terrarium measuring 24 x 18 in (60 x 45 cm) is suitable for two or three sandfish. Height is not important. They obviously need a substrate of free-running sand, which should be at least 6 in (15 cm) deep. This skink does not drink from a bowl, but water can be sprayed onto the sides of the terrarium in the evening. A heat lamp is essential, and a UV lamp may be beneficial, although there is little information on this topic.

WHAT environment?

Hot conditions, to 104°F (40°C) or even more, directly under the basking lamp. They often bask just below the surface but occasionally emerge when the heat lamp first goes on in the morning. Conditions should be mainly dry, but the sand at one end of the terrarium should be kept very slightly damp.

HOW much time?

Five minutes a day.

WHAT varieties?

There are a number of subspecies as well as three other species of *Scincus*. Identification can be difficult, but they all require similar conditions. *S. scincus* is by far the most common species in the pet trade, originating from Egypt.

WHAT care?

Daily feeding and light spraying.

WHAT food?

Insects, especially waxworms and newly molted mealworms. Crickets and other insects occasionally, although they have trouble feeding on the surface. All meals should be dusted with a vitamin and mineral supplement.

HOW easy are they to breed?

Not bred in captivity, unfortunately.

Cost				
Setup cost				
Running cost				

Size: About 6 in (15 cm)
Distribution: North Africa and the Middle East
Life span: Unknown; probably 5–10 years

Above: A sandfish doing what it does best: swimming through sand. It has several adaptations that help it to do this. These fascinating reptiles require specialized conditions.

WHAT drawbacks?

Lack of captive-bred stock. Not good display animals; most of the time they are hidden from view.

Tiliqua gigas

Giant blue-tongued skink

PROFILE

The blue-tongued skink is one of the largest species in the family and one of the most popular pets. Like most skinks, their scales are large and glossy. They are brown in color with a number of dark bands crossing their body. The characteristic that gives them their name is their bright blue tongue, which they sometimes use as a warning display, holding it out for several seconds while hissing at the same time.

basking area. If the lizard has difficulty in shedding, the hide box can be stuffed with moist chopped sphagnum, and, if the problem persists, this can be left in place.

Left: Giant blue-tongued skink from New Guinea.

WHAT temperament?

Diurnal lizards that move in a slow, deliberate manner. They are highly intelligent, taking an interest in their surroundings and usually become very tame.

WHAT accommodation?

They require large terrariums; one with a floor space measuring 5 x 2 ft (1.5 m x 60 cm) being the minimum for one or two individuals. Height is not important. The substrate can be bark chippings or coconut fiber. They require a water bowl that is large enough to soak in and a hide box. They will also need a heat lamp and a UV lamp.

WHAT environment?

A background temperature of 73–82°F (23–28°C) is required with a warmer area under the basking lamp of up to 104°F (40°C). A UV lamp is essential, and this should be directed onto the

HOW much time?

Ten to fifteen minutes a day.

WHAT varieties?

There are other species of blue-tongued skinks, but they are not freely available.

WHAT care?

Daily feeding and occasional cleaning and spraying.

WHAT food?

They eat most things, but their diet should consist of green vegetables such as kale, dandelions, insects such as locusts, and a little fruit. All meals should be dusted with a vitamin and mineral supplement. Cat food can be used in an emergency.

Cost			
Setup cost			
Running cost			

Size: To 14 in (35 cm) (other species are slightly smaller)

Distribution: New Guinea

Life span: 20–30 years

HOW easy are they to breed?

Breeding is difficult but possible. They are live-bearers.

WHAT drawbacks?

They are expensive and need large cages and considerable amounts of time. Captive-bred stock is rarely available.

Tribolonotus gracilis

Red-eyed crocodile skink

PROFILE

One of the most unusual skinks, with a wedge-shaped head and four rows of heavily keeled scales running down its back. Its tail is also armored, with rings of spiny scales and there are additional spines on its limbs and the rear of its head. It is brown in color, but the eyes are surrounded by a ring of bright orange. This very unusual skink also vocalizes when it feels threatened, and it produces one single large egg at a time. It lives in moist habitats within forests and forest clearings.

WHAT temperament?
Calm and slow-moving but secretive.

WHAT accommodation?
They need large terrariums measuring at least 40 × 18 × 18 in (100 × 45 × 45 cm). This should be filled to a depth of about 6 in (15 cm) with coconut fiber, mixed with dead leaves and a piece of wood so that the skinks can create burrows. They also need a large water bowl and are good swimmers, sometimes remaining in the water for long periods of time. Living plants are worth including if possible.

WHAT environment?
Hot and humid, with a background temperature of 73–77°F (23–25°C). A heat lamp should be turned on in the day, raising the temperature beneath it to about 86°F (30°C), and a UV lamp should also be installed. They require humid conditions, and the substrate should be moist but not waterlogged, allowing them to push through it easily.

HOW much time?
Ten to fifteen minutes a day.

WHAT varieties?
There are seven other species, none of which enters the pet trade with the possible exception of *T. novaeguineae*, which is imported very occasionally.

WHAT care?
Daily feeding and spraying.

WHAT food?
Insects such as cockroaches, crickets, and waxworms, always dusted with a vitamin and mineral powder, which is especially important for breeding females.

Cost					
Setup cost					
Running cost					

Size: To 7 in (18 cm)

Distribution: New Guinea

Life span: Unknown, probably long—perhaps 20 years or more

HOW easy are they to breed?
They will breed in captivity, but they only lay one very large egg at a time.

WHAT drawbacks?
They are rare and expensive, and the supply of captive-bred young is very limited.

Above: The red-eyed crocodile skink is a very unusual species in looks and behavior.

Tupinambis merianae

Argentine black-and-white tegu

PROFILE

Tegu lizards are outwardly similar to the monitors even though they are not closely related and come from South America (monitors are from Africa, Asia, and Australasia). They are large lizards with glossy scales that, in the case of the Argentine species, are black and white. They have long tongues that they flick out constantly to explore their surroundings and are seemingly highly intelligent and very aware of their surroundings.

essential. Heating should be by means of a spotlight positioned at one end, and a UV lamp will also be necessary.

WHAT environment?

A background temperature of 77–86°F (25–30°C) and a hot spot that reaches 104°F (40°C) or more during the day. Humidity needs to be fairly high; spray occasionally and use a large water bowl.

Cost				
Setup cost				
Running cost				

| **Size:** 3–4.5 ft (1–1.5 m); males are larger than females |
| **Distribution:** South America |
| **Life span:** 10–15 years |

WHAT care?

Daily feeding and general maintenance. The more time you spend with the tegu, the better; they like to be taken out of their terrarium and allowed to explore their surroundings.

Above: A juvenile Argentine black-and-white tegu.

WHAT food?

Insects and small rodents as hatchlings, larger rodents, chicks, and eggs as adults. Artificial diets can be made.

WHAT temperament?

Captive-bred individuals are calm and very responsive to their owner.

WHAT accommodation?

A very large terrarium is required; a minimum of 6 x 3 x 3 ft (2 x 1 x 1 m) for one or two adults. It should have a substrate of coconut fiber, orchid bark, or similar material and one or two branches or logs for interest. A hide box and a water bowl are

HOW much time?

Ten to twenty minutes a day. Time spent handling the tegu will be well rewarded as they are very responsive.

WHAT varieties?

There are no varieties, but there are several other species of tegu. The Argentine black-and-white tegu is the best one to keep and most frequently bred.

HOW easy are they to breed?

Not easy in captivity as they require large amounts of space.

WHAT drawbacks?

Large size; hatchlings soon grow into large lizards with substantial appetites. Only captive-reared young become tame enough to make suitable pets.

Eremias species

Steppe lizard

PROFILE

Steppe lizards, of which there are over thirty species, all very similar, are recent newcomers to the reptile hobby. They are fast-moving lizards with pointed heads, long legs, and a long tail. Most species have some degree of striping down their bodies. Importations often consist of *Eremias velox*, one of the more common species, which has a row of blue spots along each side. They all live in barren, open places in Central Asia, and they are thought to have very short life spans, reaching maturity within a year.

WHAT temperament?
Very fast-moving and agile; difficult to handle.

WHAT accommodation?
A large terrarium would be necessary, up to 40 x 18 in (100 x 45 cm) floor space. Height is not important but it must be covered. It should have a sandy

substrate, with scattered rocks, and a water bowl. A basking light and UV lamp are essential.

WHAT environment?
Very hot, with temperatures under the heat lamp reaching at least 104°F (40°C) but with a cooler area for the lizard to retreat to.

HOW much time?
Five to ten minutes a day.

WHAT varieties?
There are several species that could potentially appear in the pet trade, but the differences between them are often slight and exact identification may be difficult.

Cost		
Setup cost		
Running cost		

Size: About 6 in (15 cm)

Distribution: Central Asia and South China

Life span: 1–2 years

WHAT care?
Daily feeding and light spraying, as they may not drink from a water bowl.

WHAT food?
Small insects such as crickets, dusted with a vitamin and mineral supplement.

HOW easy are they to breed?
Not bred in captivity.

WHAT drawbacks?
Very difficult to handle and probably not very long lived. A challenge to keep for any length of time.

Right: Steppe lizards of various species are sometimes available, for instance, Eremias przewalskii *(above) and* E. velox *(below).*

Takydromus sexlineatus

Six-lined long-tailed lizard

PROFILE

This is a most unusual lizard belonging to the wall lizard family. Although small, its tail accounts for about three-quarters of its total length, and it uses it to help push it through dense grasses and other vegetation. It is brown or russet in color with darker and lighter stripes running along its body. Some are pale green underneath, but most are white or cream.

WHAT temperament?
Fast-moving and alert, active during the day, and a good display species.

WHAT accommodation?
A large terrarium is best, with a floor area measuring at least 24 x 12 in (60 x 30 cm) and, ideally, 24 in (60 cm) high for a pair or a small group. This gives it an opportunity to clamber around among branches, twigs, and living plants.

It needs a heat lamp and a UV lamp, both placed over a basking spot at one end of the terrarium, and a small water bowl.

WHAT environment?
Fairly undemanding, requiring a background temperature of about 68–77°F (20–25°C) and a hot spot that reaches 86°F (30°C) for basking. It should be lightly sprayed every day to raise the humidity temporarily.

HOW much time?
Five to ten minutes a day

WHAT varieties?
No varieties, although there are several other species in the genus, rarely imported.

WHAT food?
Small insects such as crickets, dusted with a vitamin and mineral supplement.

Size: To 12 in (30 cm), most of which is tail

Distribution: South Asia and China

Life span: Unknown; probably 4 years or more

WHAT care?
Daily feeding and spraying.

HOW easy are they to breed?
Breeding is rarely attempted, unfortunately, although it should be easy. They are egg layers.

Above: The six-lined long-tailed lizard is common in the pet trade. Other members of the genus are similar but rarely seen; their very long tails distinguish them from other members of the family.

WHAT drawbacks?
Lack of captive-bred stock is the biggest problem. Imported animals vary in quality, and thin ones should be avoided as they may be parasitized, dehydrated, or both.

Gerrhonotus multicarinatus

Southern alligator lizard

PROFILE

The southern alligator lizard is a medium-sized species with a slender body, long tail, and short limbs. Its scales are heavily keeled and the keels line up to form a series of low parallel ridges running the length of its body. It has dark bars across its back, white spots on its flanks, and a scattering of orange scales. It lives in grassy places, in fields or forest clearings, often in damp places, hiding under logs and in matted vegetation.

WHAT temperament?
A slow-moving, calm lizard that adapts well to captivity.

WHAT accommodation?
A terrarium measuring 40 × 18 × 18 in (100 × 45 × 45 cm) is suitable for a pair or small group, and it should be covered with a deep layer of leaf litter topped off with pieces of bark, dead branches, and sheets of moss. A water bowl is essential. It needs a heat lamp under which to bask and a UV lamp is recommended.

WHAT environment?
A background temperature of 68–77°F (20–25°C) is suitable, although it can be allowed to fall below this at night if necessary. The spot under the basking light should reach 86°F (30°C) at least, and the UV lamp should be concentrated onto the same area. The top layer of the substrate should be dry, but there should be a layer of slightly moist substrate below. This species lends itself to naturalistic setups, which provide a range of environments.

Above: Alligator lizards are attractive and undemanding species but are not always available.

HOW much time?
Five to ten minutes a day, but allow longer for occasional thorough servicing of large, complicated setups.

WHAT varieties?
There are several subspecies that vary slightly in coloration, and another species, the northern alligator lizard, *Gerrhonotus coeruleus*, that requires similar conditions. The latter is a live-bearing species, whereas the southern alligator lizard lays eggs.

WHAT care?
Daily feeding and light spraying.

WHAT food?
Slugs, snails, insects such as crickets, and small mice. They have powerful jaws and can tackle most small prey.

HOW easy are they to breed?
Rarely attempted, unfortunately.

WHAT drawbacks?
Lack of supply of captive-bred stock.

Cost			
Setup cost			
Running cost			

Size: 4–7 in (10–17 cm)

Distribution: Western North America

Life span: Many years; probably 10 or more

153

Pseudopus apodus

Glass lizard

The glass lizard is a very large, legless lizard from Eastern Europe, previously placed in the genus *Ophisaurus*. It has a large head and cylindrical body with a fold of skin running down each flank, and is overall brown, slightly paler below, with a tan head. Juveniles are grey with several dark brown bars across their body. They live in open, grassy places, often visible from many feet, and move like a snake.

Above: The presence of eyelids and ear openings distinguishes legless lizards from snakes.

Cost			
Setup cost			
Running cost			

Size: To 53 in (135 cm)

Distribution: Eastern Europe and Central Asia

Life span: Unknown; probably 10–20 years or longer

WHAT temperament?

They dislike being handled and may bite or smear their captor with the smelly contents of their gut. They also spin rapidly when held and, as a last resort, their tails will break off. They do become tame in captivity, though, and can be handled for short periods.

WHAT accommodation?

Large terrariums are required, measuring 40 × 18 × 18 in (100 × 45 × 45 cm) at least, but preferably

larger. They need a substrate they can burrow into, such as coconut fiber or leaf litter, and plenty of pieces of wood and bark to shelter under. They need a large bowl of clean water. Heating during the day can be by means of an overhead basking lamp, but room temperature is adequate at night.

WHAT environment?

A temperature of about 77°F (25°C) should be aimed for beneath a heat lamp, and UV should be provided. The substrate should be dry or slightly moist.

Left: North American legless lizards are smaller and belong to the genus *Ophisaurus*. They have similar requirements in captivity.

HOW much time?

Ten to fifteen minutes a day.

WHAT varieties?

None. Similar species include the slow worm, *Anguis fragilis*, and the North American glass lizards, *Ophisaurus* species.

WHAT care?

Daily feeding and light spraying. Cleaning as necessary.

WHAT food?

They like snails and slugs but will take a wide range of animal food, including insects, mice, and dog and cat food, which should be given only occasionally.

HOW easy are they to breed?

Not bred in captivity.

WHAT drawbacks?

The large amount of space needed and the lack of captive-bred young.

Varanus salvator

Water monitor

PROFILE

This is a very large lizard, probably the largest species in the pet trade, and looking after one is a serious business. Water monitors come from South and Southeast Asia, and are common along bodies of water where they typically bask on logs and muddy river banks and quickly slip into the water if they are disturbed. They are often common around towns and cities, where they feed on anything they can scavenge, including offal.

Above: Juvenile water monitors are attractively marked.

WHAT temperament?
Unpredictable. Large monitors are able to give nasty bites and will scratch with their claws and use their tails as whips. Wounds often become infected. If they are raised from hatchlings, they become habituated to captivity and are more easily managed.

WHAT accommodation?
Although hatchlings can be kept in terrariums measuring about 3 ft (1 m) long, they grow quickly and eventually need large walk-in enclosures. These need a substrate of wood shavings or bark chippings, several substantial branches for climbing on, and a very large water bowl—preferably large enough for the monitor to submerge itself completely. There should be a powerful heat lamp, and, although it is uncertain whether monitors require a UV lamp or not, one should be included to be on the safe side.

WHAT environment?
A background temperature of 77–86°F (25–30°C) is required, with a basking area that reaches 104°F (40°C) for part of the day. The cage should be heavily sprayed every one or two days to raise the humidity.

HOW much time?
Fifteen to thirty minutes a day.

Cost			
Setup cost			
Running cost			

Size: 6 ft (2 m) or more; males are larger than females

Distribution: South and Southeast Asia

Life span: To 25 years or more

WHAT varieties?
None. Other large monitors with similar requirements include Bosc's monitor and the Nile monitor.

WHAT care?
Daily feeding; refreshing water bowl.

WHAT food?
Dead rodents, chicks, fish, and eggs. Vitamin and mineral powder should be added to every meal.

HOW easy are they to breed?
Not bred in captivity.

WHAT drawbacks?
Size and uncertain temperament.

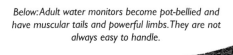

Below: Adult water monitors become pot-bellied and have muscular tails and powerful limbs. They are not always easy to handle.

Varanus acanthinurus

Spiny-tailed monitor

PROFILE

The spiny-tailed monitor, sometimes known as the ridge-tailed monitor or, in pet-trade terminology, the "ackie," is among the smallest species in this large genus and is therefore a good choice for captivity. In addition, it is easy to tame and is bred in fairly large numbers, ensuring a good supply of captive-bred young. Like all monitors, this species has a long, pointed head and a long neck. Its body is cylindrical in cross-section, and its tail, which is longer than the head and body combined, is thick at the base and covered with spiny scales, hence the name. The color is rich brown, sometimes reddish-brown, with lighter spots over the body. There is a pale line passing through the eye and onto the neck and this distinguishes the species from closely related ones.

The spiny-tailed monitor occurs in arid regions, where they are often found in small colonies around rocky outcrops. Their narrow shape enables them to squeeze into small cracks, and they can inflate their bodies to jam themselves in even more tightly, making them almost impossible to dislodge. They can use their spiny tails to protect their body, or as a weapon to lash out at enemies. They are good climbers but do not have the opportunity to climb trees to the same degree as monitors living in forests. They are very predatory and eat small lizards and mammals as well as large insects.

Above: All monitors have a long, forked tongue.

WHAT temperament?

Nervous by nature but easily tamed. All monitors are very intelligent and will respond to their owners. They prefer to be allowed to climb onto a hand or arm rather then being held tightly.

WHAT accommodation?

A large terrarium, with a floor area measuring 4.5 x 2 ft (1.5 m x 60 cm) is the minimum size for a pair or trio (one male to two females) of adults. Height is not so important, although the terrarium should be covered. Juveniles will live in small groups in smaller terrariums but grow quickly. The substrate can be sand or gravel or a mixture of the two. Piles of flat rocks should be arranged so that they can be used for climbing and basking, but care must be taken to see that they are stable; if necessary, they

Below: The spiny-tailed monitor is so-named for obvious reasons.

can be stuck together using silicone adhesive. A powerful heat lamp and a UV lamp are essential, and should be placed at one end of the terrarium to provide a thermal gradient.

WHAT environment?

Hot and dry, with a background temperature of 77–86°F (25–30°C) and a hot spot under the basking lamp that reaches at least 104°F (40°C). A bowl of clean water must be present at all times, but occasionally spraying the lizards is recommended.

HOW much time?

Fifteen minutes a day.

WHAT varieties?

The so-called "red" and "yellow" forms may be subspecies, or they may simply be regional variants. Other than this, there are several other dwarf monitors that are occasionally available. These include the argus monitor, *Varanus panoptes*, the blue tailed monitor, *Varanus doreanus*, and others. Although their care is broadly similar, their natural habits should be taken into account when designing their terrarium and creating their environment.

Right: The argus monitor is one of the more attractively marked species.

WHAT care?

Daily feeding and occasional cleaning.

WHAT food?

Large insects such as adult cockroaches and locusts, occasional nestling mice and rats, pieces of lean meat, and raw eggs. Insects should make up the major part of their diet and need to be dusted with a vitamin and mineral supplement. Monitors are inclined to become obese if too much high-protein food is given.

HOW easy are they to breed?

They breed readily in captivity.

WHAT drawbacks?

The large amount of space that must be devoted to their terrarium.

Right: The narrow head of the blue-tailed monitor, V. doreanus.

Cost					
Setup cost					
Running cost					

Size: To 30 in (75 cm), most of which is tail	
Distribution: Northern and eastern Australia	
Life span: Many years; probably more than 20	

Snakes

■ Snakes are reptiles and the 3,378 species recognized at present have an almost global distribution, with the majority of species in the tropical regions. They range in size from less than 12 in (30 cm) to more than 26 ft (8 m) in length and may be thick or slender, dull or brightly colored. Some species are venomous (they are not considered here), whereas others constrict their prey or simply grasp it and begin to swallow. All species are carnivorous, but their prey ranges from ants to antelopes, mainly depending on their size. Only a small proportion of this number are regularly kept in captivity, and some groups of species are especially favored: the boas and pythons, rat snakes, and king snakes accounting for the great majority of all those commonly kept and bred in captivity. Most of the commonly kept species eat rodents or slightly larger birds or mammals, which can most conveniently be bought frozen and thawed out when required. Snakes do not require vitamin or mineral supplements, nor do they require UV-B, except, possibly, in the case of a few rarely kept diurnal species that may benefit from it.

■ Generally speaking, snakes are secretive creatures, and many of them are strictly nocturnal. Because of this, they do not always make good display animals. Snake keepers are often content to know that the apparently empty cage of sand, wood chips, or bark in their home is actually inhabited by a snake that may only put in a voluntary appearance once every week or so. The rest of the time it hides away under a piece of cage furnishing or an artificial hide. Depriving it of somewhere to hide will not force it to become more tame but will have the opposite effect. Most snakes can be handled safely and will get used to it, but probably don't "enjoy" it as such, although some snake keepers would probably disagree. Even non-venomous snakes can bite, and bites from the larger species can be painful. Very large snakes have no place around young children.

■ Snake cages may be of many types, but plastic boxes with well-fitting ventilated lids are favored by those with large collections. These can be heated with heat strips fixed to shelves and the cages placed on them, with about one quarter to one third of the floor area in contact with the heat strip. This provides a thermal gradient, allowing the snake to choose its preferred temperature, which may vary according to whether it has fed, is about to shed its skin, or is about to lay eggs (or give birth). Depending on the background temperature of the room, a thermostat may not be necessary but is always recommended to avoid overheating.

■ Apart from substrate and a hide box, all snakes require a bowl of drinking water, which must be kept clean, and, if this is large enough for them to soak themselves in, problems in skin shedding are usually avoided. Other furnishings, such as pieces of wood, bark, rock, etc., can be added according to the owner's taste but are rarely essential. There are a few snakes, however, that have more specialized needs, and these include arboreal and semi-aquatic species, and small, burrowing species, whose lifestyles must obviously be taken into account when creating their environment.

■ Snakes are more easily bred than most other reptiles and amphibians, and there is a good supply of captive-bred young. Some species, such as certain pythons and corn snakes, are available in a kaleidoscope of different color and pattern forms. These are popular with some enthusiasts, whereas others prefer the wild forms; the important thing is to choose healthy, feeding individuals over other considerations.

Antaresia childreni

Children's python

Cost			
Setup cost			
Running cost			

Size: 24–32 in (60–80 cm), occasionally longer

Distribution: Northern Australia

Life span: At least 25 years; probably longer

PROFILE

The smallest of the commonly available pythons, this species comes from Australia. It is mid-brown in color, heavily spotted with darker markings in juveniles, but as the snake grows its markings fade and adults are sometimes uniform brown. It is a slender species with a narrow head. Its name comes from a Mr. J.G. Children, who worked at the British Museum; it does not signify that it is especially suitable for children to keep. It lives in a variety of dry habitats, including rocky hillsides, caves, grasslands, and even in towns.

WHAT temperament?
Docile and easy to handle. May bite occasionally.

WHAT accommodation?
A terrarium measuring about 24 x 18 x 18 in (60 x 45 x 45 cm) is adequate for an adult. The substrate can be wood shavings or reptile bark, and a hide box and water bowl should be included. Branches for climbing on will largely be ignored by the snake.

WHAT environment?
A temperature of 77–95°F (25–35°C) should be provided, with a thermal gradient between the warmest and coolest parts of the terrarium.

HOW much time?
Five to ten minutes a day.

Left and above: Children's python is a small species that can easily be accommodated if space is limited.

WHAT varieties?
No varieties, but a similar species, the spotted python, *Liasis maculosus*, is also available (and sometimes the two species are confused). This has similar requirements to the Children's python.

WHAT care?
Feeding every one or two weeks, refreshing the water, and cleaning as required.

WHAT food?
Small mammals such as mice. Hatchlings can sometimes be reluctant to feed on mice but usually start eventually. If necessary, a newborn mouse can be scented with a lizard.

HOW easy are they to breed?
Easy.

WHAT drawbacks?
Not very colorful but in all other respects a good choice.

Morelia viridis

Green tree python

PROFILE

The green tree python is a spectacular species that sometimes goes under the name of "chondro," in reference to its former name of *Chondropython viridis*. It is a bright green tree snake with a row of pale spots, or a pale line running down its back. It is slender (for a python) with a large head and prominent heat pits bordering its mouth. Juveniles are bright yellow or, occasionally, red, and change color as they mature. This species lives in rain forests and is highly arboreal, resting with its coils draped over a horizontal branch.

WHAT temperament?

Hatchlings sometimes bite, but adults normally calm down and can be handled safely.

WHAT accommodation?

A tall terrarium measuring 30 x 30 x 40 in (75 x 75 x 100 cm) high is the minimum size for

Above: Green tree pythons often drape themselves over a horizontal branch.

an adult. There must be several horizontal branches (broom handles are a good substitute) fixed at various heights. A heat lamp is needed, and the substrate can be wood shavings, paper towels, orchid bark, or moss. A large water bowl should be included.

WHAT environment?

A background temperature of 77–86°F (25–30°C) with an opportunity to bask is ideal. The temperature under the basking lamp should be 95°F (35°C) during the day. Humidity should be low unless the snake has problems shedding, in which case it should be thoroughly sprayed every day until shedding has occurred.

HOW much time?

Ten to twenty minutes a day.

WHAT varieties?

There are no varieties, although specimens from various Indonesian islands often differ from each other and are identified by locality, such as "Aru" and "Biak," although most of those in captivity have mixed ancestry.

WHAT care?

Feeding every one or two weeks, replenishing the water, spraying or cleaning as required.

Cost			
Setup cost			
Running cost			

| **Size:** 5–6.5 ft (1.5–2 m) |
| **Distribution:** Australia and New Guinea |
| **Life span:** 25–30 years |

Below: Juvenile green tree pythons are bright yellow for the first year or so.

WHAT food?

Small mammals such as mice or rats. Small meals are best, and food should be offered on long forceps.

HOW easy are they to breed?

Breeding requires specialist knowledge.

WHAT drawbacks?

Not always easy to handle. Some hatchlings are reluctant to feed and are more delicate than most other pythons.

Morelia spilota

Carpet and diamond python

The carpet python occurs in many forms over its wide range, which includes Australia and New Guinea. Its coloration can be predominantly grey, brown, reddish, black and yellow, or anything in between. Its pattern is usually a complex of large, interconnected, dark-edged blotches on a paler background, or it may be the other way around, i.e., light markings on a darker background. Sometimes the blotches are arranged across the body in the form of indistinct bars, and at other times they may be small, pale spots on a darker background, as in the diamond python, which is one of several subspecies. The carpet pythons in captivity have often lost their locality information and are of uncertain origin, but many have names to distinguish them, such as "jungle" carpet python, "coastal" carpet python, and "Irian Jaya" carpet python. Even so, the carpet python is an attractive snake in all its forms.

Above and below: "Jungle" carpet pythons are brightly marked in yellow and black and are among the most popular forms.

It occupies a huge variety of habitats, from rain forests to wooded grasslands. It is an agile snake with good climbing abilities and is commonly found in and around abandoned buildings and outbuildings, sometimes in roof spaces. They do not live in the very dry interior of Australia. In places that experience very cold conditions, diamond pythons hibernate for several months.

WHAT temperament?

Highly variable. Most carpet pythons can be tamed and are easy to handle, especially if they are handled carefully when they are young. Others are bad-tempered, however, and large ones can give a painful bite. There is some correlation between the various forms: "Irian Jaya" carpet pythons tend to be very gentle, whereas "jungle" carpet pythons can sometimes be snappy, for instance.

WHAT accommodation?

A large terrarium measuring at least 40 × 20 × 20 in (100 × 50 × 50 cm) is the minimum size for an adult. This should have a substrate of wood shavings, one or two hide boxes, and some stout branches for the snake to climb on. A large water dish must be included.

WHAT environment?

A thermal gradient should be created, giving a temperature range of 68–86°F (20–30°C). This can be achieved with under-cage heat mats or an overhead heat lamp, which must be well guarded to prevent the snake from burning itself. Snakes will naturally find the warmest place after they have eaten, to aid digestion. The humidity should be low.

HOW much time?

Five to fifteen minutes a day.

WHAT varieties?

As mentioned above, the carpet python occurs in numerous forms, or subspecies. There should be something for

everyone, but in case this is not enough there are a number of artificially created "morphs" on the market. The diamond python is a distinct subspecies, *Morelia spilota spilota*, and the inland carpet python, *Morelia bredli*, is a separate species. The former is rarely kept in captivity, but the latter is gaining in popularity and is a very beautiful species.

WHAT care?

Feeding every one or two weeks (hatchlings need to be fed more often than adults),

Below: The diamond python, Morelia spilota spilota, *is a subspecies of the carpet python, but it has very different requirements and is not as easy to keep and breed.*

replenishing the water every day and cleaning as required.

WHAT food?

Small mammals such as mice and rats.

HOW easy are they to breed?

They breed readily in captivity and can be quite prolific.

Cost				
Setup cost				
Running cost				

Size: 6.5–10 ft and slender*

Distribution: Australia and New Guinea

Life span: To 30 or more years

*Very large specimens are unusual, but this varies with the subspecies.

Above: The Centralian python, M. bredli, *is a very beautiful species; adults become rich brown in color.*

WHAT drawbacks?

They require large amounts of space and can sometimes be untrustworthy; choose one that is used to being handled. In many respects the carpet python is a good choice for anyone wanting a moderately large snake.

Python breitensteini

Borneo blood python

PROFILE

A very heavy-bodied snake with a small, flattened head. It has rich chestnut brown markings on a yellow or tan background. Although the shape and size of the blotches differ between individuals, there is not as much color variation in this species as in other pythons. It is a secretive species from Borneo

and is found mainly in damp habitats in forests and plantations. The very short tail (only about ten percent of the total length) is the reason for the alternative English name of Borneo short-tailed python.

WHAT temperament?

Usually very placid and not inclined to bite, although they can strike very rapidly when necessary.

WHAT accommodation?

A terrarium measuring at least 60 × 30 in (150 × 75 cm) is required for an adult. Height is not important. A substrate of wood shavings works well and there should be a hide box and bowl of clean water large enough for the snake to soak itself.

WHAT environment?

A temperature of 77–95°F (25–35°C), with the heat applied to one end to create a thermal gradient between the warmest and coolest parts of the terrarium.

HOW much time?

Five to ten minutes; longer for cleaning.

Although it is a heavy snake, the Borneo blood python is not very active and is content with a relatively small cage. Regular handling will keep it tame.

WHAT varieties?

None at present.

WHAT care?

Feeding every one or two weeks, water change every day, and occasional cleaning. This snake responds well to regular handling.

Cost				
Setup cost				
Running cost				

Size: To 6.5 ft or a little longer

Distribution: Borneo

Life span: 25 years or more

WHAT food?

Small mammals such as mice and rats. It will eat relatively large meals.

HOW easy are they to breed?

Easy to breed. Like other pythons, females coil around their eggs and brood them.

WHAT drawbacks?

Large size.

Python brongersmai

Malaysian blood python

PROFILE

The blood python, sometimes known as the short-tailed python, is a heavily-built species from the Southeast Asian mainland. It is tan, orange, or reddish above, with a series of pale blotches down the center of its back and along each flank, those on the flanks having dark centers. This species occurs in rain forests, along river courses, or in swamps. It is a typical "sit and wait" predator that remains hidden until prey comes within range.

WHAT temperament?

Some examples of this species can be bad-tempered and strike without warning, making them unpredictable, whereas others are docile and easy to handle.

WHAT accommodation?

A terrarium measuring at least 60 × 30 in (150 × 75 cm) is required for an adult. Height is unimportant. A substrate of wood shavings works well, and there should be a bowl of clean water large enough for the snake to be able to soak itself in. A large hide box is essential.

WHAT environment?

A temperature of 77–95°F (25–35°C) should be provided, with a thermal gradient between the warmest and coolest parts of the terrarium.

HOW much time?

Five to twenty minutes a day.

WHAT varieties?

The "wild" type varies in color greatly and there is also an albino strain. The Sumatran blood python, *P. curtus*, is similar in shape and size but very dark in coloration.

Cost			
Setup cost			
Running cost			

Size: 6.5 ft, very heavy-bodied

Distribution: Southeast Asia (Malaysian Peninsula and eastern Sumatra)

Life span: 25 years or more

There is often confusion between the two as they were formerly regarded as subspecies within a single species

WHAT care?

Feeding every one or two weeks, water change every day, and occasional cleaning.

WHAT food?

Mammals such as mice, rats, and rabbits and also birds such as chickens.

HOW easy are they to breed?

They breed readily.

WHAT drawbacks?

Large size and their unpredictable temperament

Left: The Malaysian blood python has distinctive markings, although it is highly variable. It tends to grow larger than other blood pythons.

Python molurus bivittatus

Burmese python

PROFILE

The Burmese python is one of the largest species in the world and is very popular among snake keepers who like their pets on the large side. It adapts well to captivity, is usually easy to tame, and comes in a variety of colors and patterns. In its natural form, it is tan or pale brown with many large, rich brown blotches down its back and sides. These are darker toward the edges. There is always a characteristic arrow-head marking on the top of its head. There are many variations of this pattern, due either to geographic origin of the snake or to selective breeding.

In nature the Burmese python lives in rain forests but may also be common around villages and other human habitations, where they are attracted by food in the form of vermin and domestic animals. Small individuals are good climbers, but as they become bulkier they tend to rest on the ground among dead leaves and low-growing vegetation, or in caves in rock outcrops. In colder parts of its range it may become dormant during the winter, and its ability to tolerate cool conditions has been instrumental in allowing escaped animals to survive, and even breed, in parts of Florida, where it has become a pest, feeding on local wildlife and domestic pets.

WHAT temperament?
Usually calm and tolerant of handling. Hatchlings occasionally bite.

WHAT accommodation?
A very large terrarium is required, with a floor space measuring at least 6.5 × 3 ft (2 × 1 m) for a medium-sized adult. Height is not so important, although the floor space can be increased by adding a shelf to the upper part of the terrarium. A range of substrates are suitable, but most people prefer easy-to-replace materials such as bark chippings, wood shavings, or newspaper. A hide box, which can range from a work of art to a simple cardboard box, should be provided, and a stout log or branch can add aesthetic appeal to the terrarium but is not essential. A large bowl of clean water should always be available.

Below: Wild type Burmese pythons are beautifully marked and, in many cases, are more attractive than the various "morphs" on the market.

Above: The "granite" form of the Burmese python.

Cost			
Setup cost			
Running cost			

Size: Potentially to 20 ft (6 m), commonly 10–13 ft (3–4 m), heavy-bodied

Distribution: Southeast Asia

Life span: 20–25 years

WHAT environment?

A temperature of 77–95°F (25–35°C) should be provided, with a thermal gradient between the warmest and coolest parts of the terrarium. This can be achieved by an overhead heat lamp or an under-cage heater.

HOW much time?

Five to twenty minutes a day.

WHAT varieties?

There are three subspecies, of which the Burmese python is one, and the Indian python, *P. molurus molurus* is another. These are not widely kept. Mutant forms, or morphs, of the Burmese python are widely kept and bred. They include the albino or "golden" Burmese python, which has yellow or orange blotches on a white background, as well as leucistic (white with black eyes), "green" (although not really

green), "granite," in which the markings are broken up into a network of smaller spots and lines, plus all the combinations of these: albino granite, albino green, etc., as well as more subtle color variations, such as "caramel," "butterscotch," and other flavors.

WHAT care?

Feeding every one to two weeks, water changes daily, and cage cleaning as required.

WHAT food?

Mammals, starting with mice and young rats and working up to large rabbits or even sheep, in the case of very large adults. Worth bearing in mind if you are thinking of keeping this species.

HOW easy are they to breed?

They breed readily, hence the availability of the many selectively bred color forms.

WHAT drawbacks?

Size. Permits may be needed for interstate transport.

Below: Golden pythons are among the most popular forms.

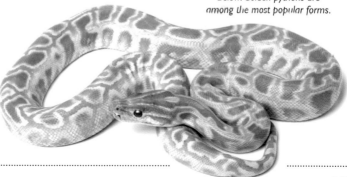

Python reticulatus

Reticulated python

The reticulated python is usually regarded as the longest snake in the world (the South American anaconda is heavier, but this is a shorter, more heavy-bodied species). It comes from Southeast Asia, where it occurs over a wide area and on many islands, large and small, giving rise to a number of regional variations in size and color, some of which may turn out to be valid species. In its most common form it has a number of fawn, black-edged blotches down its back, with areas of yellow or tan on either side. The flanks are grey with regular white spots. Superimposed on this pattern are numerous dark spots and specks, producing a complicated and colorful result. The head is often yellow or golden, and the eye is orange.

The reticulated python inhabits rain forests, often close to rivers, where it coils up in overhanging branches. It is also common around towns and villages, where it feeds on rats and domestic animals such as dogs and cats. It has been known to take humans, but very rarely. It is well camouflaged when resting among leaves, whether in trees or on the ground, and remains motionless for days on end until it feels the need to go hunting.

WHAT temperament?

Highly variable; some are extremely aggressive and resist all attempts to tame them, whereas others are docile and never attempt to bite.

WHAT accommodation?

Huge terrariums are required for adults, measuring a minimum of 6.5 x 5 ft (2 x 1.5 m) and preferably larger. Captive adults rarely climb (they are usually too bulky), and height of the terrarium is not important. A substrate of shavings is best, and it should have one or two hides. A shelf about halfway up will increase the available surface area, and the snake will often make use of a resting place off the floor. A bowl of clean water is important; some individuals have difficulty in shedding their skin unless they can soak beforehand.

Above: The wild-type reticulated python displays a kaleidoscope of colors in a geometric pattern.

Cost			
Setup cost			
Running cost			

Size: Potentially to nearly 23 ft*

Distribution: Southeast Asia

Life span: 25 or more years

Most only attain about half this length. Island forms are sometimes larger or smaller than average, depending on locality.

WHAT environment?

A choice of temperatures between 77 and 95°F (25 and 35°C) should be provided by positioning the heat source at one end of the terrarium.

HOW much time?

Five to twenty minutes a day.

WHAT varieties?

Once again, selective breeding has produced some weird and wonderful "morphs" of this species, but, probably because of the amount of space required, this has not progressed to the same point as the royal python, for instance. As with other species, the albino is the basis for many strains, and there are others missing yellow or other colors, as well as striped and patternless forms. All these have been crossed with albinos and others to produce an array of morphs. Add to this the natural variations from the many

Above and below: The "lavender" form lacks the darker pigments so that the yellows are emphasized and the black areas become purplish pink It is a popular and attractive "morph."

islands on which the species occurs and the resulting permutations are almost endless.

WHAT food?

Mammals, starting with mice and rats for hatchlings, and progressing to rabbits and eventually to farm animals for adults.

WHAT care?

Feeding every one or two weeks.

HOW easy are they to breed?

They are easy to breed, but space is often a limitation.

WHAT drawbacks?

Size, and their requirement for food that is often difficult to obtain.

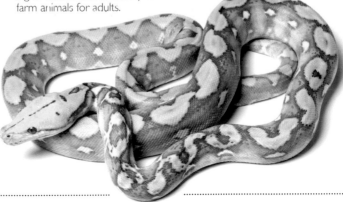

Python regius ▨▨☑

Ball python

PROFILE

The ball python is a short, heavily built python from West Africa, also known as the royal python. In its natural form it is very dark brown, almost black, with spots and bars of tan or yellowish-brown. The top of its head is usually dark with a pale line passing through its eye. Its defensive strategy is to form a tight coil protecting its head in the center of the ball.

WHAT temperament?
Very calm, if a little shy, and tolerant of handling. It rarely bites.

substrate of wood shavings or reptile bark, as well as a hide box. Other than this, cage furnishings are very much up to the taste of the individual keeper.

WHAT environment?
A temperature of 77–95°F (25–35°C) is ideal, with the heat concentrated at one end of the terrarium to provide a thermal gradient so that the snake can choose its preferred body temperature. Lights are not necessary.

Cost*				
Setup cost				
Running cost				

Some of the most desirable "designer" morphs sell for several thousand dollars each.

Size:	3–6 ft (1–1.8 m)
Distribution:	West Africa
Life span:	20–25 years

WHAT care?
Feeding once every one or two weeks, water change every day, and occasional cleaning.

Left: Wild form of the ball python.

WHAT food?
Small mammals such as mice and rats. Wild snakes are very difficult to get to feed and will often live for over a year without feeding, whereas captive-bred individuals are much easier.

HOW much time?
Five to fifteen minutes a day.

WHAT varieties?
As with several other species of snakes and lizards, ball python "morphs" have become big business. One website lists 1,323 different morphs at the time of writing, and naming all these forms is becoming increasingly creative, out of hand perhaps.

WHAT accommodation?
A terrarium measuring about 40 x 20 in (100 x 50 cm) is adequate for an adult ball python; they do not climb, so height is unimportant. It should have a

HOW easy are they to breed?
Very easy, as evidenced by the huge numbers of captive-bred young available.

WHAT drawbacks?
None, provided captive-bred young are purchased.

Xenopeltis unicolor

Sunbeam snake

PROFILE

This is a very unusual snake from tropical Asia. It is dark brown or black above and white below, with a flattened, shovel-shaped head. Its scales are large, smooth, and highly iridescent, and its eyes are small. These are all adaptations to a burrowing lifestyle, and sunbeam snakes spend almost their entire lives below the ground living in burrows and underneath objects such as rocks, logs, and debris. They are common in rice paddies and around villages, wherever there is a good supply of food.

WHAT temperament?
They never bite but may spray an evil-smelling substance from their cloacal gland.

WHAT accommodation?
A large terrarium with a floor area of 40 × 18 in (100 × 45 cm) is required for one or two sunbeam snakes. Height is not important, and they can be kept in plastic trays if required. The substrate is important, and should consist of at least 4 in (10 cm) of moist wood pulp, chopped sphagnum, or coconut fiber. Heating should be applied from below, at one end only, with a heat pad. A small water bowl should be placed at the cool end of the terrarium; no other equipment is necessary.

Below: The sunbeam snake is an unusual Asian species, only occasionally available and tricky to keep.

Cost			
Setup cost			
Running cost			

Size: To 48 in (120 cm), but usually smaller	
Distribution: Southeast Asia	
Life span: Unknown	

WHAT environment?
Warm and humid: 73–86°F (23–30°C) and 80–100 percent humidity; the substrate should not be waterlogged.

HOW much time?
Five to ten minutes a day.

WHAT varieties?
None.

WHAT care?
Feeding once a week and maintaining the correct conditions.

WHAT food?
Small rodents such as mice and young rats.

HOW easy are they to breed?
Rarely bred in captivity

WHAT drawbacks?
Only available as wild-caught adults, which are prone to parasites and skin infections. Not good display animals. Interesting rather than spectacular.

Acrantophis dumerili

Dumeril's boa

PROFILE

Dumeril's boa is a medium-sized species from Madagascar. It is a stocky snake, intricately marked in shades of buff and brown, often with a pinkish tinge, especially when young. It lives in the dry deciduous forests of western Madagascar, where it is well camouflaged when resting among dead leaves.

WHAT temperament?
A slow-moving, nocturnal snake that is good-natured in captivity and easy to handle, hardly ever attempting to bite.

WHAT accommodation?
A terrarium with a floor space measuring at least 5 x 3 ft (1.5 x 1 m) is required for an adult. Height is not important as they do not climb. Juveniles can be kept in smaller terrariums. They should have a substrate of wood shavings, one or two hide boxes and a large water bowl.

WHAT environment?
A thermal gradient of 77–95°F (25–35°C) should be created by using an under-cage heat mat or an overhead heat lamp, which must be well guarded to prevent the snake from burning itself. Humidity needs to be low.

HOW much time?
Ten to twenty minutes a day.

WHAT varieties?
There are no varieties, but a

Below: Dumeril's boas are attractively marked in shades of brown. Juveniles often have a pink or orange tinge, but this fades as they mature.

related species, the Madagascar ground boa, *A. madagascariensis*, may be available occasionally. This is larger, but in most respects its care is similar to that required by Dumeril's boa.

WHAT care?
Feeding every one or two weeks, replenishing the water in its bowl, and cleaning when necessary. They respond to regular handling.

WHAT food?
Small mammals such as mice and rats.

HOW easy are they to breed?
They usually breed readily, and there is a good supply of captive-bred young.

Cost			
Setup cost			
Running cost			

Size: To 6.5 ft, heavy-bodied

Distribution: Madagascar

Life span: 25–40 years

WHAT drawbacks?
The species is on Appendix 1 of the CITES list and cannot be traded internationally. Captive-bred individuals must be micro-chipped and registered, with the relevant certificate passed to the new owner. Always check that an animal is chipped before buying it.

Corallus caninus

Emerald boa

PROFILE

This tree boa from South America bears a remarkable resemblance to the green tree python from Australasia, being green with white markings along its back. It also coils around horizontal branches in a similar fashion. Its young are orange or brick red. The heat pits in this species are between the scales bordering its mouth, whereas those of the green tree python are in the center of the scales. They live in rain forests of the Amazon Basin and neighboring regions, and give birth to live young.

WHAT temperament?
Variable but often short-tempered. Their teeth are long and curved so they can give a painful bite.

WHAT accommodation?
A tall terrarium measuring 30 × 30 × 60 in (75 × 75 × 150 cm) high is a suitable size for an adult. There must be several horizontal branches or dowel rods fixed at various heights. A heat lamp is required, and the substrate can be wood shavings, paper towels, orchid bark, or moss. A large water bowl should be included.

WHAT environment?
Same as the green tree python (page 161). A background temperature of 77–86°F (25–30°C) with an opportunity to bask is ideal. The temperature under the basking lamp should be 95°F (35°C) during the day. Humidity should be low, although it should be thoroughly sprayed on a daily basis when it is about to shed.

Cost				
Setup cost				
Running cost				

Size: To 6 ft (1.8 m)

Distribution: Tropical South America

Life span: At least 25 years

Left: Emerald boas look like green tree pythons and have similar requirements in captivity, although they are live-bearers.

their back and yellow undersides, whereas those from Guyana and Surinam, for example, have short white bars that are separated from each other. Others lack the white markings altogether and are solid green.

HOW much time?
Ten to twenty minutes a day.

WHAT varieties?
There are regional variations, although many captives do not have locality information. Those from the Amazon Basin often have a continuous white line down

WHAT care?
Feeding once every two weeks.

WHAT food?
Small mammals.

HOW easy are they to breed?
Difficult.

WHAT drawbacks?
Inclined to bite and not always easy to feed.

Common boa

PROFILE

The common boa, or boa constrictor, is probably the best-known snake in the world. It occurs over a large part of tropical and subtropical America and exists in a number of different forms. Some of these are recognized subspecies, while others are traits peculiar to certain populations. The basic pattern consists of a buff or tan background on which there are a number of darker crossbars. These become wider on the flanks so that they are hourglass-shaped. The number and spacing of the crossbars vary, as does their color. In all forms they become darker and closer together toward the tail, and some of the most attractive forms are known as "red-tailed" boas, although boas with red or reddish tails can be found in several different populations. Common boas in captivity often come from mixed parentage and cannot be assigned to one form or another.

The common boa is an adaptable species associated with rain forests, scrub, and even semi-desert habitats. In the wild it is found from northern Mexico to Argentina and on several Caribbean islands. It often lives near rivers, where its food is more easily found, and climbs well. Even large individuals frequently rest on branches well above the ground. It also swims well.

WHAT temperament?

This is usually a well-mannered snake, although some individuals are bad-tempered and inclined to bite. Captive-bred juveniles nearly always settle down quickly, but large common boas should be handled with care.

WHAT accommodation?

A large terrarium measuring at least 5 × 3 × 3 ft (1.5 x 1 x 1 m) is the minimum size for an adult. Most grow to between 6.5 and 10 ft (2 and 3 m) and some to 13 ft (4 m), but they never get as large as the mythical boa constrictors of explorers' stories. Juveniles can be kept in terrariums with more modest dimensions but they all grow up eventually! Their terrarium should have a substrate of wood shavings and one or two hide boxes. Some individuals like to climb, whereas others hardly ever do, so it is a good idea to include some stout branches at first and simply remove them if they are not used. Make sure the branches are well anchored to prevent them from falling. A large water dish, big enough for the snake to submerge itself completely, must be included.

WHAT environment?

A thermal gradient should be created, giving a temper-ature range of 77–95°F (25–35°C). This can be achieved with under-cage heat mats or an overhead heat lamp, which must be well guarded to prevent the snake

Above: This is an attractive form of the common boa, often referred to as a "red-tailed boa" and similar to wild individuals from South America. Juveniles are usually more brightly colored than adults.

Cost				
Setup cost				
Running cost				

Size: 3–13 ft (1–4 m), depending on locality

Distribution: Central and South America

Life span: 30 years or more

from burning itself. Snakes will find the warmest place after they have eaten, to aid digestion, but they must also be able to move away from the heat. Although they are rain forest snakes, the humidity should be low.

HOW much time?

Ten to twenty minutes a day.

WHAT varieties?

Seven subspecies of the common boa are widely recognized, and another four or five are accepted by some experts but not others. The most distinctive include the red-tailed boa, *B. c. constrictor*, although not every boa with a red tail belongs to this subspecies; the Mexican common boa, *B. c. imperator*, including dwarf island forms such as the Hog Island boa; and the Argentine boa, *B. c. occidentalis*, a distinct subspecies covered with a network of fine black markings. The others are less often seen in captivity. Superimposed on these subspecies are a range of color morphs, mostly albino, missing black or missing red forms, and various permutations.

Above: A juvenile albino common boa. All dark pigment is missing from the skin.

WHAT care?

Feeding every one or two weeks, replacing the water daily, and cage cleaning as necessary.

WHAT food?

Small and large mammals such as mice, rats, and rabbits, according to size.

HOW easy are they to breed?

Frequently bred in captivity.

WHAT drawbacks?

Potential size is an important consideration when buying a young common boa. Otherwise, straightforward.

Above: A boa constrictor feeding; they can handle relatively large food items.

Below: A "salmon" form of the common boa, a variant with subtle coloration.

Epicrates cenchria

Rainbow boa

PROFILE

The rainbow boa occurs over a wide area in South America, and several subspecies are recognized. The Brazilian rainbow boa, *E. cenchria cenchria,* is the most colorful one, but all forms are popular as captives. Typically it is a brown or orange snake with a series of lighter, dark-edged circles running down its back. There is also a row of light-edged dark circles along each flank. Variations involve the brightness of the coloration and the contrast between the markings. Rainbow boas are rainforest snakes, usually found on the ground but occasionally climbing into low vegetation.

Right: The Brazilian rainbow boa is the most brightly colored form.

WHAT temperament?

Normally placid, although some are nervous and may bite.

WHAT accommodation?

A terrarium measuring 40 × 20 × 20 in (100 × 50 × 50 cm) is suitable for an adult. The substrate should be wood shavings, and there must be a water bowl large enough for the snake to soak thoroughly.

WHAT environment?

A thermal gradient giving a temperature range of 77–95°F (25–35°C) is suitable. They usually cope with a low humidity but sometimes have trouble shedding, in which case they can be sprayed or given a hide box filled with moss temporarily.

HOW much time?

Ten to twenty minutes a day.

WHAT varieties?

Nine subspecies are usually recognized but several of these have recently been raised to full species status. The most distinctive of these are the Argentine rainbow

Right: The Argentine rainbow boa has recently been re-classified as a full species, E. alvarezi.

boa, *E. alvarezi,* and the Colombian rainbow boa, *E. maurus.*

WHAT care?

Feeding once every one or two weeks, water changes daily, and occasional cleaning.

WHAT food?

Small mammals such as mice and rats.

HOW easy are they to breed?

They are bred regularly and are live-bearers.

WHAT drawbacks?

Other than the occasional bad-tempered individual, they have no real drawbacks.

Cost				
Setup cost				
Running cost				

Size: 5–6.5 ft (1.5–2 m), depending on subspecies	
Distribution: Central and South American	
Life span: 25–40 years	

Lichanura trivirgata

Rosy boa

PROFILE

The rosy boa is a small, semi-burrowing species from southwestern North America. It is a cream or grey snake with three longitudinal stripes of brown, orange, or dark brown, and these may be ragged or crisp, according to the subspecies and individual variation. Its scales are small and shiny, and it has a silky texture. It lives in rocky outcrops, where it can remain hidden in crevices and venture out in the evening in search of food.

WHAT temperament?
Very gentle, slow-moving, and easy to handle.

WHAT accommodation?
A terrarium with a floor area of 24 x 12 in is suitable for an adult. Height is not important as they rarely climb. A substrate of wood shavings, at least 2 in deep, should be provided, and at least one small hide box, as this species likes to jam itself into small spaces. A water bowl is required.

WHAT environment?
A thermal gradient of 68–86°F (20–30°C) should be arranged, using an under-cage heat mat at one end. The humidity should be low at all times, and lighting is not required. If necessary, the temperature can be allowed to fall to 59°F (15°C) in the winter, especially if the snake stops feeding, as they sometimes do.

Above: The desert rosy boa, often known as Lichanura trivirgata gracia, *is one of several forms from the US southwest.*

HOW much time?
Five to ten minutes a day.

WHAT varieties?
Several subspecies, the status of which is uncertain. There are also various types of albino and similar strains.

WHAT care?
Feeding once every one or two weeks, daily water changes, and cage cleaning as necessary.

WHAT food?
Mice.

Cost			
Setup cost			
Running cost			

Size: 20–40 in, depending, to a degree, on subspecies
Distribution: Southwest United States and northwest Mexico
Life span: 20–30 years; possibly longer

Above: The Baja California rosy boa, L. t. saslowi, *is probably the most desirable subspecies.*

HOW easy are they to breed?
They usually require a cooling-off period in the winter in order to breed.

WHAT drawbacks?
The supply of captive-bred young is poor.

Eryx colubrinus loveridgei

Kenyan sand boa

PROFILE

The sand boas are burrowing snakes that live in dry habitats, mainly deserts. This species comes from East Africa, and the Kenyan subspecies, *loveridgei*, is the most colorful form and the one most often kept in captivity. It is yellow, tan, or orange with large chocolate-brown blotches. Its body is cylindrical and its scales smooth and shiny, both characteristic of burrowing species. It spends most of its life below the surface or under stones and logs.

WHAT temperament?
Easy to handle and rarely attempts biting.

WHAT accommodation?
A terrarium with a floor space measuring at least 24 x 12 in (60 x 30 cm) is required. Height is not important. It should have at least 2 in (5 cm) of loose substrate such as free-running sand or wood shavings, and a water bowl. No other furnishings are required.

Below: The orange coloration indicates that this is the Kenyan subspecies of the sand boa, E. c. loveridgei.

WHAT environment?
A thermal gradient of 73–86°F (23–30°C) is suitable, with the heat applied at one end by an under-cage heat mat. The humidity should be low, and there is no need for lighting.

HOW much time?
Five to ten minutes a day.

WHAT varieties?
There is some natural color variation as well as several albino strains and an anerythristic (lacking red) strain.

Cost				
Setup cost				
Running cost				

Size: 6–10 in (15–25 cm), females are much larger than males

Distribution: East Africa

Life span: To 25 years or more

WHAT care?
Feeding once a week and changing the water as required. The substrate can be cleaned piecemeal (spot-cleaned), but a complete change will be needed occasionally.

WHAT food?
Small mammals such as mice. They are inclined to refuse food for weeks or months at a time, usually because they have been overfed previously. Fasting is not usually a cause for alarm.

HOW easy are they to breed?
They usually breed readily. The females give birth to six to fifteen live young, which usually begin to feed without problems.

WHAT drawbacks?
They are not good display animals as they rarely appear on the surface; this is more important to some people than to others.

Dasypeltis scabra

Common egg-eating snake

PROFILE

This is one of the more unusual snakes. It is grey, brown, or reddish-brown, with a long, slender body and rounded snout. It has a row of blotches down its back, and its scales are heavily keeled and rough to the touch. It lives in southern Africa and feeds exclusively on birds' eggs; it will not eat any other food.

WHAT temperament?

Usually docile, but when alarmed it may form a horse-shoe shaped coil and produce a hissing sound by rubbing its keeled scales together, mimicking the venomous saw-scaled viper. It sometimes strikes, but this is purely display as it doesn't have functional teeth.

WHAT accommodation?

A terrarium measuring 24 × 12 × 12 in (60 × 30 × 30 cm) is adequate for an adult. They are mainly terrestrial but will also climb, so a taller terrarium can be used if available but is not essential. They need a substrate of wood shavings, a hide box, and a water bowl large enough to soak in.

WHAT environment?

A temperature of 68–77°F (18–25°C) is required, and a thermal gradient, with under-cage heating applied at one end only, is the best arrangement. Humidity should be low and lighting is unnecessary.

HOW much time?

Five to ten minutes a day.

Below: The common or rhombic egg eater has heavily keeled scales, giving it a rough appearance and feel.

Cost			
Setup cost			
Running cost			

Size: 20–32 in, very slender

Distribution: Southern Africa

Life span: Unknown; probably 15 years or more

WHAT varieties?

They vary somewhat in color and there are other species of egg eaters, but this is the most common one. It is sometimes called the rhombic egg eater.

WHAT care?

Feeding, refreshing the water in the bowl, and occasional cleaning.

WHAT food?

Birds' eggs. Large adults will take a small hen's egg, while small adults will take quail eggs. Juveniles will only eat finch eggs. They can be force-fed with beaten egg through a rubber tube attached to a syringe, but this is not very satisfactory.

HOW easy are they to breed?

They breed easily, but raising the young is a problem because of the food situation.

WHAT drawbacks?

Finding enough suitable eggs can be difficult.

Euprepriophis mandarinus

Mandarin rat snake

PROFILE

A small rat snake with an unusual pattern. Typically it is grey with a series of jet-black spots down its back. Each of these spots has a yellow center and the head is similarly marked in yellow and black. Some individuals have a red or pink tinge to the background color. It apparently lives in montane forests and thick scrub but also in fields and among rocks. It probably spends much of its life below ground, in rodent burrows.

WHAT temperament?
Usually docile, hardly ever attempting to bite.

WHAT accommodation?
A terrarium with a floor space of 24 × 18 in (60 × 45 cm) is adequate for an adult. They need a deep substrate of wood shavings, one or two hide boxes, and a water bowl large enough to soak in. One box can be filled with moist moss, as this species seems to do better if the humidity is moderately high.

WHAT environment?
They must not be kept too warm. Room temperature is often sufficient, at most 68–79°F (20–25°C), but preferably less than this.

HOW much time?
Five to ten minutes a day.

WHAT varieties?
There is variation, but whether this correlates with their place of origin is uncertain.

WHAT care?
Feeding once a week. Wild mandarin rat snakes are very difficult to feed and should be

Cost			
Setup cost			
Running cost			

Size: 3–4 ft (1–1.2 m); often smaller, occasionally larger

Distribution: Southern China and neighboring countries

Life span: Uncertain, potentially to 10–15 years

Above and below: This species is one of the most distinctive rat snakes.

avoided. Captive-bred juveniles usually feed readily and grow well. Food should be placed in a hide box at first as they prefer to feed in confined spaces. Otherwise, water changes and occasional cage cleaning.

WHAT food?
Small mice. Even adults are reluctant to take mice larger than their own body diameter.

HOW easy are they to breed?
Not difficult but requires some specialist knowledge.

WHAT drawbacks?
Sometimes rather delicate. Best left to experienced snake keepers.

Gonyosoma oxycephalum

Red-tailed green rat snake

PROFILE

This is a large and spectacular rat snake from Asia. It occurs over a wide range in Southeast Asia, including Borneo and many other islands, and is quite variable, but most specimens are bright green with an orange, red, or grey tail. It is slender with a narrow pointed head, and its scales are smooth and shiny. It is highly arboreal and often coils up in leafy branches overhanging water. When angered, it flattens its neck and can strike very quickly.

WHAT temperament?

Nervous and inclined to bite. Not an easy snake to handle.

WHAT accommodation?

A large terrarium is required, measuring 3 x 3 x 3 ft (1 x 1 x 1 m) minimum. This arboreal snake needs to climb, and the cage should contain branches for it to do so. The substrate can be wood shavings, and a large water bowl is essential.

WHAT environment?

A temperature of 77–82°F (25–28°C) is required during the day, and this can be provided by an overhead basking lamp. Background temperature can be slightly lower at nighttime. A high humidity is required, and the terrarium should be sprayed every day, but must also be well ventilated.

HOW much time?

Ten to twenty minutes a day

WHAT varieties?

Many regional variations, some of which are yellow and others blue-grey. Similarly, the tail may be grey or yellow. Imported snakes rarely have reliable locality information.

WHAT care?

Daily spraying, preferably onto the leaves of living or artificial plants so that the snake can lap water from them. The water bowl should be kept full of clean water, however. Feeding once a week; cleaning as required.

WHAT food?

Mice, although some apparently will only eat birds. Offering food on long forceps often works better than leaving it in the terrarium.

HOW easy are they to breed?

Possible but not easy.

Cost			
Setup cost			
Running cost			

Size: 5¼–6.5 ft (1.6–2 m)
Distribution: Southeast Asia
Life span: Unknown; probably 10–15 years

Above: Red-tailed green rat snakes are highly arboreal and must be kept in spacious, high terrariums. They are alert, diurnal snakes that make a fine display.

WHAT drawbacks?

Captive-bred young are rarely available, and wild-caught animals are often full of parasites, fail to feed, and may be aggressive.

Below: This species varies somewhat in color. This bright green individual is using its blue tongue to explore its surroundings.

Western hognose snake

PROFILE

A distinctive little snake with a stocky body, short tail, wide head, and upturned snout. It may be brown, grey, greenish, or reddish in color, with dark markings on a paler background. Its scales are heavily keeled. It lives in semi-desert regions, grasslands, farmlands, etc., but prefers areas with loose sandy soil in which it can use its snout to dig up buried toads, which are its main natural food.

WHAT temperament?
Usually very calm and adapts easily to captivity. It sometimes puffs up its body and hisses and makes mock strikes if alarmed but rarely bites.

WHAT accommodation?
A terrarium with a floor area measuring 24 x 18 in (60 x 45 cm) is adequate for an adult. Height is not important as it does not climb. They need a substrate of wood shavings deep enough to burrow into, one or two hide boxes, and a water bowl large enough to soak in.

WHAT environment?
A temperature of 64–77°F (18–25°C) is suitable, although it will tolerate colder conditions. A thermal gradient, with under-cage heating applied at one end only, is the best arrangement, and it can hibernate in the winter. Humidity should be low, and lighting is unnecessary.

HOW much time?
Five to ten minutes a day.

WHAT varieties?
There are three subspecies, the plains hognose, *H. n. nasicus*, the dusty hognose, *H. n. gloydi*, and the Mexican hognose, *H. n. kennerlyi*. There are also two other species, but they will not eat mice. Albino strains are also being selectively bred.

WHAT care?
Feeding once a week, refreshing the water bowl daily, and cleaning as necessary.

WHAT food?
Mice. Captive-bred individuals will nearly always accept mice, and some prefer them to be slightly "high." They can take relatively large food items and sometimes swallow them sideways!

HOW easy are they to breed?
Very easy, and there is a good supply of captive-bred young.

WHAT drawbacks?
None, although it is not a good idea to allow them to chew on your finger as their saliva is slightly toxic. Probably best kept away from children.

Cost				
Setup cost				
Running cost				

Size:	16–24 in, rarely to 35 in
Distribution:	North America
Life span:	15–20 years

Above: Hognose snakes have stocky bodies and bold markings, although their coloration varies.

Lampropeltis alterna

Grey-banded kingsnake

PROFILE

This is a highly variable snake with two distinct color forms: "Blair's phase" are light or dark grey with wide saddles of orange or red, edged in black, whereas "alterna phase" are grey with narrow dark bands. Sometimes these narrow bands have a small amount of orange in their centers, and sometimes they have a narrow border of white scales. There are several intermediate forms, but they are all the same species. Its head is flattened, and its eyes are slightly bulbous. This species lives in arid habitats, often among rocks, and is nocturnal and secretive.

WHAT temperament?
A gentle species, rarely attempting to bite and easily handled.

WHAT accommodation?
A terrarium with a floor space of 30 × 18 in (75 × 45 cm) is adequate for an adult. They need a deep substrate of wood shavings, and the availability of one or two hide boxes is especially important as this species prefers to rest in a confined space. A water bowl is essential, but other cage furnishings are optional.

WHAT environment?
A temperature of 64–77°F (18–25°C) is ideal, and a thermal gradient, with under-cage heating applied at one end only, suits them best. Humidity should be low, and lighting is unnecessary.

HOW much time?
Five to ten minutes a day.

WHAT varieties?
Several color forms, as described above. Some are rarer than others, and the orange-banded form is probably the most common and the most popular.

WHAT care?
Feeding once a week, changing the water daily, and cleaning the terrarium as necessary.

Cost			
Setup cost			
Running cost			

Size: 20–35 in (50–90 cm)

Distribution: South Texas and adjacent parts of Mexico

Life span: 15–25 years

WHAT food?
Mice. Some individuals are not good feeders, although captive-bred animals are trouble-free once they have started to feed.

HOW easy are they to breed?
Fairly easy.

"Blair's phase" of the grey-banded kingsnake.

WHAT drawbacks?
Feeding the young, as described above, and obtaining a good enough supply. They seem to have become less popular in recent years, and there are fewer breeders and they may be hard to find.

Lampropeltis getula

Common kingsnake

PROFILE

The common kingsnake is divided into numerous subspecies, many of which are disputed by some experts. The Californian kingsnake, *Lampropeltis getula californiae*, has been elevated to a full species, *Lampropeltis californiae*, and this includes at least two of the former subspecies. In other words, the situation is complicated. Whatever names are used, however, this kingsnake (or these kingsnakes) are basically black or dark brown with a range of different markings in white, cream, or yellow. The behavior and captive

Above: The brown and cream coastal form of the Californian kingsnake. Below: The black and white desert form.

care of all these forms are similar. They are cylindrical in cross-section, with smooth, glossy scales. Their heads are narrow and the same width as their necks. They occur from coast to coast in North America and from the northern states south into Mexico, living in a range of habitats that includes deserts, foothills, prairies,

and swamps. It is equally adaptable in diet and feeds on other snakes, lizards, rodents, turtles' eggs, and birds' eggs. In places it eats venomous snakes such as rattlesnakes, to whose venom it is supposedly immune. It is a powerful constrictor and often feeds in confined places, crushing its prey against a hard surface such as the sides of a burrow.

WHAT temperament?

The vast majority of common kingsnakes are docile and easily handled. They have a strong feeding reflex, however, and if they think food is on the way they may strike at a hand by mistake. If they latch on, they are sometimes difficult to dislodge.

WHAT accommodation?

A terrarium of 40 × 20 in (100 × 50 cm) is adequate for an adult. Height is not so important as they are not climbers. Kingsnakes have been known to eat one another, so they cannot be housed together, especially after they have been fed. The substrate may be wood shavings, and they should be given a hide box and a bowl of clean water. Other cage furnishings are optional.

WHAT environment?

A thermal gradient ranging from 68–82°F (20–28°C) and produced by an under-cage heat mat at one

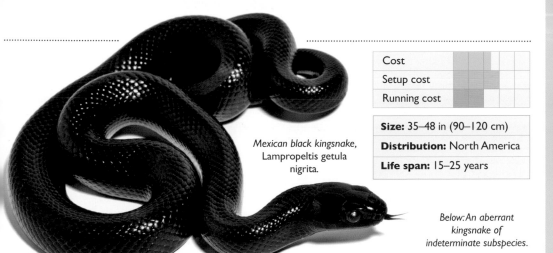

Mexican black kingsnake,
Lampropeltis getula
nigrita.

Cost			
Setup cost			
Running cost			

Size: 35–48 in (90–120 cm)

Distribution: North America

Life span: 15–25 years

Below: An aberrant
kingsnake of
indeterminate subspecies.

end of the cage is the best way of heating. Lighting is unnecessary and the humidity should be low, even for species from humid environments.

HOW much time?

Five to ten minutes a day; longer periods for cleaning. They can be allowed to hibernate in the winter in which case they do not need to be fed and time spent is minimal.

WHAT varieties?

The patterns vary with locality and may consist of broad bands (Californian kingsnakes), blotches (desert kingsnake and others), or speckles (speckled kingsnake and others). There are also intermediate forms, and in the past many different subspecies were named. Many of these are now considered to be intergrades between neighboring forms. Californian kingsnakes are probably the most popular, and they can be black with chalky white bands (desert form), or brown with yellow or white bands (coastal form). There is also a naturally occurring striped form of the black-and-white variety, in which the white markings take the form of a wide stripe down the center of the snake's back. In addition, there is, as usual, a multitude of selectively bred "morphs" mostly based on albinos of various types: "lavender," "ruby-eyed," "blizzard," etc.

WHAT care?

Feeding once a week, water changes, and cleaning as necessary.

WHAT food?

Mice. Note the remarks about their cannibalistic tendencies.

HOW easy are they to breed?

Very easy. The young of most Californian kingsnakes, and the majority of other forms, begin feeding without problems.

WHAT drawbacks?

None, but do not be tempted to keep more than one in a cage.

Lampropeltis triangulum

Milk snake

PROFILE

The milk snake is a wide-ranging species with numerous subspecies; up to 25 are recognized. The eastern milk snake, *L. triangulum triangulum*, is grey or brown with a series of large brown blotches running down its back. All the other subspecies are colored in red, white, and black, with bands of various widths. In many the red bands are wide, and the triads of black-white-black are narrow. The number and spacing of the triads are variable, even within a subspecies. There is a tendency in most subspecies for the coloration to become darker as the snake ages, and very few, if any, retain the bright hatchling markings throughout their lives. In addition, some subspecies are much larger than others. With such a wide geographical range (Canada to Ecuador!), this species may occur in a wide variety of habitats, including temperate woodland, farmlands, mountain slopes, and arid deserts. In captivity, all species can be treated similarly, although the smallest forms are difficult to keep and breed because the hatchlings are too small to eat mice. In practice, species on offer are most likely to be medium to large forms, which are relatively easy to cater for.

Above: An orange-banded Pueblan milk snake with her newly laid clutch of eggs.

WHAT temperament?

This varies. Most are relatively easy to handle and rarely bite, but they all tend to be nervous, quick-moving, and dislike being restrained. They often thrash about if not held firmly. They are nocturnal and secretive.

Below: Stuart's milk snake, Lampropeltis triangulum stuarti, *is one of the more evenly marked forms and often has bright coloration.*

WHAT accommodation?

The size of the terrarium depends on the subspecies. Small forms can be kept in a terrarium with a floor space of 24 × 12 in (60 × 30 cm) whereas larger ones, such as the Honduran milk snake, require terrariums up to twice this length. Height is not important as they are terrestrial snakes that rarely climb. They need a substrate of wood shavings, one or two hide boxes and a water bowl large enough to soak in.

WHAT environment?

A temperature of 64–82°F (18–28°C) is required, although it will depend on the origin of the subspecies in question; northern forms prefer cooler conditions than southern and subtropical forms, and can sometimes be kept at room temperature. A thermal gradient, with under-cage heating applied at one end only, is the best arrangement.

Right: Typical Pueblan milk snake, L. t. campbelli.

Cost			
Setup cost			
Running cost			

Size: 20 in–6.5 ft (50 cm–2 m), depending on subspecies

Distribution: North, Central, and northern South America

Life span: 15–25 years

The humidity should be low, and there is no need for lighting as they are nocturnal.

HOW much time?

Five to ten minutes a day.

WHAT varieties?

There are up to 25 subspecies. These range from the small scarlet kingsnake, *L. triangulum elapsoides*, which grows to 20 in (50 cm), to the large Honduran milk snake, *L. t. hondurensis*, and other tropical subspecies, which can reach over 6.5 ft (2 m). Among the most popular are the Sinaloan milk snake, *L. t. sinaloae*, with wide red bands separating the triads, Stuart's milk snake, which is similar but in which the red bands are not as wide, the Pueblan milk snake, *L. t. campbelli*, with bands of roughly equal width, and the Mexican milk snake, *L. t. annulata*, in which the pale rings are often yellow, but many other forms have their following. There are forms in which the pale bands are orange, such as the "tangerine" Honduran milk snakes, strains that have been selected for especially bright coloration, and others that have produced albinos.

WHAT care?

Feeding once a week, changing the water daily, and cleaning as necessary.

WHAT food?

Mice, but note the remarks above about small subspecies that are reluctant to eat mice when they are young.

HOW easy are they to breed?

Very easy, and there is a good supply of captive-bred young.

WHAT drawbacks?

Small hatchlings of some subspecies, but this can be avoided by choosing the more popular forms.

Lampropeltis pyromelana

Sonoran mountain kingsnake

PROFILE

This snake – sometimes called the Arizona mountain kingsnake – is a colorful "tricolored" species with rings of white, bordered with black, on a red background. It is sometimes known as a false coral snake because it mimics the venomous coral snakes, although the arrangement of the rings or "triads" is slightly different. Its snout is white, which separates it from a similar species, the Californian mountain kingsnake, which has a black snout. It lives among rocks in mountain ranges, often in places that are lightly wooded with conifer trees.

WHAT temperament?
Placid and easy to handle and only rarely bites. Quite secretive.

WHAT accommodation?
A terrarium with a floor space of 30 × 18 in (75 × 45 cm) is adequate for an adult. Height is not important as they rarely climb. They need a deep substrate of wood shavings, one or two hide boxes and a water bowl large enough to soak in.

WHAT environment?
A temperature of 64–77°F (18–25°C) is ideal and room temperature is often sufficient. A thermal gradient, with under-cage heating applied at one end only, is the best arrangement. Humidity should be low, and lighting is unnecessary.

HOW much time?
Five to ten minutes a day.

WHAT varieties?
There are several subspecies, but the differences are slight. The Californian mountain kingsnake, *Lampropeltis zonata*, is similar but is not so common in captivity.

WHAT care?
Feeding once per week during the spring and summer, changing the water, and cleaning as necessary. This species often refuses to feed in the winter, in which case it helps to allow it to hibernate at 46–50°F (8–10°C).

Cost			
Setup cost			
Running cost			

Size: 20–40 in (50–100 cm)

Distribution: American southwest and adjacent parts of Mexico

Life span: 25 years or more

WHAT food?
Mice.

HOW easy are they to breed?
They are easy to breed but require a cool winter period.

WHAT drawbacks?
Not always easy to obtain as they are not prolific breeders.

Above: This is subspecies L. p. pyromelana.

Right: This is subspecies L. p. woodini.

Pantherophis bairdi

Baird's rat snake

PROFILE

Baird's rat snakes are grey in color with orange edges to their scales, orange on their head, and four dusky lines running down their body. A very attractive form from Mexico has a yellow body and a grey head. Juveniles of both forms have darker blotches down their back, but these fade as they grow. Its scales are smoother than those of most rat snakes, which usually have a central keel. Baird's rat snakes live in rocky canyons and hillsides in arid mountain ranges in a small area of Texas and northeastern Mexico, and are rarely seen in the wild.

Cost		
Setup cost		
Running cost		

Size: 33–53 in (85–135 cm)	
Distribution: North America	
Life span: 15–20 years	

Above left: The Mexican form of Baird's rat snake is not as common as the Texas form and is very distinctive, with its grey head and yellow body. Both forms are grey with dark blotches as juveniles, and the adult coloration takes from one to two years to develop.

Below left: A sub-adult Texas Baird's rat snake in which the juvenile blotches have not quite disappeared.

WHAT temperament?
Nearly always placid and easy to handle.

WHAT accommodation?
A terrarium with a floor space of 30 × 18 in (75 × 45 cm) is the minimum requirement for an average adult; large adults require more room. They need a substrate of wood shavings, a hide box and a water bowl large enough to soak in. Other cage furnishings are optional.

WHAT environment?
A thermal gradient ranging from 68–82°F (20–28°C) and produced by an under-cage heat mat at one end of the cage is the best way of heating. Lighting is unnecessary, and the humidity should be low.

HOW much time?
Five to ten minutes a day, longer periods for cleaning. They can be allowed to hibernate in the winter, in which case they do not need to be fed, and time spent is minimal.

WHAT varieties?
Just the two races mentioned above: Texas Baird's and Mexican Baird's.

WHAT care?
Feeding once a week, water changes, and cleaning as necessary.

HOW easy are they to breed?
Very easy. Hatchlings tend to be vigorous and start feeding without any problems.

WHAT food?
Mice.

WHAT drawbacks?
None.

Pantherophis guttatus

Corn snake

PROFILE

The corn snake is a type of rat snake and one of the most popular snakes with reptile keepers, and rightly so. It is attractive, occurs in many natural and unnatural color forms, is a good size, is easy to handle, and breeds readily in captivity. Wild corn snakes are grey, tan, or straw colored with large saddles of red or reddish-brown. Each saddle is edged in black. The underside is a checkerboard of black-and-white squares. Like most rat snakes, the corn snake is loaf-shaped in cross section with a flat underside. It is slender and its tail is long. Variation in color concerns both the background and the saddles. Individuals from South Carolina, often known as "Okeetee corns" tend to have the brightest red colors, with broad black borders to the saddles and are sought after. "Miami corns" are grey or silver with narrow orange-red saddles. These are two extremes, and most corn snakes fall somewhere in between. However, the species has been widely bred in captivity for longer than any other snake, and geo-graphical races have inevitably become mixed up in the hunt for new varieties. Pure strains from specific localities are almost impossible to obtain.

Corn snakes climb well but are most commonly found on the ground, in a variety of habitats, including open woodland, rocky hillsides, and abandoned buildings. It feeds mainly on rodents, which it hunts and eats underground.

WHAT temperament?

Although a few are nervous and inclined to bite, corn snakes are usually docile and easily handled. They are sometimes restless in captivity and experts at escaping.

WHAT accommodation?

A terrarium with a floor space of 24 x 18 in (60 x 45 cm) is the minimum requirement for an adult. The height is not so important, although they will climb given the opportunity. Many breeders keep them in shallow plastic trays or boxes to save space. They need a substrate of wood shavings, a hide box, and a water bowl large enough for the snake to soak itself. Other cage furnishings are optional.

WHAT environment?

A thermal gradient is important; it should range from 68–82°F (20–28°C). An undercage heat mat is the best way of providing this, placed at one end of the cage. Lighting is unnecessary, and the humidity should be low.

HOW much time?

Five to ten minutes a day; longer periods for cleaning. Corn snakes can be allowed to hibernate in the winter, in which case they do not need to be fed, and time spent is minimal.

Left and above: The amelanistic form (above) lacks black pigment whereas the Okeetee form occurs in the wild.

Below: Striped anerythristic corn snake. The cloudy eyes show that it will shed its skin soon.

Cost		
Setup cost		
Running cost		

Size: 30–48 in (75–120 cm)

Distribution: Eastern North America

Life span: 15–20 years

WHAT varieties?

Corn snakes were the original "designer" snakes. Apart from the geographical races mentioned above, there are forms in which the black pigment is missing (amelanistic); the red pigment is missing (anerythristic); all pigment is missing ("snow" and "blizzard" corns); the black pigment is faded (hypomelanistic); and various selectively bred variants and combinations of these, many of which have rather fanciful names. Then there are pattern variations, such as striped corn snakes, and these can also be combined with any of the color variations. The list is endless. Selection of a corn snake should be based mainly on health and vigor; choice of color and pattern is secondary. A weak snake of a spectacular strain will not give as much pleasure as a healthy snake from a less colorful one that feeds well.

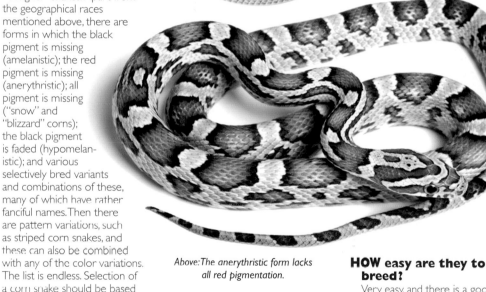

Above: The anerythristic form lacks all red pigmentation.

WHAT care?

Feeding once a week, water changes, and cleaning out as necessary.

WHAT food?

Mice.

HOW easy are they to breed?

Very easy, and there is a good supply of captive-bred hatchlings.

WHAT drawbacks?

None, although some hatchlings are small and reluctant to feed at first.

Pantherophis obsoletus

American rat snake

PROFILE

This is a variable species, with several subspecies recognized. They all start out greyish, with dark blotches down their back. The grey rat snake (sometimes regarded as a separate species) remains this color all its life; the black rat snake turns solid black, the yellow rat snake becomes yellow with four dark lines down its back, and the Everglades rat snake is similar to the yellow form but is orange. It is a large, powerful snake and an efficient constrictor. It occurs in a variety of habitats from rocky hillsides, farms, and open woodlands to swamps.

WHAT temperament?
Usually calm, but some individuals are bad-tempered and may bite.

WHAT accommodation?
A terrarium with a floor space of 40 × 18 in (100 × 45 cm) is the minimum requirement for an adult. They like to climb and can be given a tall cage with branches, but this is not essential. They need a substrate of wood shavings, a hide box, and a water bowl that is large enough to soak in.

WHAT environment?
A thermal gradient ranging from 68–82°F (20–28°C) and produced by an undercage heat mat at one end of the cage is the best way of heating. Lighting is unnecessary and the humidity should be low.

HOW much time?
Five to ten minutes a day; longer periods for cleaning.

Cost			
Setup cost			
Running cost			

Size: 5–6.5 ft (1.5–2m)

Distribution: Eastern North America

Life span: 15–20 years

They can be allowed to hibernate in the winter, in which case they do not need to be fed, and time spent is minimal.

WHAT varieties?
The subspecies as listed above: grey, black, yellow, and Everglades, and another, the Texas rat snake, which is rarely kept. There are also albino, leucistic (with reduced pigmentation), and other strains.

WHAT care?
Feeding once a week, water changes, and cleaning as necessary.

WHAT food?
Mice and rats. Large adults will eat adult rats.

HOW easy are they to breed?
They breed easily, and the hatchlings usually start feeding without problems.

WHAT drawbacks?
May become too large for some setups, and a small minority can be aggressive.

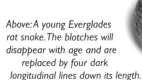

Above: A young Everglades rat snake. The blotches will disappear with age and are replaced by four dark longitudinal lines down its length.

Pituophis catenifer

Gopher snake

PROFILE

The gopher snake is related to the pine snake and the bull snake, and they used to be classed as the same species. It is a large, heavily built snake with a tan or cream body and many large, irregular darker brown blotches down its back. Its scales are keeled, giving it a rough appearance. It lives in deserts, farmland, scrub, and gardens, and is often common on the outskirts of towns. When alarmed it vibrates its tail, and if it is coiled among dead leaves this can produce a sound that may be mistaken for a rattlesnake.

Above: The bull snake, Pituophis catenifer sayi, is the largest subspecies and makes a handsome pet.

WHAT temperament?
Wild adults can be aggressive, hissing loudly and striking, but captive-bred animals are usually easy to handle.

WHAT accommodation?
Adults can be kept in a terrarium with a floor space of 40 × 12 in (100 × 30 cm), but larger terrariums are better. Height is not important. They need a substrate of wood shavings, a hide box, and a water bowl large enough to soak in.

WHAT environment?
A temperature of 68–82°F (20–28°C) is required, with a thermal gradient produced by undercage heating applied at one end only. The humidity should be low and there is no need for lighting as they are nocturnal. They can hibernate during the winter.

HOW much time?
Five to ten minutes a day.

WHAT varieties?
There are up to ten subspecies, all differing slightly in size, coloration, and pattern. The most popular subspecies are the San Diego gopher snake, *P. c. annectens*, and the Arizona gopher snake, *P. c. affinis*. Both of these have produced albino strains, which are also popular.

WHAT care?
Feeding once a week, changing water every day, and cleaning as required.

WHAT food?
Mice and small rats. They can handle quite large prey.

HOW easy are they to breed?
They breed readily in captivity, and there is usually an ample supply of young.

WHAT drawbacks?
They get a little large for some setups and the occasional one can be aggressive, but generally an easy and pleasant snake to keep.

Cost		
Setup cost		
Running cost		

Size: 3–5 ft (1–1.5 m), sometimes up to 6.5 ft (2 m)

Distribution: Western North America

Life span: 15–25 years

Above: A particularly colorful form of the albino San Diego gopher snake, P. c. annectens.

193

Pituophis melanoleucus

Pine snake

PROFILE

Closely related to the gopher snake, the pine snake is a large, heavy-bodied species and a powerful constrictor. It has a pointed snout and very heavily keeled scales. Its markings are variable, according to subspecies. It is a terrestrial species, and females dig burrows in sandy soil in which to lay their eggs. It is also common around farms, attracted there by rodents. The pine snake raises the front part of its body, forms an S-shaped coil, and gives off a loud and intimidating hiss when threatened.

WHAT accommodation?

Depending on their size, adults can be kept in a terrarium with a floor space of 40 × 12 in (100 × 30 cm) but larger terrariums are needed for very large individuals. Height is not important. They need a substrate of wood shavings, a hide box, and a water bowl large enough to soak in.

WHAT environment?

A temperature of 68–82°F (20–28°C) is ideal in summer, with a thermal gradient produced by under-cage heating applied at one end only. The humidity should be low, and there is no need for lighting as they are nocturnal. They can hibernate during the winter.

HOW much time?

Five to ten minutes a day.

WHAT temperament?

Captive-bred pine snakes rarely bite, but they can sometimes be nervous and seem to dislike being handled.

WHAT varieties?

There are three subspecies. The northern pine snake, *P. m. melanoleucus*, is white or cream with brown or black markings; the Florida pine snake, *P. m. mugitus,* may be a faded version of the northern pine or it may be plain buff; and the black pine,

Cost			
Setup cost			
Running cost			

Size: 5–7.5 ft (1.5–2.3 m)

Distribution: Eastern North America

Life span: 15–25 years

Below and left: Both of these are the patternless Florida subspecies, P. m. mugitus.

P. m. lodingi, is completely black. The rare Louisiana pine snake is now a separate species, *Pituophis ruthveni.*

WHAT care?

Feed once a week, change the water daily, and clean as needed.

WHAT food?

Mice and small rats.

HOW easy are they to breed?

They breed easily but lay fewer eggs than gopher snakes.

WHAT drawbacks?

Rather large and may be aggressive.

Zamenis longissimus

Aesculapian snake

PROFILE

A very graceful and handsome snake despite its drab coloration, which is typically brown or olive with a yellowish collar and lower jaw. Juveniles have white flecks on their scales, which fade as they mature. Some populations include black (melanistic) individuals. This species lives in a range of different habitats, in mountains, scrub, and agricultural areas. It is a good climber and often coils up in stone walls, hedges, or in holes in old trees.

WHAT temperament?

Wild-caught individuals are often nervous and inclined to bite, but captive-bred ones are easily tamed and have calmed down by the time they are sub-adults.

WHAT accommodation?

They do not do well in box- or tray-type setups; a terrarium of about 40 × 20 × 20 in (100 × 50 × 50 cm) is needed. They like to climb and should be given one or two sloping branches, a hide box, and a water bowl. The substrate can be wood shavings.

WHAT environment?

A background temperate of 68–77°F (20–25°C) suits them, and a basking lamp can provide a hot spot of up to 86°F (30°C); they will use this when they have fed. They can occasionally be lightly sprayed provided the terrarium is well ventilated, but it is not strictly necessary unless they have trouble shedding their skin.

HOW much time?

Five to ten minutes a day.

WHAT varieties?

The melanistic form mentioned above, and there is also a striped form, now elevated to a full species, *Zamenis lineata*, from southern Italy.

WHAT care?

Feeding once a week in summer, regular water changes, and cleaning when necessary. If they are allowed to hibernate they require almost no care during this time.

WHAT food?

Mice. They sometimes refuse to eat in mid-summer and in winter, when they can hibernate.

HOW easy are they to breed?

Easy, although a larger terrarium is required.

WHAT drawbacks?

They dislike constant handling and may bite occasionally.

Cost			
Setup cost			
Running cost			

Size: 3–5 ft (1–1.5 m)

Distribution: Most of southern, central, and eastern Europe

Life span: 15–20 years

Left: The Aesculapian snake is a slender, elegant, and undemanding species that is not as popular as it deserves to be.

Zamenis situla

Leopard snake

PROFILE

A small, pretty rat snake with a pattern of red, reddish-brown, or brown blotches on a speckled cream or grey background. These are usually, but not always, edged in black, and there is a black bar across the top of the head, between the eyes. In some regions there is also a striped variety, in which the red markings take the form of longitudinal stripes, also edged in black. It is a native of southern Italy, some Mediterranean islands, eastern Europe, and western Asia. Well-marked leopard snakes are among the most attractive colubrids. They are usually found in rocky places, such as loose scree and dry stone walls, but may also live in overgrown cemeteries, gardens, and ruins. They are most active in the spring and early summer, when it is diurnal, becoming nocturnal and more secretive later in the year, when the days are very hot. In captivity, they often refuse food in mid-summer but eat heartily in the spring and autumn, so feeding should be concentrated at these times.

Above: This striped leopard snake appears to have eaten recently, judging by the substantial bulge visible in its stomach region.

WHAT temperament?

Wild individuals are nervous and inclined to bite, but captive-bred individuals are docile and easy to handle. Like many other snakes, they are more likely to become tame if they are given places to hide. Forcing them out into the open only serves to make them more nervous and, in some cases, aggressive.

WHAT accommodation?

A terrarium measuring about 24 x 12 x 12 in (60 x 30 x 30 cm) is adequate for an average-sized adult. It should have a substrate of wood shavings and at least one hide box. It would also be possible to set this species up in a semi-naturalistic way, using dead leaves as a substrate and employing pieces of flat stone or driftwood to create places for them to hide.

WHAT environment?

A temperature of 68–77°F (20–25°C), with the heat being applied to one end only: this may be by means of a heat strip that covers, at most, one-third of the floor area, or a low-power basking light directed onto a flat rock, for instance. In most households, however, they can also be kept at (warm) room temperature. UV is not necessary, although a light spraying occasionally may be beneficial.

HOW much time?

Five to ten minutes a day.

WHAT varieties?

Spotted and striped, as described above. There are numerous other slight variations, often associated with specific localities. Some individuals, for instance, lack the black borders to their markings.

Left: Leopard snakes are arguably the most beautiful of all European species.

Cost			
Setup cost			
Running cost			

Size: 28–40 in (70–100 cm), usually 28 in (70 cm) or less

Distribution: Southern Italy, Mediterranean islands, eastern Europe, western Asia

Life span: 15–20 years at least

Above: A well-marked leopard snake of the spotted form.

Below: Striped individuals are less common than the spotted ones.

WHAT care?

Feeding once a week and cleaning as necessary. If they stop feeding in the autumn, it is best to let them hibernate by removing heat altogether and moving them to a cool place.

WHAT food?

Small mice. Meals should be relatively small, and even adults are reluctant to eat full-grown mice, preferring half-grown juveniles or even nestling mice. They often prefer to feed in a confined space; placing the food inside their hide box often encourages reluctant feeders to start eating. This species may not feed during winter, nor in mid-summer, so food should be given regularly when they are willing to eat, i.e., in the spring and autumn.

HOW easy are they to breed?

They breed readily as long as they have been hibernated for several months the previous winter but are not prolific, laying three to six elongated eggs.

WHAT drawbacks?

Lack of supply, which makes them expensive compared to similar species. They can also be rather temperamental feeders until their natural feeding habits are taken into account.

Checkered garter snake

PROFILE

A very distinctive species with a thin pale line down its back and large black markings arranged on either side in a staggered pattern on a pale olive background. It usually has a black collar. This species is very adaptable and has spread into desert regions by following irrigation systems. It also occurs in grasslands, farmlands, and lightly wooded areas, as long as there is water nearby. In very hot regions it is active at night. It is disappearing over much of its range due to modern farming practices.

WHAT temperament?
Nervous and quick, like all garter snakes, but becomes tamer than most.

WHAT accommodation?
Same as the common garter snake, although this species tends to remain smaller and may be kept in slightly smaller terrariums.

WHAT environment?
Same as the common garter snake (pages 200-201). A temperature gradient is important.

HOW much time?
Ten to fifteen minutes a day.

WHAT varieties?
There is an albino strain, one of the first albino garter snakes to be available.

WHAT care?
Feeding once or twice a week, refreshing the water bowl daily, and cleaning as necessary.

Cost			
Setup cost			
Running cost			

Size: 20–40 in (50–100 cm), females are much larger

Distribution: South-central North America

Life span: 10–15 years

WHAT food?
This species is easier to cater for than other garter snakes, as it will often eat mice in addition to the usual food. They are very greedy and newborn snakes grow quickly, occasionally reaching breeding size in less than a year if well fed.

HOW easy are they to breed?
Very easy. Females will breed twice in a single season, and hibernation is not essential with this species.

WHAT drawbacks?
They need rather large terrariums and are not as easy to handle as some other snakes, such as rat and kingsnakes, but out of all the garter snakes that are readily available, this is probably the easiest one to keep.

Left: The checkered garter snake is an attractive and adaptable species that usually does well in captivity.

Thamnophis radix

Plains garter snake

PROFILE

This is one of the more colorful garter snakes, with a bright orange or yellow stripe down the center of its back. Otherwise, it is olive-green, becoming paler on the flanks, with two rows of black markings on either side and black bars below its eyes. It lives in prairies and farmlands, usually staying close to marshes, streams, and ponds. Like other garter snakes, it gives birth to live young, numbering up to 90 in extreme cases.

Right: The wide orange or yellow stripe down the center of its back helps to distinguish the plains garter snake from other species.

WHAT temperament?

Nervous and fast-moving but perhaps easier to handle than some other garter snakes; less inclined to expel the contents of their anal glands.

WHAT accommodation?

Same as for the common garter snake (pages 200-201) although this species tends to remain smaller and may be kept in slightly smaller terrariums.

WHAT environment?

Same as the common garter snake. A temperature gradient is important.

HOW much time?

Ten to twenty minutes a day.

Cost			
Setup cost			
Running cost			

Size: 20–28 in (50–70 cm)

Distribution: Central North America

Life span: 10–15 years

WHAT varieties?

Two subspecies, the eastern, *T. radix radix*, and the western plains garter snake, *T. radix haydeni*. The latter has smaller black spots between the stripes. There are also albinos and various other color mutations.

WHAT care?

Feeding once or twice a week, refreshing the water bowl daily, and cleaning as necessary.

WHAT food?

Same as the common garter snake. This species probably eats more frogs than fish in the wild but will take artificial garter snake food in captivity.

HOW easy are they to breed?

They will breed given the right conditions. They probably need a long period of hibernation.

WHAT drawbacks?

Feeding can be time-consuming unless they will take mice. Not a snake that enjoys being handled.

Thamnophis sirtalis

Common garter snake

PROFILE

This garter snake is found over a wide area in North America and in a range of different habitats. It has a white or yellow stripe down the center of its back and another stripe on each flank. Other colors and markings are variable and depend to some extent on the subspecies, about twelve of which are recognized. Subspecies from the west of the United States often have red markings on their backs and heads, whereas those from the eastern states are more likely to be grey, brown, pinkish, or blue. Many individuals are intermediate in their colors and markings, and it can be difficult to assign them to a particular subspecies.

It is associated with water and is usually found close to lakes, ponds, ditches, and rivers. Its natural diet includes frogs, newts, fish, and earthworms. It can be very common in places, but some forms, such as the San Francisco garter snake, have become endangered due to habitat destruction. Some of these rare types are bred in captivity and can be legally obtained through breeders.

WHAT temperament?

Nervous and fast-moving. Garter snakes dislike being handled and try to escape, sometimes producing a foul-smelling fluid from their anal glands. Long-term captives, however, usually lose this habit. They are diurnal and very alert, especially when they can smell food.

WHAT accommodation?

Garter snakes require large terrariums because they are very active. One with a floor area measuring 40 x 20 in (100 x 50 cm) is the minimum size for a pair or small group of adults. Height is not so important as they do not normally climb. The cage should have a substrate of wood shavings and plenty of hiding places, including hide boxes, pieces of curved bark, or broken plant

pots. A large water bowl is essential, but the substrate in the cage should remain dry.

WHAT environment?

Depending on their origin, they need a temperature gradient of 64–82°F (18–28°C), although they will tolerate cooler conditions. Heating can be by under-cage heat mats, an overhead lamp, or both. The humidity should be low. There is some evidence that garter snakes benefit from UV lighting, and natural daylight lamps are recommended.

Above: The San Francisco garter snake, T. s. tetrataenia, *is endangered in the wild but widely bred in captivity.*

Cost				
Setup cost				
Running cost				

Size: 20–50 in (50–130 cm), depending on subspecies

Distribution: North America, from Canada to Mexico

Life span: 10–15 years

Above: The eastern garter snake occurs in many color forms but always has a series of longitudinal stripes.

HOW much time?

Ten to twenty minutes a day.

WHAT varieties?

Many subspecies as described above. The most popular are the San Francisco garter snake, *T. s. tetrataenia*, the Californian red-sided garter snake, *T. s. infernalis*, and the Florida blue garter snake, *T. s. similis*, but almost any form can be available from time to time. In addition, there are selectively bred albino and melanistic strains, and some very colorful orange forms known as "flame" garter snakes.

WHAT care?

Feeding once or twice a week. The water bowl should be washed and replenished every day, especially after a feed, and cleaning will be necessary on a regular basis.

WHAT food?

Fish, earthworms, and, sometimes, mice. The nutrition of garter snakes and other fish-eating snakes can be a problem. Some artificial garter snake foods contain a balanced diet, including vitamin and mineral supplements. Artificial diets can also be homemade, using trout as the main ingredient. Those individuals that will eat mice are less of a problem. Earthworms are only suitable for the short-term feeding of newborn garter snakes for the first few weeks.

HOW easy are they to breed?

Breeding is relatively easy. Garter snakes are live-bearers, and some subspecies of the common garter snake are very prolific.

WHAT drawbacks?

Feeding can be time-consuming, and they need cleaning more often than many other snakes. They are not suitable for people who like to handle their snakes regularly.

Above: The Californian red-sided garter snake is arguably the most colorful form but is rarely seen in captivity. The blue stripe and red blotches down the sides are typical.

Opheodrys aestivus

Rough green snake

PROFILE

The rough green snake is a beautiful, slender species that lives among dense vegetation, where its coloration makes it difficult to see. It is solid green on the back, paler below, and has a pale yellow chin. Its scales are slightly keeled, separating it from another species, the smooth green snake, of the same region. It is partially arboreal, climbing into trees and bushes, and often lays its eggs in holes in rotting tree trunks. It is one of the few insectivorous snakes available to reptile keepers.

WHAT temperament?
Diurnal. Active and alert, quite nervous, but very gentle.

WHAT accommodation?
Being arboreal, a tall terrarium is necessary, and one with a floor space of about 24 × 18 in (60 × 45 cm) and a height of at

Cost			
Setup cost			
Running cost			

Size: 20–32 in (50–80 cm)

Distribution: Eastern North America

Life span: Unknown

Above and top: The rough green snake is a pretty small species suitable for a naturalistic set-up with living plants.

least 24 in (60 cm) would be adequate for one or two adults. It should have plenty of branches of various diameters and living or artificial plants for it to climb in and hide among. The substrate can be wood shavings, but dead leaves look more natural, and a bowl of clean water should be available.

WHAT environment?
A thermal gradient of 68–86°F (20–30°C) is ideal, and this can be provided by an under-cage heat mat in conjunction with a basking light to raise the daytime temperature in one part of the cage. A UV or natural daylight lamp may be beneficial, and this can be positioned near the basking light. The terrarium can be sprayed daily but must be well ventilated.

HOW much time?
Ten to fifteen minutes a day.

WHAT varieties?
None.

WHAT care?
Daily feeding, refreshing the water bowl, and cleaning as required.

WHAT food?
Insects such as crickets, grasshoppers, waxworms, caterpillars, spiders, and other species from the garden.

HOW easy are they to breed?
Rarely attempted.

WHAT drawbacks?
Wild individuals sometimes fail to adapt and will not feed, and there is almost no source of captive-bred young. An interesting project for someone.

Boaedon fuliginosus

Brown house snake

PROFILE

The brown house snake is an elegant African species, with smooth, silky scales and a narrow head. When young it has mottled markings on the front half of its body, but it gradually changes to uniform brown as it grows. There is usually a white or cream line through each eye. It is very adaptable and lives in semi-deserts, grasslands, farmlands, and, as their name implies, in human dwellings.

Above: A pale form of one of the house snake species.

WHAT temperament?

Usually docile and a pleasure to handle, although some can be nervous and aggressive.

WHAT accommodation?

A terrarium measuring around 30 x 18 x 12 in (75 x 45 x 30 cm) is adequate for an adult. They are mainly terrestrial but will climb given the opportunity. They need a substrate of wood shavings, one or two hide boxes, and a water bowl large enough to soak in.

WHAT environment?

A temperature of 64–77°F (18–25°C) is required, and a thermal gradient, with under-cage heating applied at one end only, is the best arrangement. Humidity should be low, and lighting is unnecessary.

HOW much time?

Five to ten minutes a day.

WHAT varieties?

There is some dispute over their taxonomy, and they are still listed under the genus *Lamprophis* in some literature. The striped house snake, *B. lineatus*, is similar to *B. fuliginosus* but has a cream stripe along its flanks, *B. capensis* is probably a local form of *B. fuliginosus*, and the desert house snake, *B. fuliginosus mentalis*, may be a full species. There are also albinos and other "morphs" on the market occasionally.

WHAT care?

Feeding once a week, refreshing the water bowl daily, and cleaning as necessary.

Cost			
Setup cost			
Running cost			

Size: 24–48 in and slender	
Distribution: Southern Africa	
Life span: 12–15 years	

Above: A typical brown house snake.

WHAT food?

Mice. They are powerful constrictors and will swallow relatively large mice, but it is best to give fairly small meals.

HOW easy are they to breed?

Very. Females will continue to lay fertile eggs long after they have been separated from the male.

WHAT drawbacks?

None. An underrated species.

Index of common names

A

Aesculapian snake 195
African bullfrog 67
African clawed frog 29
African grey tree frog 69
African spurred tortoise 91
Amazonian milk frog 43
American green tree frog 39
American rat snake 192
Argentine black-and-white tegu 150
Asian bullfrog 63
Asian foam-nest tree frog 72
Asian horned frog 36
Asian painted frog 63
Axolotl 12-13

B

Baird's rat snake 189
Ball python 170
Barking tree frog 40
Black and yellow poison dart frog 58
Blue poison dart frog 59
Borneo blood python 164
Bright-eyed frog 68
Brown anole 120
Brown house snake 203
Budgett's frog 47
Bumblebee toad 55
Burmese python 166-167

C

Cane toad 56
Carpet python 162-163

Checkered garter snake 198
Children's python 160
Chinese butterfly lizard 112
Chinese crocodile newt 24
Chinese soft-shell turtle 93
Collared lizard 121
Common boa 174-175
Common egg-eating snake 179
Common garden lizard 104
Common garter snake 200-201
Common kingsnake 184-185
Common map turtle 84
Common musk turtle 97
Common newt 19
Common snapping turtle 80
Common spadefoot toad 34
Corn snake 190-191
Couch's spadefoot toad 35
Crested gecko 138-139
Cuban tree frog 42

D

Desert horned lizard 124
Diamond python 162-163
Dumeril's boa 172
Dwarf aquarium frog 28

E

Eastern spiny-tailed gecko 137
Eastern water dragon 106
Electric blue day gecko 131
Emerald boa 173
European common frog 77
European green tree frog 38
European pond turtle 82

F

Fat-tailed gecko 142
Fire salamander 22-23
Fire skink 146
Frilled lizard 103
Frog-eyed gecko 143

G

Giant blue-tongued skink 148
Giant day gecko 134-135
Glass lizard 154
Golden mantella 70-71
Gopher snake 193
Green and gold poison dart frog 57
Green anole 119
Green iguana 122-123
Green tree python 161
Grey tree frogs 41
Grey-banded kingsnake 183

H

Helmeted chameleon 113
Hermann's tortoise 94-95
Horsfield's tortoise 89

I

Inland bearded dragon 108-109

J

Japanese red-bellied newt 18

K

Kenyan sand boa 178

L

Leopard gecko 140-141
Leopard snake 196-197
Leopard tortoise 92

M

Madagascan leaf-tailed gecko 136

Malaysian blood python 165

Mandarin rat snake 180

Marbled newt 21

Marbled salamander 14

Marbled tree frog 37

Marine toad 56

Mascarene grass frog 66

Matamata 98

Milk snake 186-187

Mississippi map turtle 85

Mossy frog 73

Mountain horned dragon 102

Mourning gecko 130

N

Neon day gecko 133

Northern leopard frog 76

O

Oriental fire-bellied toad 30-31

P

Painted big-headed gecko 132

Painted frog 33

Panther chameleon 116-117

Phantasmal poison dart frog 60

Pied mossy frog 74

Pine snake 194

Pink-bellied shortneck turtle 99

Pink-tongued skink 145

Plains garter snake 199

Plains toad 53

R

Rainbow boa 176

Rankin's bearded dragon 107

Razorback musk turtle 96

Red Niger Uromastyx 110-111

Red-eyed crocodile skink 149

Red-eyed leaf frog 44-45

Red-footed tortoise 90

Red-tailed green rat snake 181

Reticulated python 168-169

Rosy boa 177

Rough green snake 202

S

Sandfish 147

Sharp-ribbed newt 20

Short-tailed leaf chameleon 118

Six-lined long-tailed lizard 152

Slimy salamander 15

Smooth newt 19

Sonoran mountain kingsnake 188

South American horned frogs 50-51

Southern alligator lizard 153

Spiny-tailed monitor 156-157

Spotted puddle frog 75

Spotted reed frog 64

Spotted turtle 81

Square-marked toad 52

Steppe lizard 151

Sunbeam snake 171

T

Taliang knobbly newt 25

Thai water dragon 105

Tiger salamander 16-17

Tinker reed frog 65

Tokay gecko 126-127

Tomato frog 62

Turkish gecko 128

V

Veiled chameleon 114-115

Viper gecko 129

W

Water monitor 155

Waxy frog 46

Western fence lizard 125

Western green toad 54

Western hognose snake 182

White's tree frog 48-49

Wood turtle 83

Y

Yellow poison dart frog 61

Yellow-bellied toad 32

Yellow-bellied turtle 86-87

Yellow-margined box turtle 88

Z

Zimbabwe girdle-tailed lizard 144

Index of Latin names

A

Acanthosaura crucigera 102
Acrantophis dumerili 172
Agalychnis callidryas 44-45
Agrionemys horsfieldii 89
Ambystoma mexicanum 12-13
Ambystoma opacum 14
Ambystoma tigrinum 16-17
Amietophrynus regularis 52
Anaxyrus cognatus 53
Anaxyrus debilis 54
Anolis carolinensis 119
Anolis sagrei 120
Antaresia childreni 160

B

Boa constrictor 174-175
Boaedon fuliginosus 203
Bombina orientalis 30-31
Bombina maxima 31
Bombina variegata 32
Boophis rappiodes 68

C

Calotes versicolor 104
Ceratophrys cranwelli 50-51
Ceratophrys ornata 50-51
Chamaeleo calyptratus 114-115
Chelonoides carbonaria 90
Chelus fimbriatus 98
Chelydra serpentina 80
Chiromantis xerampelina 69
Chlamydosaurus kingii 103
Clemmys guttata 81
Corallus caninus 173

Cordylus rhodesianus 144
Crotaphytus collaris 121
Cuora flavomarginata 88
Cynops pyrrhogaster 18

D

Dasypeltis scabra 179
Dendrobates auratus 57
Dendrobates leucomelas 58
Dendrobates tinctorius azureus 59
Dendropsophus marmoratus 37
Discoglossus pictus 33
Dyscophus guineti 62

E

Emydura subglobosa 99
Emys orbicularis 82
Epicrates cenchria 176
Epipedobates tricolor 60
Eremias przewalskii 151
Eremias velox 151
Eryx colubrinus loveridgei 178
Eublepharus macularius 140-141
Euprepriophis mandarinus 180

F

Furcifer pardalis 116-117

G

Gekko gecko 126-127
Geochelone sulcata 91
Gerrhonotus multicarinatus 153

Glyptemys insculpta 83
Gonyosoma oxycephalum 181
Graptemys geographica 84
Graptemys pseudogeographica
    kohnii 85

H

Hemidactylus imbricatus 129
Hemidactylus turcicus 128
Hemisphaeriodon gerrardii 145
Hemitheconyx caudicinctus 142
Heterodon nasicus 182
Hyla arborea 38
Hyla chrysoscelis 41
Hyla cinerea 39
Hyla gratiosa 40
Hyla versicolor 41
Hymenochirus boettgeri 28
Hyperolius puncticulatus 64
Hyperolius tuberilinguis 65

I

Iguana iguana 122-123

K

Kaloula pulchra 63

L

Lampropeltis alterna 183
Lampropeltis getula 184-185
Lampropeltis pyromelana 188
Lampropeltis triangulum 186-187
Lamprophis fuliginosus 203
Leiolepis reevesii 112
Lepidobatrachus laevis 47
Lepidodactylus lugubris 130
Lepidothyris fernandi 146

Lichanura trivirgata 177
Lissotriton vulgaris 19
Lithobates pipiens 76
Litoria caerulea 48-49
Litoria infrafrenata 49
Lygodactylus williamsii 131
M
Mantella aurantiaca 70-71
Megophrys nasuta 36
Melanophryniscus stelzneri 55
Morelia spilota 162-163
Morelia viridis 161
O
Occidozyga lima 75
Opheodrys aestivus 202
Osteopilus septentrionalis 42
P
Pantherophis bairdi 189
Pantherophis guttatus 190-191
Pantherophis obsoletus 192
Paroedura pictus 132
Pelobates fuscus 34
Pelodiscus sinensis 93
Phelsuma klemmeri 133
Phelsuma madagascariensis 134-135
Phrynosoma platyrhinos 124
Phyllobates terribilis 61
Phyllomedusa sauvagii 46
Physignathus cocincinus 105
Physignathus lesueurii 106
Pituophis catenifer 193
Pituophis melanoleucus 194
Plethodon glutinosus 15

Pleurodeles waltl 20
Pogona henrylawsoni 107
Pogona vitticeps 108-109
Polypedates leucomystax 72
Pseudopus apodus 154
Ptychadena mascareniensis 66
Python breitensteini 164
Python brongersmai 165
Python curtus 165
Python molurus bivittatus 166-167
Python regius 170
Python reticulatus 168-169
Pyxicephalus adspersus 67
Pyxicephalus edulis 67
R
Rana temporaria 77
Rhacodactylus ciliatus 138-139
Rhinella marinus 56
Rieppeleon brevicaudatus 118-119
S
Salamandra salamandra 22-23
Scaphiopus couchii 35
Sceloporus occidentalis 125
Scincus scincus 147
Sternotherus carinatus 96
Sternotherus odoratus 97
Stigmochelys pardalis 92
Strophurus williamsi 137

T
Takydromus sexlineatus 152
Teratolepis fasciata 129
Teratoscincus scincus 143
Testudo hermanni 94-95
Thamnophis marcianus 198
Thamnophis radix 199
Thamnophis sirtalis 200-201
Theloderma aspera 74
Theloderma corticale 73
Tiliqua gigas 148
Trachemys scripta 86-87
Trachycephalus resinifictrix 43
Tribolonotus gracilis 149
Trioceros hoehnelii 113
Triturus marmoratus 21
Tupinambis merianae 150
Tylototriton kweichowensis 24
Tylototriton taliangensis 25
U
Uromastyx geyri 110-111
Uromastyx ocellata 111
Uroplatus fimbriatus 136
V
Varanus acanthinurus 156-157
Varanus salvator 155
X
Xenopeltis unicolor 171
Xenopus laevis 29
Z
Zamenis longissimus 195
Zamenis situla 196-197

Picture Credits

Most of the photographs reproduced in this book are the work of the author, **Chris Mattison**, who owns their copyright. The publishers would like to express their thanks to him for permission to reproduce them. The exceptions are those listed and credited below:

Shutterstock.com

alslutsky: 43 right.
Sira Anamwong: 155 bottom.
Ryan M. Bolton: 17 top, 96 bottom left, 113 top.
Steve Bower: 40 right, 202 bottom left.
Katrina Brown: 62 left.
Andrew Burgess: 12 bottom left.
Sasha Burkard: 45 top, jacket (front cover: leaf frog).
Steve Byland: 125 bottom left.
Kate Connes: 46 right.
A Cotton Photo: 42 top.
David Dohnal: 121 top.
EcoPrint: 67 top, 69 bottom, 71 bottom.
Dirk Ercken: 57 right.
fivespots: 6 top, 61 bottom right, 64 bottom left,
    81 bottom, 83 bottom right, 87 top, 88 bottom left,
    90 top, 97 center right, 99 center left, 137 bottom,
    157 bottom, 160 top, 163 bottom, 176 bottom right,
    180 top, 188 top, 193 top, 194 center right,
    203 center left, 205 top.
Karel Gallas: 92 top.
iliuta goean: 34 bottom left.
Michael C. Gray: 161 bottom left.
Arto Hakola: 120 bottom left.
Gabriela Insuratelu: 196 top.
IrinaK: 3 (frog), 39 top.
Eric Isselée: 1 (tortoise), 1 (frog), 3 (gecko), 3 (frilled
    lizard), 5, 14 bottom, 21 bottom, 22 top, 30 top,
    36 top, 59 top, 60 bottom, 73 top, 82 top, 91 bottom
    right, 103 bottom, 109 top, 110 bottom, 114 top,

167 top, 126 top, 134 top, 138 bottom, 175 top,
    181 top, 185 center right, 206 bottom, 208, jacket
    (front cover: fire-bellied toad, corn snake, turtle;
    back cover: common boa, mantella frog).
Matt Jeppson: 54 top, 154 bottom left, 177 top.
Kletr: 58 top.
D. Kucharski and K. Kucharski: 20 bottom, 63 top.
Kuttelvaserova: 77 top.
Hugh Lansdown: 136 top.
Brian Lasenby: 124 top.
LuckyKeeper: 49 top, jacket (back cover: tree frog).
mikeledray: 102 top.
Jeffrey Moore: 53 top.
NatalieJean: 3 (snake), 183 top.
Maxim Petrichuk: 89 center right.
Psychotic Nature: 84 top.
RamonaS: 145 bottom right.
Dr Morley Read: 37 left.
Peter Reijners: 129 center right.
Arun Roisri: 24 top.
Ron Rowan Photography: 76 center right.
s-eyerkaufer: 95 center right.
SF photo: 80 top.
Audrey Snider-Bell: 50 top.
Ilias Strachinis: 128 top.
TiberiusSahlean: 72 top.
tongdang: 112 bottom.
tratong: 122 top, jacket (back flap).
Xpixel: 2 (tortoise), 38 top, 39 top, 94 top.
Zenotri: 106 center right.

Wikimedia Commons

Andrew S. Gardner, from *Mapping the terrestrial
    reptile distributions in Oman and the United Arab
    Emirates:* 143 top.
Alastair Rae: 151 top.